D0899693

Stories
of
Louisiana

"TONTON."

[*From a portrait now in the possession of Mme. Veuve Alcibiade De Blanc.*]

Strange
True
Stories
of
Louisiana

Original and Unabridged

By George W. Cable

RIVER
ROAD
PRESS

New Orleans 2015

First published in 1888 by Charles Scribner's Sons
First River Road Press Printing, 2015

The name and logo for "River Road Press" are trademarks of
River Road Press LLC and are registered with the
U.S. Patent and Trademark Office.

ISBN: 978-1-941879-04-7

For more information on other River Road Press titles,
please visit www.riverroadpress.com

Original cover illustration by Julie Dupré Buckner

Printed in the United States of America
Published by River Road Press LLC
P.O. Box 125
Metairie, LA 70001

TO MY FRIEND

JAMES BIRNEY GUTHRIE

CONTENTS.

LIST OF ILLUSTRATIONS.

*From photographs of the originals, in possession of
Mr. George W. Cable.*

Court papers in Miller vs. Belmonti.   The "Alix MS."
Louisa Cheval's letter.   Letter from Suzanne.   The War Diary (underneath).

SOME OF THE MANUSCRIPTS,

François's Pages.

STRANGE TRUE STORIES

OF LOUISIANA.

HOW I GOT THEM.

1882–89.

TRUE stories are not often good art. The relations
and experiences of real men and women rarely fall
in such symmetrical order as to make an artistic
whole. Until they have had such treatment as we
give stone in the quarry or gems in the rough they
seldom group themselves with that harmony of values
and brilliant unity of interest that result when art
comes in — not so much to transcend nature as to
make nature transcend herself.

Yet I have learned to believe that good stories happen oftener than once I thought they did. Within
the last few years there have dropped into my hands
by one accident or another a number of these natural
crystals, whose charms, never the same in any two,
are in each and all enough at least to warn off all
tampering of the fictionist. Happily, moreover, without being necessary one to another, they yet have a

coherent sequence, and follow one another like the days of a week. They are mine only by right of discovery. From various necessities of the case I am sometimes the story-teller, and sometimes, in the reader's interest, have to abridge; but I add no fact and trim naught of value away. Here are no unconfessed "restorations," not one. In time, place, circumstance, in every essential feature, I give them as I got them — strange stories that truly happened, all partly, some wholly, in Louisiana.

In the spring of 1883, being one night the guest of my friend Dr. Francis Bacon, in New Haven, Connecticut, and the conversation turning, at the close of the evening, upon wonderful and romantic true happenings, he said:

"You are from New Orleans; did you never hear of Salome Müller?"

"No."

Thereupon he told the story, and a few weeks later sent me by mail, to my home in New Orleans, whither I had returned, a transcription, which he had most generously made, of a brief summary of the case — it would be right to say tragedy instead of case — as printed in "The Law Reporter" some forty years ago. That transcription lies before me now, beginning, "The Supreme Court of the State of Louisiana has lately been called upon to investigate and decide one of the most interesting cases which has ever come under the cognizance of a judicial tribunal." This episode, which had been the cause of public excitement within the memory of men still living on the scene, I, a native resident of New Orleans and student of its history, stumbled upon for the first time nearly two thousand miles from home.

I mentioned it to a number of lawyers of New Orleans, one after another. None remembered ever having heard of it. I appealed to a former chief-justice of the State, who had a lively personal remembrance of every member of the bench and the bar concerned in the case; but of the case he had no recollection. One of the medical experts called in by the court for evidence upon which the whole merits of the case seemed to hang was still living — the distinguished Creole physician, Dr. Armand Mercier. He could not recall the matter until I recounted the story, and then only in the vaguest way. Yet when my friend the former chief-justice kindly took down from his shelves and beat free of dust the right volume of supreme court decisions, there was the terse, cold record, No. 5623. I went to the old newspaper files under the roof of the city hall, and had the pleasure speedily to find, under the dates of 1818 and 1844, such passing allusions to the strange facts of which I was in search as one might hope to find in those days when a serious riot was likely to receive no mention, and a steamboat explosion dangerously near the editorial rooms would be recorded in ten lines of colorless statement. I went to the courts, and, after following and abandoning several false trails through two days' search, found that the books of record containing the object of my quest had been lost, having unaccountably disappeared in — if I remember aright — 1870.

e was one chance left: it was to find the origi-
apers. I employed an intelligent gentleman at
much a day to search till he should find them. In
the dusty garret of one of the court buildings — the
old Spanish Cabildo, that faces Jackson Square — he
rummaged for ten days, finding now one desired document and now another, until he had gathered all but
one. Several he drew out of a great heap of papers
lying in the middle of the floor, as if it were a pile of
rubbish; but this one he never found. Yet I was content. Through the perseverance of this gentleman and
the intervention of a friend in the legal profession,
and by the courtesy of the court, I held in my hand
the whole forgotten story of the poor lost and found
Salome Müller. How through the courtesy of some of
the reportorial staff of the " New Orleans Picayune "
I found and conversed with three of Salome's still
surviving relatives and friends, I shall not stop to
tell.

WHILE I was still in search of these things, the
editor of the " New Orleans Times-Democrat " handed
me a thick manuscript, asking me to examine and
pronounce upon its merits. It was written wholly in
French, in a small, cramped, feminine hand. I replied,
when I could, that it seemed to me unfit for the pur-
poses of transient newspaper publication, yet if he
declined it I should probably buy it myself. He
replied that he had already examined it and decided
to decline it, and it was only to know whether I, not
he, could use it that I had been asked to read it.

I took it to an attorney, and requested him, under certain strict conditions, to obtain it for me with all its rights.

"What is it?"

"It is the minute account, written by one of the travelers, a pretty little Creole maiden of seventeen, of an adventurous journey made, in 1795, from New Orleans through the wilds of Louisiana, taking six weeks to complete a tour that could now be made in less than two days."

"But this is written by some one else; see, it says

Voyage de ma grand'mère

"Yes," I rejoined, "it purports to be a copy. We must have the little grandmother's original manuscript, written in 1822; that or nothing."

So a correspondence sprang up with a gentle and refined old Creole lady with whom I later had the honor to become acquainted and now count among my esteemed friends — grand-daughter of the grandmother who, after innumerable recountings by word of mouth to mother, sisters, brothers, friends, husband, children, and children's children through twenty-seven years of advancing life, sat down at last and wrote the oft-told tale for her little grand-children, one of whom, inheriting her literary instinct and herself become an aged grandmother, discovers the manuscript among some old family papers and recognizes its value. The first exchange of letters disclosed the fact that the "New Orleans Bee" ("L'Abeille") had bought the right to publish the manuscript in French; but the moment its editors had proper assurance that there was impending another arrangement more profitable to her, they chivalrously yielded all they had bought, on merely being reimbursed.

The condition that required the delivery of the original manuscript, written over sixty years before, was not so easily met. First came the assurance that its spelling was hideous, its writing bad and dimmed by time, and the sheets tattered and torn. Later followed the disclosure that an aged and infirm mother of the grandmother owned it, and that she had some time before compelled its return to the private drawer from which the relic-loving daughter had abstracted it. Still later came a letter saying that since the attorney was so relentlessly exacting, she had written to her mother praying her to part with the manuscript. Then followed another communication, — six large, closely written pages of despair, — inclosing a letter from the mother. The wad of papers, always more and more in the way and always "smelling bad," had been put into the fire. But a telegram followed on the heels of the mail, crying joy! An old letter had been found and forwarded which would prove that such a manuscript had existed. But it was not in time to intercept the attorney's letter saying that, the original manuscript being destroyed, there could be no purchase or any need of further correspondence. The old letter came. It was genuine beyond a doubt, had been written by one of the party making the journey, and was itself forty-seven years old. The paper was poor and sallow, the hand-writing large, and the orthography —!

Ma bien chair nuice je ressoit ta lette ce mattin

But let us translate:

                      st. john baptist [1] 10 august 1836

My VERY DEAR NIECE. I received your letter this morning in which you ask me to tell you what I remember of the journey to Attakapas made in 1795 by papa, M. ——, [and] my younger sister Françoise afterward your grandmother. If it were with my tongue I could answer more favorably; but writing is not my forte; I was never calculated for a public writer, as your grandmother was. By the way, she wrote the journey, and very prettily; what have you done with it? It is a pity to lose so pretty a piece of writing. ... We left New Orleans to go to the Atta-kapas in the month of May, 1795, and in an old barge ["vieux chalant qui senté le rat mord a plien nez"]. We were Françoise and I Suzanne, pearl of the family, and Papa, who went to buy lands; and one Joseph Charpentier and his dear and pretty little wife Alix [whom] I love so much; 3 Irish, father mother and son [fice]; lastly Mario, whom you knew, with Celeste, formerly lady's maid to Marianne — who is now my sister-in-law. ... If I knew better how to write I

---

[1] Name of the parish, or county. — TRANSLATOR.

would tell you our adventures the alligators tried to devour us. We barely escaped perishing in Lake Chicot and many other things. . . .. At last we arrived at a pretty village St. Martinville called also little Paris and full of barons, marquises, counts and countesses[1] that were an offense to my nose and my stomach. your grandmother was in raptures. it was there we met the beautiful Tonton, your aunt by marriage. I have a bad finger and must stop. . . . Your loving aunty [ta tantine qui temme]

Suzanne ——— née ———

The kind of letter to expect from one who, as a girl of eighteen, could shoot and swim and was called by her father "my son"; the antipode of her sister Françoise. My attorney wrote that the evidence was sufficient.

His letter had hardly got into the mail-bag when another telegram cried hold! that a few pages of the original manuscript had been found and forwarded by post. They came. They were only nine in all — old, yellow, ragged, torn, leaves of a plantation account-book whose red-ruled columns had long ago faded to a faint brown, one side of two or three of them pre-occupied with charges in bad French of yards of cottonade, "mouslin à dames," "jaconad," dozens of soap, pounds of tobacco, pairs of stockings, lace, etc.; but to our great pleasure each page corresponding closely, save in orthography and syntax, with a page of the new manuscript, and the page numbers of the

---

[1] Royalist refugees of '93. — TRANSLATOR.

old running higher than those of the new! Here was evidence which one could lay before a skeptical world that the transcriber had not expanded the work of the original memoirist. The manuscript passed into my possession, our Creole lady-correspondent reiterating to the end her inability to divine what could be wanted with "an almost illegible scrawl" (griffonage), full of bad spelling and of rather inelegant diction. But if old manuscript was the object of desire, why, here was something else; the very document alluded to by Françoise in her memoir of travel — the autobiography of the dear little countess, her beloved Alix de Morainville, made fatherless and a widow by the guillotine in the Reign of Terror.

"Was that all?" inquired my agent, craftily, his suspicions aroused by the promptness with which the supply met the demand. "Had she not other old and valuable manuscripts?"

"No, alas! only that one."

Thus reassured, he became its purchaser. It lies before me now, in an inner wrapper of queer old black paper, beside its little tight-fitting bag, or case of a kind of bright, large-flowered silken stuff not made in these days, and its outer wrapper of discolored brief-paper; a pretty little document of sixty-eight small pages in a feminine hand, perfect in its slightly archaic grammar, gracefully composed, and, in spite of its flimsy yellowed paper, as legible as print: "Histoire d'Alix de Morainville écrite à la Louisiane ce 22 Aout 1795. Pour mes chères amies, Suzanne et Françoise Bossier."

One day I told the story to Professor Charles Eliot
Norton of Harvard University. He generously offered
to see if he could find the name of the Count de
Morainville on any of the lists of persons guillotined
during the French Revolution. He made the search,
but wrote, "I am sorry to say that I have not been
able to find it either in Prudhomme, 'Dictionnaire des
Individues envoyés à la Mort judiciairement, 1789–
1796,' or in the list given by Wallon in the sixth
volume of his very interesting 'Histoire du Tribunal
Revolutionnaire de Paris.' Possibly he was not put
to death in Paris," etc. And later he kindly wrote
again that he had made some hours' further search,
but in vain.

Here was distress. I turned to the little manuscript
roll of which I had become so fond, and searched its
pages anew for evidence of either genuineness or its
opposite. The wrapper of black paper and the close-
fitting silken bag had not been sufficient to keep it
from taking on the yellowness of age. It was at least
no modern counterfeit. Presently I noticed the total
absence of quotation marks from its passages of conversation. Now, at the close of the last century,
the use of quotation marks was becoming general, but
had not become universal and imperative. Their
entire absence from this manuscript of sixty-eight
pages, abounding in conversations, meant either age or
cunning pretense. But would a pretender carry his
or her cunning to the extreme of fortifying the manuscript in every possible way against the sallowing
touch of time, lay it away in a trunk of old papers, lie

down and die without mentioning it, and leave it for some one in the second or third generation afterward to find ? I turned the leaves once more, and lo ! one leaf that had had a large corner torn off had lost that much of its text; it had been written upon before it was torn; while on another torn leaf, for there are two, the writing reads — as you shall see — uninterruptedly around the torn edge; the writing has been done after the corner was torn off. The two rents, therefore, must have occurred at different times; for the one which mutilates the text is on the earlier page and surely would not have been left so by the author at the time of writing it, but only by some one careless of it, and at some time between its completion and the manifestly later date, when it was so carefully bestowed in its old-fashioned silken case and its inner wrapper of black paper. The manuscript seemed genuine. Maybe the name De Morainville is not, but was a convenient fiction of Alix herself, well understood as such by Françoise and Suzanne. Everything points that way, as was suggested at once by Madame Sidonie de la Houssaye — There ! I have let slip the name of my Creole friend, and can only pray her to forgive me ! " Tout porte à le croire " (Everything helps that belief), she writes; although she also doubts, with reason, I should say, the exhaustive completeness of those lists of the guillotined. " I recall," she writes in French, " that my husband has often told me the two uncles of his father, or grandfather, were guillotined in the Revolution ; but though search was made by an advocate, no trace of them was found in any records."

An assumed name need not vitiate the truth of the story; but discoveries made since, which I am still investigating, offer probabilities that, after all, the name is genuine.

We see, however, that an intention to deceive, were it supposable, would have to be of recent date.

Now let me show that an intention to deceive could not be of recent date, and at the same time we shall see the need of this minuteness of explanation. Notice, then, that the manuscript comes directly from the lady who says she found it in a trunk of her family's private papers. A prominent paper-maker in Boston has examined it and says that, while its age cannot be certified to from its texture, its leaves are of three different kinds of paper, each of which might be a hundred years old. But, bluntly, this lady, though a person of literary tastes and talent, who recognized the literary value of Alix's *history*, esteemed original *documents* so lightly as, for example, to put no value upon Louisa Cheval's thrilling letter to her brother. She prized this Alix manuscript only because, being a simple, succinct, unadorned narrative, she could use it, as she could not Françoise's long, pretty story, for the foundation of a nearly threefold expanded romance. And this, in fact, she had written, copyrighted, and arranged to publish when our joint experience concerning Françoise's manuscript at length readjusted her sense of values. She sold me the little Alix manuscript at a price still out of all proportion below her valuation of her own writing, and counting it a mistake that the expanded romance should go unpreferred and unpublished.

But who, then, wrote the smaller manuscript? Madame found it, she says, in the possession of her very aged mother, the daughter and namesake of Françoise. Surely she was not its author; it is she who said she burned almost the whole original draft of Françoise's "Voyage," because it was "in the way and smelt bad." Neither could Françoise have written it. Her awkward handwriting, her sparkling flood of words and details, and her ignorance of the simplest rules of spelling, make it impossible. Nor could Suzanne have done it. She wrote and spelled no better at fifty-nine than Françoise at forty-three. Nor could any one have imposed it on either of the sisters. So, then, we find no intention to deceive, either early or recent. I translated the manuscript, it went to the magazine, and I sat down to eat, drink, and revel, never dreaming that the brazen water-gates of my Babylon were standing wide open.

For all this time two huge, glaring anachronisms were staring me, and half a dozen other persons, squarely in the face, and actually escaping our notice by their serene audacity. But hardly was the pie — I mean the magazine — opened when these two birds began to sing. Was n't that — interesting? Of course Louis de la Houssaye, who in 1786 "had lately come from San Domingo," had *not* "been fighting the insurgents" — who did not revolt until four or five years afterward! And of course the old count, who so kindly

left the family group that was bidding Madelaine de
Livilier good-bye, was not the Prime Minister Maurepas, who was *not* "only a few months returned from
exile," and who was *not* then "at the pinnacle of royal
favor"; for these matters were of earlier date, and
this "most lovable old man in the world" was n't any
longer in the world at all, and had not been for eight
years. He was dead and buried.

And so, after all, fraudulent intent or none, *this*
manuscript, just as it is, could never have been written
by Alix. On "this 22d of August, 1795," she could
not have perpetrated such statements as these two.
Her memory of persons and events could not have
been so grotesquely at fault, nor could she have hoped
so to deceive any one. The misstatements are of later
date, and from some one to whom the two events were
historical. But the manuscript is all in one simple,
undisguised, feminine handwriting, and with no inter-
lineation save only here and there the correction of a
miswritten word.

Now in translating madame's "Voyage de ma
Grandmère," I noticed something equivalent to an in-
terlineation, but in her own writing like all the rest,
and added in a perfectly unconcealed, candid manner,
at the end of a paragraph near the close of the story.
It struck me as an innocent gloss of the copyist, justified in her mind by some well-credited family tradition.
It was this: "Just as we [Françoise and Alix] were
parting, she [Alix] handed me the story of her life." I
had already called my friend's attention to the anachronisms, and she was in keen distress, because totally

unable to account for them. But as I further pon-
dered them, this gloss gained new significance and I
mentioned it. My new inquiry flashed light upon her
aged memory. She explained at once that, to connect
the two stories of Françoise and Alix, she had thought
it right to impute these few words to Françoise rather
than for mere exactness to thrust a detailed explanation of her own into a story hurrying to its close. My
question called back an incident of long ago and resulted first in her rummaging a whole day among her
papers, and then in my receiving the certificate of a
gentleman of high official standing in Louisiana that,
on the 10th of last April (1889), this lady, in his presence, took from a large trunk of written papers, vari-
ously dated and " appearing to be perfectly genuine,"
a book of memoranda from which, writes he, "I copy
the following paragraph written by Madame S. de la
Houssaye herself in the middle of the book, on page
29." Then follows in French:

JUNE 20, 1841. — M. Gerbeau has dined here again. What
a singular story he tells me. We talked of my grandmother
and Madame Carpentier, and what does M. Gerbeau tell me but
that Alix had not finished her history when my grandmother and
my aunt returned, and that he had promised to get it to them.
"And I kept it two years for want of an opportunity," he added.
How mad Grandmamma must have been! How the delay must
have made her suffer!

Well and good! Then Alix did write her story!
But if she wrote for both her " dear and good friends,"
Suzanne and Françoise, then Françoise, the younger
and milder sister, would the more likely have to be

content, sooner or later, with a copy. This, I find no reason to doubt, is what lies before me. Indeed, here (crossed out in the manuscript, but by me restored and italicized) are signs of a copyist's pen: "Mais helas! il desesperoit de reussir quand' *il desespe* rencontra," etc. Is not that a copyist's repetition? Or this: "— et lui, mon mari apres tout se fit mon *mari m* domestique." And here the copyist misread the original: "Lorsque le maire entendit les noms et les *personnes* prenoms de la mariée," etc. In the manuscript personnes is crossed out, and the correct word, prenoms, is written above it.

Whoever made this copy it remains still so simple and compact that he or she cannot be charged with many embellishments. And yet it is easy to believe that some one, with that looseness of family tradition and largeness of ancestral pride so common among the Creoles, in half-knowledge and half-ignorance should have ventured aside for an instant to attribute in pure parenthesis to an ancestral De la Houssaye the premature honor of a San Domingan war; or, incited by some tradition of the old Prime Minister's intimate friendship with Madelaine's family, should have imputed a gracious attention to the wrong Count de Maurepas, or to the wrong count altogether.

I find no other theory tenable. To reject the whole matter as a forgery flies into the face of more incontestable facts than the anachronisms do. We know, from Suzanne and Françoise, without this manuscript, that there was an Alix Carpentier, daughter of a count, widow of a viscount, an *emigrée* of the Revolution, married to a Norman peasant, known to M. Gerbeau, beloved of Suzanne and Françoise, with whom they journeyed to Attakapas, and who wrote for them the history of her strange life. I hold a manuscript carefully kept by at least two generations of Françoise's descendants among their valuable private papers. It professes to be that history — a short, modest, unadorned narrative, apparently a copy of a paper of like compass, notwithstanding the evident insertion of two impossible statements whose complete omission does not disturb the narrative. I see no room to doubt that it contains the true story of a real and lovely woman.

But to come back to my attorney.

WHILE his grave negotiations were still going on, there met me one evening at my own gate a lady in black, seeking advice concerning her wish to sell to some publisher a private diary never intended for publication.

"That kind is the best," I said. "Did you write it during the late war?" I added at a guess.

"Yes."

"I suppose, then, it contains a careful record of each day's public events."

"No, I'm sorry to say —"

"Nay, don't be sorry; that lack may save it from the waste-basket." Then my heart spoke. "Ah! madam, if you had only done what no woman seems to have seen the importance of doing — written the women's side of that awful war —"

"That's just what I have done," she interrupted.

" I was a Union woman, in the Confederacy. I
could n't talk ; I had to write. I was in the siege of
Vicksburg from beginning to end."

" Leave your manuscript with me," I said. " If, on
examining it, I find I can recommend it to a publisher,
I will do so. But remember what I have already told
you — the passage of an unknown writer's work
through an older author's hands is of no benefit to it
whatever. It is a bad sign rather than a good one.
Your chances of acceptance will be at least no less
if you send this to the publishers yourself."

No, she would like me to intervene.

How my attorney friend and I took a two days'
journey by rail, reading the manuscript to each other
in the Pullman car; how a young newly married
couple next us across the aisle, pretending not to
notice, listened with all their might ; how my friend
the attorney now and then stopped to choke down
tears ; and how the young stranger opposite came at
last, with apologies, asking where this matter would
be published and under what title, I need not tell. At
length I was intercessor for a manuscript that publishers would not lightly decline. I bought it for
my little museum of true stories, at a price beyond
what I believe any magazine would have paid — an
amount that must have filled the widow's heart
with joy, but as certainly was not beyond its worth
to me. I have already contributed a part of this
manuscript to " The Century " as one of its " War
papers." But by permission it is restored here to its
original place.

JUDGE FARRAR, with whom I enjoyed a slight but valued acquaintance, stopped me one day in Carondelet street, New Orleans, saying, "I have a true story that I want you to tell. You can dress it out — "

I arrested him with a shake of the head. "Dress me no dresses. Story me no stories. There's not one of a hundred of them that does not lack something essential, for want of which they are good for naught. Keep them for after-dinner chat; but for the novelist they are good to smell, not to eat. And yet — tell me your story. I have a use for it — a cabinet of true things that have never had and shall not have a literary tool lifted up against them; virgin shells from the beach of the sea of human events. It may be I shall find a place for it there." So he told me the true story which I have called "Attalie Brouillard," because, having forgotten the woman's real name, it pleased his fancy to use that name in recounting the tale: "Attalie Brouillard." I repeated the story to a friend, a gentleman of much reading.

His reply dismayed me. "I have a faint impression," he said, "that you will find something very much like that in one of Lever's novels."

But later I thought, "Even so, what then? Good stories repeat themselves." I remembered having twice had experiences in my own life the accounts of which, when given, would have been great successes only that they were old anecdotes — great in their day, but long worn out in the club-rooms and abandoned to clergymen's reunions. The wise thing was not to find out or care whether Lever had somewhere

told something like it, but whether the story was ever
a real event in New Orleans, and, if so, to add it to my
now, to me, priceless collection. Meeting the young
judge again, I asked boldly for the story's full authen-
tication. He said promptly that the man who told
it of his own knowledge was the late Judge T. Whar-
ton Collins; that the incidents occurred about 1855,
and that Judge McCaleb could doubtless give the
name of the notary public who had been an actor in
the affair. "Let us go to his office right now," said
my obliging friend.

We went, found him, told him our errand. He remembered the story, was confident of its entire verity,
and gave a name, which, however, he begged I would
submit for verification to an aged notary public in
another street, a gentleman of the pure old Creole
type. I went to him. He heard the story through in
solemn silence. From first to last I mentioned no
name, but at the end I asked:

"Now, can you tell me the name of the notary in
that case?"

"Yes."

I felt a delicious tingling as I waited for the disclosure. He slowly said:

"Dthere eeze wan troub' 'bout dat. To *which* case
do you *riffer?* '*Cause, you know, dey got t'ree, four
case' like dat.* An' you better not mention no name,
'cause you don't want git nobody in troub', you know.
Now dthere's dthe case of ——. And dthere's dthe
case of ——. And dthere's the case of ——. *He*
had to go away; yes; 'cause when *he* make dthe dade

man make his will, he git *behine* dthe dade man in bade, an' hole 'im up in dthe bade."

I thanked him and departed, with but the one regret that the tale was true so many more times than was necessary.

IN all this collection the story of the so-called haunted house in Royal street is the only one that must ask a place in literature as partly a twice-told tale. The history of the house is known to thousands in the old French quarter, and that portion which antedates the late war was told in brief by Harriet Martineau as far back as when she wrote her book of American travel. In printing it here I fulfill an oft-repeated promise; for many a one has asked me if I would not, or, at least, why I did not, tell its dark story.

So I have inventoried my entire exhibit — save one small matter. It turned out after all that the dear old Creole lady who had sold us the ancient manuscript, finding old paper commanding so much more per ton than it ever had commanded before, raked together three or four more leaves — stray chips of her lovely little ancestress Françoise's workshop, or rather the shakings of her basket of cherished records, — to wit, three Creole African songs, which I have used elsewhere; one or two other scraps, of no value; and, finally, a long letter telling its writer's own short story — a story so tragic and so sad that I can only say pass it, if you will. It stands first be-

cause it antedates the rest. As you will see, its time
is something more than a hundred years ago. The
writing was very difficult to read, owing entirely to
the badness — mainly the softness — of the paper. I
have tried in vain to find exactly where Fort Latourette was situated. It may have had but a momentary existence in Galvez's campaign against the English. All along the Gulf shore the sites and remains
of the small forts once held by the Spaniards are
known traditionally and indiscriminately as "Spanish
Fort." When John Law, — author of that famed
Mississippi Bubble, which was in Paris what the
South Sea Bubble was in London, — failed in his
efforts at colonization on the Arkansas, his Arkansas
settlers came down the Mississippi to within some
sixty miles of New Orleans and established themselves
in a colony at first called the *Côte Allemande* (German Coast), and later, owing to its prosperity, the
Côte d'Or, or Golden Coast. Thus the banks of the
Mississippi became known on the Rhine, a goodly
part of our Louisiana Creoles received a German tincture, and the father and the aunt of Suzanne and
Françoise were not the only Alsatians we shall meet
in these wild stories of wild times in Louisiana.

THE YOUNG AUNT WITH WHITE HAIR.

1782.

THE date of this letter — I hold it in one hand as I write, and for the first time noticed that it has never in its hundred years been sealed or folded, but only doubled once, lightly, and rolled in the hand, just as the young Spanish officer might have carried it when he rode so hard to bear it to its destination — its date is the last year but one of our American Revolution. France, Spain, and the thirteen colonies were at war with Great Britain, and the Indians were on both sides.

Galvez, the heroic young governor of Louisiana, had just been decorated by his king and made a count for taking the forts at Manchac, Baton Rouge, Natchez, and Mobile, and besieging and capturing the strong-hold of Pensacola, thus winning all west Florida, from the Mississippi to the Appalachicola, for Spain. But this vast wilderness was not made safe; Fort Pan-mure (Natchez) changed hands twice, and the land was full of Indians, partly hireling friends and partly enemies. The waters about the Bahamas and the Greater and Lesser Antilles were fields for the move-

ments of hostile fleets, corsairs, and privateers. Yet
the writer of this letter was tempted to run the
gauntlet of these perils, expecting, if all went well,
to arrive in Louisiana in midsummer.

"How many times," says the memorandum of her
brother's now aged great-granddaughter,—"How many
times during my childhood has been told me the story
of my aunt Louise. It was not until several years after
the death of my grandmother that, on examining the
contents of the basket which she had given me, I
found at the bottom of a little black-silk bag the letter
written by my grand-aunt to her brother, my own
ancestor. Frankly, I doubt that my grandmother had
intended to give it to me, so highly did she prize it,
though it was very difficult to read. The orthography
is perfect; the difficulty is all owing to the paper and,
moreover, to the situation of the poor wounded suf-
ferer." It is in French:

> *To my brother mister Pierre Bossier.*
> *In the parish[1] of St. James.*
>
> Fort Latourette,
> The 5 August, 1782.

My Good Dear Brother: Ah! how shall I tell
you the frightful position in which I am placed! I
would that I were dead! I seem to be the prey of a
horrible nightmare! O Pierre! my brother! hasten
with all speed to me. When you left Germany, your
little sister was a blooming girl, very beautiful in

[1] County.

your eyes, very happy! and to-day! ah! to-day, my brother, come see for yourself.

After having received your letter, not only my husband and I decided to leave our village and go to join you, but twelve of our friends united with us, and the 10 May, 1782, we quitted Strasbourg on the little vessel *North Star* [Étoile du Nord],[1] which set sail for New Orleans, where you had promised to come to meet us. Let me tell you the names of my fellow-travelers. O brother! what courage I need to write this account: first my husband, Leonard Cheval, and my son Pierre, poor little angel who was not yet two years old! Fritz Newman, his wife Nina, and their three children; Irwin Vizey; William Hugo, his wife, and their little daughter; Jacques Lewis, his daughter, and their son Henry. We were full of hope: we hoped to find fortune in this new country of which you spoke with so much enthusiasm. How in that moment did I bless my parents, and you my brother, for the education you had procured me. You know how good a musician my Leonard was, and our intention was on arriving to open a boarding-school in New Orleans; in your last letter you encouraged the project — all of us, movables with us, all our savings, everything we owned in this world.

This paper is very bad, brother, but the captain of the fort says it is all he has; and I write lying down, I am so uncomfortable.

[1] If this was an English ship, — for her crew was English and her master's name seems to have been Andrews, — she was probably not under British colors. — TRANSLATOR.

The earlier days of the voyage passed without accident, without disturbance, but often Leonard spoke
to me of his fears. The vessel was old, small, and
very poorly supplied. The captain was a drunkard
[here the writer attempted to turn the sheet and
write on the back of it], who often incapacitated himself with his first officers [word badly blotted]; and
then the management of the vessel fell to the mate,
who was densely ignorant. Moreover, we knew that
the seas were infested with pirates. I must stop, the
paper is too bad.

THE captain has brought me another sheet.

Our uneasiness was great. Often we emigrants assembled on deck and told each other our anxieties.
Living on the frontier of France, we spoke German
and French equally well; and when the sailors heard
us, they, who spoke only English, swore at us, accused
us of plotting against them, and called us Saurkrouts.
At such times I pressed my child to my heart and
drew nearer to Leonard, more dead than alive. A
whole month passed in this constant anguish. At its
close, fevers broke out among us, and we discovered,
to our horror, there was not a drop of medicine on
board. We had them lightly, some of us, but only a
few; and [bad blot] Newman's son and William Hugo's
little daughter died, . . . and the poor mother soon
followed her child. My God! but it was sad. And
the provisions ran low, and the captain refused to turn
back to get more.

One evening, when the captain, his lieutenant, and

two other officers were shut in their cabin drinking,
the mate, of whom I had always such fear, presented
himself before us surrounded by six sailors armed,
like himself, to the teeth, and ordered us to surrender
all the money we had. To resist would have been
madness; we had to yield. They searched our trunks
and took away all that we possessed: they left us
nothing, absolutely nothing. Ah! why am I not
dead? Profiting by the absence of their chiefs they
seized the [or some — the word is blotted] boats and
abandoned us to our fate. When, the next day, the
captain appeared on deck quite sober, and saw the
cruelty of our plight, he told us, to console us, that
we were very near the mouth of the Mississippi, and
that within two days we should be at New Orleans.
Alas! all that day passed without seeing any land,[1]
but towards evening the vessel, after incredible efforts,
had just come to a stop — at what I supposed should
be the mouth of the river. We were so happy to have
arrived that we begged Captain Andrieux to sail all
night. He replied that our men, who had worked all
day in place of the sailors, were tired and did not
understand at all sufficiently the handling of a vessel
to sail by night. He wanted to get drunk again. As
in fact our men were worn out, we went, all of us, to
bed. O great God! give me strength to go on. All
at once we were awakened by horrible cries, not human sounds: we thought ourselves surrounded by
ferocious beasts. We poor women clasped our chil-

[1] The treeless marshes of the Delta would be very slow coming into
view. — TRANSLATOR.

dren to our breasts, while our husbands armed themselves with whatever came to hand and dashed forward to meet the danger. My God! my God! we saw
ourselves hemmed in by a multitude of savages yelling and lifting over us their horrible arms, grasping
hatchets, knives, and tomahawks. The first to fall was
my husband, my dear Leonard; all, except Irwin Vizey,
who had the fortune to jump into the water unseen,
all were massacred by the monsters. One Indian tore
my child from me while another fastened my arms
behind my back. In response to my cries, to my
prayers, the monster who held my son took him by one
foot and, swinging him several times around, shattered
his head against the wall. And I live to write these
horrors! . . . I fainted, without doubt, for on opening
my eyes I found I was on land [blot], firmly fastened
to a stake. Nina Newman and Kate Lewis were
fastened as I was: the latter was covered with blood
and appeared to be dangerously wounded. About
daylight three Indians came looking for them and
took them God knows where! Alas! I have never
since heard of either of them or their children.

I remained fastened to the stake in a state of delirium, which saved me doubtless from the horrors of
my situation. I recall one thing: that is, having seen
those savages eat human flesh, the members of a child
— at least it seemed so.   Ah! you see plainly I must
have been mad to have seen all that without dying!
They had stripped me of my clothing and I remained
exposed, half naked, to a July sun and to clouds of
mosquitoes. An Indian who spoke French informed

me that, as I was young and fat, they were reserving
me for the dinner of the chief, who was to arrive
next day. In a moment I was dead with terror; in
that instant I lost all feeling. I had become indifferent to all. I saw nothing, I heard nothing. Towards
evening one of the sub-chiefs approached and gave me
some water in a gourd. I drank without knowing
what I did; thereupon he set himself to examine me
as the butcher examines the lamb that he is about to
kill; he seemed to find me worthy to be served on the
table of the head-chief, but as he was hungry and did
not wish to wait [blot], he drew from its sheath the
knife that he carried at his belt and before I had had
time to guess what he intended to do [Enough to
say, in place of literal translation, that the savage,
from the outside of her right thigh, flayed off a large
piece of her flesh.] It must be supposed that I again
lost consciousness. When I came to myself, I was
lying some paces away from the stake of torture on a
heap of cloaks, and a soldier was kneeling beside me,
while I was surrounded by about a hundred others.
The ground was strewed with dead Indians. I learned
later that Vizey had reached the woods and by chance
had stumbled into Fort Latourette, full of troops.
Without loss of time, the brave soldiers set out, and
arrived just in time to save me. A physician dressed
my wound, they put me into an ambulance and brought
me away to Fort Latourette, where I still am. A
fierce fever took possession of me. My generous protectors did not know to whom to write; they watched
over me and showed every care imaginable.

Now that I am better, I write you, my brother, and close with these words : I await you ! make all haste !
Your sister,   LOUISA CHEVAL.

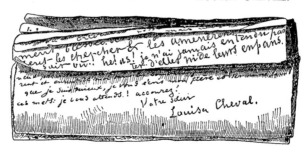

"MY grandmother," resumes the memorandum of the Creole great-grandniece, "had often read this letter, and had recounted to me the incidents that followed its reception. She was then but three years old, but as her aunt lived three years in her (*i.e.,* the aunt's) brother's family, my grandmother had known her, and described her to me as a young woman with white hair and walking with a staff. It was with difficulty that she used her right leg. My great-grandfather used to tell his children that his sister Louise had been blooming and gay, and spoke especially of her beautiful blonde hair. A few hours had sufficed to change it to snow, and on the once charming countenance of the poor invalid to stamp an expression of grief and despair.

"It was Lieutenant Rosello, a young Spaniard, who came on horseback from Fort Latourette to carry to my great-grandfather his sister's letter. . . . Not to

lose a moment, he [the brother] began, like Lieutenant
Rosello, the journey on horseback, procuring a large
ambulance as he passed through New Orleans. . . .
He did all he could to lighten the despair of his poor
sister. . . . All the members of the family lavished
upon her every possible care and attention; but alas!
the blow she had received was too terrible. She
lingered three years, and at the end of that time
passed peaceably away in the arms of her brother, the
last words on her lips being ' Leonard!—my child!'"

So WE make way for the bright and happy story of
how Françoise made Evangeline's journey through
the dark wilds of Atchafalaya.

THE ADVENTURES OF FRANÇOISE
AND SUZANNE.

1795.

YEARS passed by. Our war of the Revolution was over. The Indians of Louisiana and Florida were all greedy, smiling gift-takers of his Catholic Majesty. So were some others not Indians; and the Spanish governors of Louisiana, scheming with them for the acquisition of Kentucky and the regions intervening, had allowed an interprovincial commerce to spring up. Flatboats and barges came floating down the Mississippi past the plantation home where little Suzanne and Françoise were growing up to womanhood. Many of the immigrants who now came to Louisiana were the royalist *noblesse* flying from the horrors of the French Revolution. Governor Carondelet was strengthening his fortifications around New Orleans; for Creole revolutionists had slipped away to Kentucky and were there plotting an armed descent in flatboats upon his little capital, where the rabble were singing the terrible songs of bloody Paris. Agents of the Revolution had come from France and so "contaminated," as he says, "the greater part of the province" that he kept order only "at the cost of sleepless nights, by frightening some, punishing others, and driving several out of the colony." It looks as though Suzanne had caught a touch of dis-relish for *les aristocrates*, whose necks the songs of the day were promising to the lampposts. To add to all these commotions, a hideous revolution had swept over San Domingo; the slaves in Louisiana had heard of it, insurrection was feared, and at length, in 1794, when Susanne was seventeen and Françoise fifteen, it broke out on the Mississippi no great matter over a day's ride from their own home, and twenty-three blacks were gibbeted singly at intervals all the way down by their father's plantation and on to New Orleans, and were left swinging in the weather to insure the peace and felicity of the `land. Two other matters are all we need notice for the ready compre-hension of Françoise's story. Immigration was knock-ing at every gate of the province, and citizen Étienne de Boré had just made himself forever famous in the history of Louisiana by producing merchantable sugar; land was going to be valuable, even back on the wild prairies of Opelousas and Attakapas, where, twenty years before, the Acadians, — the cousins of Evange-line, — wandering from far Nova Scotia, had settled. Such was the region and such were the times when it began to be the year 1795.

By good fortune one of the undestroyed fragments of Françoise's own manuscript is its first page. She was already a grandmother forty-three years old when in 1822 she wrote the tale she had so often told. Part of the dedication to her only daughter and namesake — one line, possibly two — has been torn off, leaving only the words, "ma fille unique a la grasse [meaning 'grace'] de dieu [sic]," over her signature and the date, "14 Julet [sic], 1822."

I.

THE TWO SISTERS.

It is to give pleasure to my dear daughter Fannie and to her children that I write this journey. I shall be well satisfied if I can succeed in giving them this pleasure: by the grace of God, Amen.

Papa, Mr. Pierre Bossier, planter of St. James parish, had been fifteen days gone to the city (New Orleans) in his skiff with two rowers, Louis and Baptiste, when, returning, he embraced us all, gave us some caramels which he had in his pockets, and announced that he counted on leaving us again in four or five days to go to Attakapas. He had long been speaking of going there. Papa and mamma were German, and papa loved to travel. When he first came to Louisiana it was with no expectation of staying. But here he saw mamma; he loved her, married her, and bought a very fine plantation, where he cultivated indigo. You know they blue clothes with that drug, and dye cottonade and other things. There we, their eight children, were born. . . .

When my father used to go to New Orleans he went in his skiff, with a canopy over his head to keep off the ma fille unique, a la grasse de dieu

Françoise Palin de Bossier

ce 14 Julled - 1822.

C' pour faire du plisire a ma chaire
fille Fanniel - a ses penfons que je
veux ecrir se voyage je selug bien son
tente si je fait rendrig a leur fair
ce plisire a la grasse du bon dieu
cause soit il - depuid - 18 fois papa

PART OF FRANÇOIS'S FIRST PAGE.

sun, and two rowers, who sang as they rowed. Sometimes papa took me with him, and it was very entertaining. We would pass the nights of our voyage at the houses of papa's friends [des zami de papa]. Sometimes mamma would come, and Suzanne always — always. She was the daughter next older than I. She barely missed being a boy. She was eighteen years of age, went hunting with our father, was skillful with a gun, and swam like a fish. Papa called her "my son." You must understand the two boys were respectively but two years and three months old, and papa, who greatly desired a son, had easily made one of Suzanne. My father had brought a few books with him to Louisiana, and among them, you may well suppose, were several volumes of travel. For myself, I rarely touched them; but they were the only books that Suzanne read. And you may well think, too, that my father had no sooner spoken of his intention than Suzanne cried:

"I am going with you, am I not, papa?"

"Naturally," replied my father; "and Françoise shall go also."

Françoise — that was I; poor child of sixteen, who had but six months before quitted the school-bench, and totally unlike my sister — blonde, where Suzanne was dark; timid, even cowardly, while she had the hardihood and courage of a young lioness; ready to cry at sight of a wounded bird, while she, gun in hand, brought down as much game as the most skillful hunter.

I exclaimed at my father's speech. I had heard

there were many Indians in Attakapas; the name means man-eaters. I have a foolish terror of Indians, and a more reasonable one for man-eaters. But papa and Suzanne mocked at my fears; and as, after all, I burned with desire for the journey, it was decided that I should go with them.

Necessarily we wanted to know how we were to go — whether we should travel by skiff, and how many negroes and negresses would go with us. For you see, my daughter, young people in 1795 were exactly what they are in 1822; they could do nothing by themselves, but must have a domestic to dress and undress them. Especially in traveling, where one had to take clothes out of trunks and put them back again, assistance became an absolute necessity. Think, then, of our astonishment, of our vexation, when papa assured us that he would not take a single slave; that my sister and I would be compelled to help each other, and that the skiff would remain behind, tied up at the landing where it then lay.

"But explain yourself, Papa, I beg of you," cried Suzanne, with her habitual petulance.

"That is what I am trying to do," said he. "If you will listen in silence, I will give you all the explanation you want."

Here, my daughter, to save time, I will borrow my father's speech and tell of the trip he had made to New Orleans; how he had there found means to put into execution his journey to Attakapas, and the companions that were to accompany him.

II.

MAKING UP THE EXPEDITION.

In 1795 New Orleans was nothing but a mere market town. The cathedral, the convent of the Ursulines, five or six cafés, and about a hundred houses were all of it.[1] Can you believe, there were but two dry-goods stores! And what fabulous prices we had to pay! Pins twenty dollars a paper. Poor people and children had to make shift with thorns of orange and *amourette* [honey locust?]. A needle cost fifty cents, very indifferent stockings five dollars a pair, and other things accordingly.

On the levee was a little pothouse of the lowest sort; yet from that unclean and smoky hole was destined to come one of the finest fortunes in Louisiana. They called the proprietor "Père la Chaise."[2] He was a little old marten-faced man, always busy and smiling, who every year laid aside immense profits. Along the crazy walls extended a few rough shelves covered with bottles and decanters. Three planks placed on boards formed the counter, with Père la Chaise always behind it. There were two or three small tables, as many

---

[1] An extreme underestimate, easy for a girl to make of a scattered town hidden among gardens and groves. — TRANSLATOR.

[2] Without doubting the existence of the *cabaret* and the nickname, the De la Chaise estate, I think, came from a real De la Chaise, true nephew of Pere la Chaise, the famous confessor of Louis XIV. The nephew was royal commissary under Bienville, and one of the worthiest fathers of the colony of Louisiana. — TRANSLATOR.

chairs, and one big wooden bench. Here gathered the city's working-class, and often among them one might find a goodly number of the city's élite; for the wine and the beer of the old *cabaretier* were famous, and one could be sure in entering there to hear all the news told and discussed.

By day the place was quiet, but with evening it became tumultuous. Père la Chaise, happily, did not lose his head; he found means to satisfy all, to smooth down quarrels without calling in the police, to get rid of drunkards, and to make delinquents pay up.

My father knew the place, and never failed to pay it a visit when he went to New Orleans. Poor, dear father! he loved to talk as much as to travel. Père la Chaise was acquainted with him. One evening papa entered, sat down at one of the little tables, and bade Père la Chaise bring a bottle of his best wine. The place was already full of people, drinking, talking, and singing. A young man of twenty-six or twenty-seven entered almost timidly and sat down at the table where my father was — for he saw that all the other places were occupied — and ordered a half-bottle of cider. He was a Norman gardener. My father knew him by sight; he had met him here several times without speaking to him. You recognized the peasant at once; and yet his exquisite neatness, the gentleness of his face, distinguished him from his kind. Joseph Carpentier was dressed[1] in a very ordinary gray woolen coat; but his coarse shirt

[1] In all likelihood described here as seen by the writer herself later, on the journey. — TRANSLATOR.

was very white, and his hair, when he took off his broad-brimmed hat, was well combed and glossy.

As Carpentier was opening his bottle a second frequenter entered the *cabaret.* This was a man of thirty or thirty-five, with strong features and the frame of a Hercules. An expression of frankness and gayety overspread his sunburnt face. Cottonade pantaloons, stuffed into a pair of dirty boots, and a *vareuse* of the same stuff made up his dress. His vareuse, unbuttoned, showed his breast, brown and hairy; and a horrid cap with long hair covered, without concealing, a mass of red locks that a comb had never gone through. A long whip, the stock of which he held in his hand, was coiled about his left arm. He advanced to the counter and asked for a glass of brandy. He was a drayman named John Gordon — an Irishman.

But, strange, John Gordon, glass in hand, did not drink; Carpentier, with his fingers round the neck of the bottle, failed to pour his cider; and my father himself, his eyes attracted to another part of the room, forgot his wine. Every one was looking at an individual gesticulating and haranguing in the middle of the place, to the great amusement of all. My father recognized him at first sight. He was an Italian about the age of Gordon; short, thick-set, powerful, swarthy, with the neck of a bull and hair as black as ebony. He was telling rapidly, with strong gestures, in an almost incomprehensible mixture of Spanish, English, French, and Italian, the story of a hunting party that he had made up five years before. This was Mario Carlo. A Neapolitan

by birth, he had for several years worked as a black-
smith on the plantation of one of our neighbors, M.
Alphonse Perret.   Often papa had heard him tell of
this hunt, for nothing could be more amusing than to
listen to Carlo.   Six young men, with Carlo as sailor
and cook, had gone on a two-months' expedition into
the country of the Attakapas.

"Yes," said the Italian, in conclusion, "game never
failed us; deer, turkeys, ducks, snipe, two or three
bears a week.   But the sublimest thing was the rich
land.   Ah! one must see it to believe it.   Plains and
forests full of animals, lakes and bayous full of fish.
Ah! fortune is there. · For five years I have dreamed,
I have worked, with but one object in view; and to-
day the end is reached.   I am ready to go.   I want
only two companions to aid me in the long journey,
and those I have come to look for here."

John Gordon stepped forward, laid a hand upon the
speaker's shoulder, and said:

"My friend, I am your man."

Mario Carlo seized the hand and shook it with all
his force.

"You will not repent the step.   But " — turning
again to the crowd — " we want one more."

Joseph Carpentier rose slowly and advanced to the
two men.   "Comrades, I will be your companion if
you will accept me."

Before separating, the three drank together and
appointed to meet the next day at the house of
Gordon, the Irishman.

When my father saw Gordon and Carpentier leave

the place, he placed his hand on Mario's shoulder and said in Italian, " My boy, I want to talk with you."

At that time, as now, parents were very scrupulous as to the society into which they introduced their children, especially their daughters; and papa knew of a certain circumstance in Carlo's life to which my mother might greatly object. But he knew the man had an honest and noble heart. He passed his arm into the Italian's and drew him to the inn where my father was stopping, and to his room. Here he learned from Mario that he had bought one of those great barges that bring down provisions from the West, and which, when unloaded, the owners count themselves lucky to sell at any reasonable price. When my father proposed to Mario to be taken as a passenger the poor devil's joy knew no bounds; but it disappeared when papa added that he should take his two daughters with him.

The trouble was this: Mario was taking with him in his flatboat his wife and his four children; his wife and four children were simply — mulattoes. However, then as now, we hardly noticed those things, and the idea never entered our minds to inquire into the conduct of our slaves. Suzanne and I had known Celeste, Mario's wife, very well before her husband bought her. She had been the maid of Marianne Perret, and on great occasions Marianne had sent her to us to dress our hair and to prepare our toilets. We were therefore enchanted to learn that she would be with us on board the flatboat, and that papa had engaged her services in place of the attendants we had to leave behind.

It was agreed that for one hundred dollars Mario

Carlo would receive all three of us as passengers, that he would furnish a room simply but comfortably, that papa would share this room with us, that Mario would supply our table, and that his wife would serve as maid and laundress. It remained to be seen now whether our other fellow-travelers were married, and, if so, what sort of creatures their wives were.

[THE next day the four intended travelers met at Gordon's house. Gordon had a wife, Maggie, and a son, Patrick, aged twelve, as unlovely in outward aspect as were his parents. Carpentier, who showed himself even more plainly than on the previous night a man of native refinement, confessed to a young wife without offspring. Mario told his story of love and alliance with one as fair of face as he, and whom only cruel law forbade him to call wife and compelled him to buy his children; and told the story so well that at its close the father of Françoise silently grasped the narrator's hand, and Carpentier, reaching across the table where they sat, gave his, saying:

"You are an honest man, Monsieur Carlo."

"Will your wife think so?" asked the Italian.

"My wife comes from a country where there are no prejudices of race."

Françoise takes the pains to say of this part of the story that it was not told her and Suzanne at this time, but years afterward, when they were themselves wives and mothers. When, on the third day, her father saw Carpentier's wife at the Norman peasant's lodgings, he was greatly surprised at her appearance

and manner, and so captivated by them that he proposed that their two parties should make one at table
during the projected voyage — a proposition gratefully
accepted. Then he left New Orleans for his plantation home, intending to return immediately, leaving
his daughters in St. James to prepare for the journey
and await the arrival of the flatboat, which must pass
their home on its way to the distant wilds of Attakapas.]

III.

THE EMBARKATION.

You see, my dear child, at that time one post-office
served for three parishes : St. James, St. John the
Baptist, and St. Charles. It was very far from us, at
the extremity of St. John the Baptist, and the mail
came there on the first of each month.

We had to pay — though the price was no object —
fifty cents postage on a letter. My father received
several journals, mostly European. There was only one
paper, French and Spanish, published in New Orleans —
"The Gazette." [1] To send to the post-office was an
affair of state. Our father, you see, had not time to
write; he was obliged to come to us himself. But such
journeys were a matter of course in those days.

"And above all things, my children," said my father,
"don't have too much baggage."

[1] Another error easy to make. For " Gazette " read " Moniteur "; " The
Gazette " appeared a little later. — TRANSLATOR.

I should not have thought of rebelling; but Suzanne raised loud cries, saying it was an absolute necessity that we go with papa to New Orleans, so as not to find ourselves on our journey without traveling-dresses, new neckerchiefs, and a number of things. In vain did poor papa endeavor to explain that we were going into a desert worse than Arabia; Suzanne put her two hands to her ears and would hear nothing, until, weary of strife, poor papa yielded.

Our departure being decided upon, he wished to start even the very next day; and while we were instructing our sisters Elinore and Marie concerning some trunks that we should leave behind us, and which they must pack and have ready for the flatboat, papa recommended to mamma a great slaughter of fowls, etc., and especially to have ready for embarkation two of our best cows. Ah! in those times if the planter wished to live well he had to raise everything himself, and the poultry yard and the dairy were something curious to see. Dozens of slaves were kept busy in them constantly. When my mother had raised two thousand chickens, besides turkeys, ducks, geese, guinea-fowls, and pea-fowls, she said she had lost her crop.[1] And the quantity of butter and cheese! And all this without counting the sauces, the jellies, the preserves, the gherkins, the syrups, the brandied fruits. And not a ham, not a chicken, not a pound of butter was sold; all was served on the master's table, or, very often, given to those who stood in need of them.

---

[1] The translator feels constrained to say that he was not on the spot.

Where, now, can you find such profusion? Ah! commerce has destroyed industry.

The next day, after kissing mamma and the children, we got into the large skiff with papa and three days later stepped ashore in New Orleans. We remained there a little over a week, preparing our traveling-dresses. Despite the admonitions of papa, we went to the fashionable modiste of the day, Madame Cinthelia Lefranc, and ordered for each a suit that cost one hundred and fifty dollars. The costume was composed of a petticoat of *camayeu*, very short, caught up in puffs on the side by a profusion of ribbons; and a very long-pointed black velvet jacket (*casaquin*), laced in the back with gold and trimmed on the front with several rows of gilt buttons. The sleeves stopped at the elbows and were trimmed with lace. Now, my daughter, do you know what camayeu was? You now sometimes see an imitation of it in door and window curtains. It was a stuff of great fineness, yet resembling not a little the unbleached cotton of to-day, and over which were spread very brilliant designs of prodigious size. For example, Suzanne's petticoat showed bunches of great radishes — not the short kind — surrounded by long, green leaves and tied with a yellow cord; while on mine were roses as big as a baby's head, interlaced with leaves and buds and gathered into bouquets graced with a blue ribbon. It was ten dollars an ell; but, as the petticoats were very short, six ells was enough for each. At that time real hats were unknown. For driving or for evening they placed on top of the high, powdered hair what they called a *catogan*, a little bonnet of gauze or lace trimmed with ribbons; and during the day a sunbonnet of silk or velvet. You can guess that neither Suzanne nor I, in spite of papa's instructions, forgot these.

Our traveling-dresses were gray *cirsacas,* — the skirt all one, short, without puffs; the jacket coming up high and with long sleeves, — a sunbonnet of cirsacas, blue stockings, embroidered handkerchief or blue cravat about the neck, and high-heeled shoes.

As soon as Celeste heard of our arrival in New Orleans she hastened to us. She was a good creature; humble, respectful, and always ready to serve. She was an excellent cook and washer, and, what we still more prized, a lady's maid and hairdresser of the first order. My sister and I were glad to see her, and overwhelmed her with questions about Carlo, their children, their plans, and our traveling companions.

"Ah! Momzelle Suzanne, the little Madame Carpentier seems to me a fine lady, ever so genteel; but the Irish woman! Ah! *grand Dieu!* she puts me in mind of a soldier. I'm afraid of her. She smokes — she swears — she carries a pistol, like a man."

At last the 15th of May came, and papa took us on board the flatboat and helped us to find our way to our apartment. If my father had allowed Carlo, he would have ruined himself in furnishing our room; but papa stopped him and directed it himself. The flatboat had been divided into four chambers. These were covered by a slightly arching deck, on which the boat was managed by the moving of immense sweeps that sent her forward. The room in the stern, surrounded by a sort of balcony, which Monsieur Carpentier himself had made, belonged to him and his wife; then came ours, then that of Celeste and her family, and the one at the bow was the Irishwoman's. Carlo and Gordon had crammed the provisions, tools, carts, and plows into the corners of their respective apartments. In the room which our father was to share with us he had had Mario make two wooden frames mounted on feet. These were our beds, but they were supplied with good bedding and very white sheets. A large cypress table, on which we saw a pile of books and our workboxes; a washstand, also of cypress, but well furnished and surmounted by a mirror; our trunks in a corner; three rocking-chairs — this was all our furniture. There was neither carpet nor curtain.

All were on board except the Carpentier couple. Suzanne was all anxiety to see the Irishwoman. Poor Suzanne! how distressed she was not to be able to speak English! So, while I was taking off my *capotte* — as the sun-bonnet of that day was called — and smoothing my hair at the glass, she had already tossed her capotte upon papa's bed and sprung up the ladder that led to the deck. (Each room had one.) I followed a little later and had the satisfaction of seeing Madame Margaretto Gordon, commonly called "Maggie" by her husband and "Maw" by her son Patrick. She was seated on a coil of rope, her son on the boards at her feet. An enormous dog crouched beside them, with his head against Maggie's knee. The mother and son were surprisingly clean. Maggie had on a simple brown calico dress and an apron of blue ticking. A big red kerchief was crossed on her breast and its twin brother covered her well combed and greased black hair. On her feet were blue stockings and heavy leather shoes. The blue ticking shirt and pantaloons and waistcoat of Master Pat were so clean that they shone; his black cap covered his hair — as well combed as his mother's; but he was barefooted. Gordon, Mario, and Celeste's eldest son, aged thirteen, were busy about the deck; and papa, his cigar in his mouth and his hands in his pockets, stood looking out on the levee. I sat down on one of the rough benches that had been placed here and there, and presently my sister came and sat beside me.

"Madame Carpentier seems to be a laggard," she said. She was burning to see the arrival of her whom we had formed the habit of calling "the little French peasant."

[PRESENTLY Suzanne begins shooting bonbons at little Patrick, watching the effect out of the corners of her eyes, and by and by gives that smile, all her own, — to which, says Françoise, all flesh invariably surrendered, — and so became dumbly acquainted; while Carlo was beginning to swear "fit to raise the dead," writes the memoirist, at the tardiness of the Norman pair. But just then —]

A CARRIAGE drove up to within a few feet of our *cha-land* and Joseph Carpentier alighted, paid the driver, and lifted from it one so delicate, pretty, and small that you might take her at first glance for a child of ten years. Suzanne and I had risen quickly and came and leaned over the balustrade. To my mortification my sister had passed one arm around the waist of the little Irishman and held one of his hands in hers. Suzanne uttered a cry of astonishment. "Look, look, Françoise!" But I was looking, with eyes wide with astonishment.

The gardener's wife had alighted, and with her little gloved hand shook out and re-arranged her toilet. That toilet, very simple to the eyes of Madame Carpentier, was what petrified us with astonishment. I am going to describe it to you, my daughter.

We could not see her face, for her hood of blue silk, trimmed with a light white fur, was covered with a veil of white lace that entirely concealed her features. Her traveling-dress, like ours, was of cirsacas, but ours was cotton, while hers was silk, in broad rays of gray and blue; and as the weather was a little cool that morning, she had exchanged the unfailing casaquin for a sort of *camail* to match the dress, and trimmed, like the capotte, with a line of white fur. Her petticoat was very short, lightly puffed on the sides, and ornamented only with two very long pockets trimmed like the camail. Below the folds of the robe were two Cinderella feet in blue silk stockings and black velvet slippers. It was not only the material of this toilet that astonished us, but the way in which it was made.

"Maybe she is a modiste. Who knows?" whispered Suzanne.

Another thing: Madame Carpentier wore a veil and gloves, two things of which we had heard but which we had never seen. Madame Ferrand had mentioned them, but said that they sold for their weight in gold in Paris, and she had not dared import them, for fear she could not sell them in Louisiana. And here was the wife of a laboring gardener, who avowed himself possessor of but two thousand francs, dressed like a duchess and with veil and gloves!

I could but notice with what touching care Joseph assisted his wife on board. He led her straight to her room, and quickly rejoined us on deck to put himself at the disposition of his associates. He explained to Mario his delay, caused by the difficulty of finding a carriage; at which Carlo lifted his shoulders and grimaced. Joseph added that madame — I noticed that he rarely called her Alix — was rather tired, and would keep her room until dinner time. Presently our heavy craft was under way.

Pressing against the long sweeps, which it required a herculean strength to move, were seen on one side Carlo and his son Celestino, or 'Tino, and on the other Joseph and Gordon. It moved slowly; so slowly that it gave the effect of a great tortoise.

IV.

ALIX CARPENTIER.

TOWARDS noon we saw Celeste come on deck with her second son, both carrying baskets full of plates, dishes, covers, and a tablecloth. You remember I have often told you of an awning stretched at the stern of the flatboat? We found that in fine weather our dining-room was to be under this. There was no table; the cloth was simply spread on the deck, and those who ate had to sit *à la Turque* or take their plates on their knees. The Irish family ate in their room. Just as we were drawing around our repast Madame Carpentier, on her husband's arm, came up on deck.

Dear little Alix! I see you yet as I saw you then. And here, twenty-seven years after our parting, I have before me the medallion you gave me, and look tenderly on your dear features, my friend!

She had not changed her dress; only she had replaced her camail with a scarf of blue silk about her neck and shoulders and had removed her gloves and *capuche*. Her rich chestnut hair, unpowdered, was combed back *à la Chinoise*, and the long locks that descended upon her shoulders were tied by a broad blue ribbon forming a rosette on the forepart of her head. She wore no jewelry except a pearl at each ear and her wedding ring. Suzanne, who always saw everything, remarked afterward that Madame Carpentier wore two.

"As for her earrings," she added, "they are nothing great. Marianne has some as fine, that cost, I think, ten dollars."

Poor Suzanne, a judge of jewelry! Madame Carpentier's earrings were two great pearls, worth at least two hundred dollars. Never have I met another so charming, so lovely, as Alix Carpentier. Her every movement was grace. She moved, spoke, smiled, and in all things acted differently from all the women I had ever met until then. She made one think she had lived in a world all unlike ours; and withal she was simple, sweet, good, and to love her seemed the most natural thing on earth. There was nothing extraordinary in her beauty; the charm was in her intelligence and her goodness.

Maggie, the Irishwoman, was very taciturn. She never mingled with us, nor spoke to any one except Suzanne, and to her in monosyllables only when addressed. You would see her sometimes sitting alone at the bow of the boat, sewing, knitting, or saying her beads. During this last occupation her eyes never quitted Alix. One would say it was to her she addressed her prayers; and one day, when she saw my regard fixed upon Alix, she said to me:

"It does me good to look at her; she must look like the Virgin Mary."

Her little form, so graceful and delicate, had, however, one slight defect; but this was hidden under the folds of her robe or of the scarf that she knew how to arrange with such grace. One shoulder was a trifle higher than the other.

After having greeted my father, whom she already knew, she turned to us, hesitated a moment, and then, her two little hands extended, and with a most charming smile, she advanced, first to me and then to Suzanne, and embraced us both as if we had been old acquaintances. And from that moment we were good friends.

It had been decided that the boat should not travel by night, notwithstanding the assurance of Carlo, who had a map of Attakapas. But in the Mississippi there was no danger; and as papa was pressed to reach our plantation, we traveled all that first night.

The next day Alix — she required us to call her by that name — invited us to visit her in her room. Suzanne and I could not withhold a cry of surprise as we entered the little chamber. (Remember one thing: papa took nothing from home, not knowing even by what means we should return; but the Carpentiers were going for good and taking everything.) Joseph had had the rough walls whitewashed. A cheap carpet — but high-priced in those times — of bright colors covered the floor; a very low French bed occupied one corner, and from a sort of dais escaped the folds of an embroidered bobbinet mosquito-bar. It was the first mosquito-bar of that kind we had ever seen. Alix explained that she had made it from the curtains of the same bed, and that both bed and curtains she had brought with her from England. New mystery!

Beside the bed a walnut dressing-table and mirror, opposite to it a washstand, at the bed's foot a *priedieu,*

a center-table, three chairs — these were all the furniture; but [an enumeration follows of all manner of
pretty feminine belongings, in crystal, silver, gold,
with a picture of the crucifixion and another of the
Virgin]. On the shelves were a rich box of colors,
several books, and some portfolios of music. From a
small peg hung a guitar.

But Suzanne was not satisfied. Her gaze never
left an object of unknown form enveloped in green
serge. Alix noticed, laughed, rose, and, lifting the
covering, said:

"This is my harp, Suzanne; later I will play it for
you."

The second evening and those that followed, papa,
despite Carlo's representation and the magnificent
moonlight, opposed the continuation of the journey
by night; and it was not until the morning of the
fifth day that we reached St. James.

You can fancy the joy with which we were received
at the plantation. We had but begun our voyage,
and already my mother and sisters ran to us with
extended arms as though they had not seen us for
years. Needless to say, they were charmed with
Alix; and when after dinner we had to say a last
adieu to the loved ones left behind, we boarded the
flatboat and left the plantation amid huzzas,[1] waving
handkerchiefs, and kisses thrown from finger-tips. No
one wept, but in saying good-bye to my father, my
mother asked:

---

[1] According to a common habit of the Southern slaves. — TRANSLATOR.

"Pierre, how are you going to return?"

"Dear wife, by the mercy of God all things are possible to the man with his pocket full of money."

During the few days that we passed on the Mississippi each day was like the one before. We sat on the deck and watched the slow swinging of the long sweeps, or read, or embroidered, or in the chamber of Alix listened to her harp or guitar; and at the end of another week, we arrived at Plaquemine.

V.

DOWN BAYOU PLAQUEMINE — THE FIGHT WITH WILD NATURE.

PLAQUEMINE was composed of a church, two stores, as many drinking-shops, and about fifty cabins, one of which was the court-house. Here lived a multitude of Catalans, Acadians, negroes, and Indians. When Suzanne and Maggie, accompanied by my father and John Gordon, went ashore, I declined to follow, preferring to stay aboard with Joseph and Alix. It was at Plaquemine that we bade adieu to the old Mississippi. Here our flatboat made a détour and entered Bayou Plaquemine.[1]

Hardly had we started when our men saw and were frightened by the force of the current. The enormous flatboat, that Suzanne had likened to a giant tortoise,

---

[1] Flowing, not into, but out of, the Mississippi, and, like it, towards the Gulf. — TRANSLATOR.

darted now like an arrow, dragged by the current. The people of Plaquemine had forewarned our men and recommended the greatest prudence. "Do everything possible to hold back your boat, for if you strike any of those tree-trunks of which the bayou is full it would easily sink you." Think how reassuring all this was, and the more when they informed us that this was the first time a flatboat had ventured into the bayou!

Mario, swearing in all the known languages, sought to reassure us, and, aided by his two associates, changed the manœuvring, and with watchful eye found ways to avoid the great uprooted trees in which the lakes and bayous of Attakapas abound. But how clouded was Carpentier's brow! And my father? Ah! he repented enough. Then he realized that gold is not always the vanquisher of every obstacle. At last, thanks to Heaven, our flatboat came off victor over the snags, and after some hours we arrived at the Indian village of which you have heard me tell.

If I was afraid at sight of a dozen savages among the Spaniards of Plaquemine, what was to become of me now? The bank was entirely covered with men, their faces painted, their heads full of feathers, moccasins on their feet, and bows on shoulder — Indians indeed, with women simply wrapped in blankets, and children without the shadow of a garment; and all these Indians running, calling to one another, making signs to us, and addressing us in incomprehensible language. Suzanne, standing up on the bow of the flatboat, replied to their signs and called with all the force of her lungs every Indian word that — God knows where — she had learned :

"Chacounam finnan ! O Choctaw ! Conno Poposso !" And the Indians clapped their hands, laughing with pleasure and increasing yet more their gestures and cries.

The village, about fifty huts, lay along the edge of the water. The unfortunates were not timid. Presently several came close to the flatboat and showed us two deer and some wild turkeys and ducks, the spoils of their hunting. Then came the women laden with sacks made of bark and full of blackberries, vegetables, and a great quantity of baskets; showing all, motioning us to come down, and repeating in French and Spanish, "Money, money!"

It was decided that Mario and Gordon should stay on board and that all the rest of the joyous band should go ashore. My father, M. Carpentier, and 'Tino loaded their pistols and put them into their belts. Suzanne did likewise, while Maggie called Tom, her bulldog, to follow her. Celeste declined to go, because of her children. As to Alix and me, a terrible contest was raging in us between fright and curiosity, but the latter conquered. Suzanne and papa laughed so at our fears that Alix, less cowardly than I, yielded first, and joined the others. This was too much. Grasping my father's arm and begging him not to leave me for an instant, I let him conduct me, while Alix followed me, taking her husband's arm in both her hands. In front marched 'Tino, his gun on his shoulder; after him went Maggie, followed by Tom;

and then Suzanne and little Patrick, inseparable friends.

Hardly had we gone a few steps when we were surrounded by a human wall, and I realized with a shiver how easy it would be for these savages to get rid of us and take all our possessions. But the poor devils certainly never thought of it: they showed us their game, of which papa bought the greater part, as well as several sacks of berries, and also vegetables.

But the baskets! They were veritable wonders. As several of those that I bought that day are still in your possession, I will not lose much time telling of them. How those half-savage people could make things so well contrived and ornamented with such brilliant colors is still a problem to us. Papa bought for mamma thirty-two little baskets fitting into one another, the largest about as tall as a child of five years, and the smallest just large enough to receive a thimble. When he asked the price I expected to hear the seller say at least thirty dollars, but his humble reply was five dollars. For a deer he asked one dollar; for a wild turkey, twenty-five cents. Despite the advice of papa, who asked us how we were going to carry our purchases home, Suzanne and I bought, between us, more than forty baskets, great and small. To papa's question, Suzanne replied with an arch smile:

"God will provide."

Maggie and Alix also bought several; and Alix, who never forgot any one, bought two charming little baskets that she carried to Celeste. Each of us, even

Maggie, secured a broad parti-colored mat to use on the deck as a couch *à la Turque.* Our last purchases were two Indian bows painted red and blue and adorned with feathers; the first bought by Celestino Carlo, and the other by Suzanne for her chevalier, Patrick Gordon.

An Indian woman who spoke a little French asked if we would not like to visit the queen. We assented, and in a few moments she led us into a hut thatched with palmetto leaves and in all respects like the others. Its interior was disgustingly unclean. The queen was a woman quite or nearly a hundred years old. She sat on a mat upon the earth, her arms crossed on her breast, her eyes half closed, muttering between her teeth something resembling a prayer. She paid no attention to us, and after a moment we went out. We entered two or three other huts and found the same poverty and squalor. The men did not follow us about, but the women — the whole tribe, I think — marched step by step behind us, touching our dresses, our *capuches,* our jewelry, and asking for everything; and I felt well content when, standing on our deck, I could make them our last signs of adieu.

Our flatboat moved ever onward. Day by day, hour by hour, every minute it advanced — slowly it is true, in the diminished current, but it advanced. I no longer knew where I was. We came at times where I thought we were lost; and then I thought of mamma and my dear sisters and my two pretty little brothers, whom I might never see again, and I was swallowed up. Then Suzanne would make fun of me and Alix would caress me, and that did me good. There were many bayous, — a labyrinth, as papa said, — and Mario had his map at hand showing the way. Sometimes it seemed impracticable, and it was only by great efforts of our men ["no zomme," says the original] that we could pass on. One thing is sure — those who traverse those same lakes and bayous to-day have not the faintest idea of what they were [il zété] in 1795.

Great vines hung down from lofty trees that shaded the banks and crossed one another a hundred — a thousand — ways to prevent the boat's passage and retard its progress, as if the devil himself was mixed in it; and, frankly, I believe that he had something to do with us in that cavern. Often our emigrants were forced to take their axes and hatchets in hand to open a road. At other times tree-trunks, heaped upon one another, completely closed a bayou. Then think what trouble there was to unbar that gate and pass through. And, to make all complete, troops of hungry alligators clambered upon the sides of our flatboat with jaws open to devour us. There was much outcry; I fled, Alix fled with me, Suzanne laughed. But our men were always ready for them with their guns.

VI.

THE TWICE-MARRIED COUNTESS.

But with all the sluggishness of the flatboat, the toils, the anxieties, and the frights, what happy times, what gay moments, we passed together on the rough deck of our rude vessel, or in the little cells that we called our bedrooms.

It was in these rooms, when the sun was hot on deck, that my sister and I would join Alix to learn from her a new stitch in embroidery, or some of the charming songs she had brought from France and which she accompanied with harp or guitar.

Often she read to us, and when she grew tired put the book into my hands or Suzanne's, and gave us precious lessons in reading, as she had in singing and in embroidery. At times, in these moments of intimacy, she made certain half-disclosures that astonished us more and more. One day Suzanne took between her own two hands that hand so small and delicate and cried out all at once:

"How comes it, Alix, that you wear two wedding rings?"

"Because," she sweetly answered, "if it gives you pleasure to know, I have been twice married."

We both exclaimed with surprise.

"Ah!" she said, "no doubt you think me younger [bocou plus jeune] than I really am. What do you suppose is my age?"

Suzànne replied: "You look younger than Françoise, and she is sixteen."

"I am twenty-three," replied Alix, laughing again
and again.

Another time my sister took a book, haphazard,
from the shelves. Ordinarily [audinaremend] Alix
herself chose our reading, but she was busy embroider-
ing. Suzanne sat down and began to read aloud a
romance entitled "Two Destinies."

"Ah!" cried my sister, "these two girls must be
Françoise and I."

"Oh no, no!" exclaimed Alix, with a heavy sigh,
and Suzanne began her reading. It told of two sisters of noble family. The elder had been married to
a count, handsome, noble, and rich; and the other,
against her parents' wish, to a poor workingman who
had taken her to a distant country, where she died of
regret and misery. Alix and I listened attentively;
but before Suzanne had finished, Alix softly took the
book from her hands and replaced it on the shelf.

"I would not have chosen that book for you; it is
full of exaggerations and falsehoods."

"And yet," said Suzanne, "see with what truth the
lot of the countess is described! How happy she was
in her emblazoned coach, and her jewels, her laces,
her dresses of velvet and brocade! Ah, Françoise!
of the two destinies I choose that one."

Alix looked at her for a moment and then dropped
her head in silence. Suzanne went on in her giddy way:

"And the other: how she was punished for her
plebeian tastes!"

"So, my dear Suzanne," responded Alix, "you would not marry —"

"A man not my equal — a workman? Ah! certainly not."

Madame Carpentier turned slightly pale. I looked at Suzanne with eyes full of reproach; and Suzanne remembering the gardener, at that moment in his shirt sleeves pushing one of the boat's long sweeps, bit her lip and turned to hide her tears. But Alix — the dear little creature! — rose, threw her arms about my sister's neck, kissed her, and said:

"I know very well that you had no wish to give me pain, dear Suzanne. You have only called up some dreadful things that I am trying to forget. I am the daughter of a count. My childhood and youth were passed in châteaux and palaces, surrounded by every pleasure that an immense fortune could supply. As the wife of a viscount I have been received at court; I have been the companion of princesses. To-day all that is a dreadful dream. Before me I have a future the most modest and humble. I am the wife of Joseph the gardener; but poor and humble as is my present lot, I would not exchange it for the brilliant past, hidden from me by a veil of blood and tears. Some day I will write and send you my history; for I want to make it plain to you, Suzanne, that titles and riches do not make happiness, but that the poorest fate illumined by the fires of love is very often radiant with pleasure."

We remained mute. I took Alix's hand in mine and silently pressed it. Even Suzanne, the inquisitive Suzanne, spoke not a word. She was content to kiss Alix and wipe away her tears.

If the day had its pleasures, it was in the evenings, when we were all reunited on deck, that the moments of gayety began. When we had brilliant moonlight the flatboat would continue its course to a late hour. Then, in those calm, cool moments, when the movement of our vessel was so slight that it seemed to slide on the water, amid the odorous breezes of evening, the instruments of music were brought upon deck and our concerts began. My father played the flute delightfully; Carlo, by ear, played the violin pleasantly; and there, on the deck of that old flatboat, before an indulgent audience, our improvised instruments waked the sleeping creatures of the centuriesold forest and called around us the wondering fishes and alligators. My father and Alix played admirable duos on flute and harp, and sometimes Carlo added the notes of his violin or played for us cotillons and Spanish dances. Finally Suzanne and I, to please papa, sang together Spanish songs, or songs of the negroes, that made our auditors nearly die a-laughing; or French ballads, in which Alix would mingle her sweet voice. Then Carlo, with gestures that always frightened Patrick, made the air resound with Italian refrains, to which almost always succeeded the Irish ballads of the Gordons.

But when it happened that the flatboat made an early stop to let our men rest, the programme was changed. Celeste and Maggie went ashore to cook the two suppers there. Their children gathered wood and lighted the fires. Mario and Gordon, or Gordon and 'Tino, went into the forest with their guns. Sometimes my father went along, or sat down by M. Carpentier, who was the fisherman. Alix, too, generally sat near her husband, her sketch-book on her knee, and copied the surrounding scene. Often, tired of fishing, we gathered flowers and wild fruits. I generally staid near Alix and her husband, letting Suzanne run ahead with Patrick and Tom. It was a strange thing, the friendship between my sister and this little Irish boy. Never during the journey did he address one word to me ; he never answered a question from Alix ; he ran away if my father or Joseph spoke to him ; he turned pale and hid if Mario looked at him. But with Suzanne he talked, laughed, obeyed her every word, called her Miss Souzie, and was never so happy as when serving her. And when, twenty years afterward, she made a journey to Attakapas, the wealthy M. Patrick Gordon, hearing by chance of her presence, came with his daughter to make her his guest for a week, still calling her Miss Souzie, as of old.

VII.

ODD PARTNERS IN THE BOLERO DANCE.

ONLY one thing we lacked — mass and Sunday prayers. But on that day the flatboat remained moored, we put on our Sunday clothes, gathered on deck, and papa read the mass aloud surrounded by our whole party, kneeling; and in the parts where the choir is heard in church, Alix, my sister, and I, seconded by papa and Mario, sang hymns.

One evening — we had already been five weeks on our journey — the flatboat was floating slowly along, as if it were tired of going, between the narrow banks of a bayou marked in red ink on Carlo's map, "Bayou Sorrel." It was about six in the afternoon. There had been a suffocating heat all day. It was with joy that we came up on deck. My father, as he made his appearance, showed us his flute. It was a signal: Carlo ran for his violin, Suzanne for Alix's guitar, and presently Carpentier appeared with his wife's harp. Ah! I see them still: Gordon and 'Tino seated on a mat; Celeste and her children; Mario with his violin; Maggie; Patrick at the feet of Suzanne; Alix seated and tuning her harp; papa at her side; and M. Carpentier and I seated on the bench nearest the musicians.

My father and Alix had already played some pieces, when papa stopped and asked her to accompany him in a new bolero which was then the vogue in New Orleans. In those days, at all the balls and parties, the boleros, fandangos, and other Spanish dances had their place with the French contra-dances and waltzes. Suzanne had made her entrance into society three years before, and danced ravishingly. Not so with me. I had attended my first ball only a few months before, and had taken nearly all my dancing-lessons from Suzanne. What was to become of me, then, when I heard my father ask me to dance the bolero

which he and Alix were playing! . . . Every one
made room for us, crying, " *Oh, oui, Mlle. Suzanne;
dancez! Oh, dancez, Mlle. Françoise!* " I did not
wish to disobey my father. I did not want to diso-
blige my friends. Suzanne loosed her red scarf and
tossed one end to me. I caught the end of the shawl
that Suzanne was already waving over her head and
began the first steps, but it took me only an instant to
see that the task was beyond my powers. I grew confused, my head swam, and I stopped. But Alix did
not stop playing; and Suzanne, wrapped in her shawl
and turning upon herself, cried, "Play on!"

I understood her intention in an instant.

Harp and flute sounded on, and Suzanne, ever gliding, waltzing, leaping, her arms gracefully lifted above
her head, softly waved her scarf, giving it a thousand
different forms. Thus she made, twice, the circuit of
the deck, and at length paused before Mario Carlo.
But only for a moment. With a movement as quick
as unexpected she threw the end of her scarf to him.
It wound about his neck. The Italian with a shoulder movement loosed the scarf, caught it in his left
hand, threw his violin to Celeste, and bowed low to
his challenger. All this as the etiquette of the bolero
inexorably demanded. Then Maestro Mario smote
the deck sharply with his heels, let go a cry like an
Indian's war-whoop, and made two leaps into the air,
smiting his heels against each other. He came down
on the points of his toes, waving the scarf from his
left hand; and twining his right arm about my sister's waist, he swept her away with him. They

danced for at least half an hour, running the one after the other, waltzing, tripping, turning, leaping. The children and Gordon shouted with delight, while my father, M. Carpentier, and even Alix clapped their hands, crying, "Hurrah!"

Suzanne's want of dignity exasperated me; but when I tried to speak of it, papa and Alix were against me.

"On board a flatboat," said my father, "a breach of form is permissible." He resumed his flute with the first measures of a minuet.

"Ah, our turn!" cried Alix; "our turn, Françoise! I will be the cavalier!"

I could dance the minuet as well as I could the bolero — that is, not at all; but Alix promised to guide me: and as, after all, I loved the dance as we love it at sixteen, I was easily persuaded, and fan in hand followed Alix, who for the emergency wore her husband's hat; and our minuet was received with as much enthusiasm as Suzanne's bolero. This ball was followed by others, and Alix gave me many lessons in the dance, that some weeks later were very valuable in the wilderness towards which we were journeying.

VIII.

A BAD STORM IN A BAD PLACE.

THE flatboat continued its course, and some slight signs of civilization began to appear at long intervals. Towards the end of a beautiful day in June, six weeks after our departure from New Orleans, the flatboat stopped at the pass of Lake Chicot.[1] The sun was setting in a belt of gray clouds. Our men fastened their vessel securely and then cast their eyes about them.

"Ah!" cried Mario, "I do not like this place; it is inhabited." He pointed to a wretched hut half hidden by the forest. Except two or three little cabins seen in the distance, this was the first habitation that had met our eyes since leaving the Mississippi.[2]

A woman showed herself at the door. She was scarcely dressed at all. Her feet were naked, and her tousled hair escaped from a wretched handkerchief that she had thrown upon her head. Hidden in the bushes and behind the trees half a dozen half-nude children gazed at us, ready to fly at the slightest sound. Suddenly two men with guns came out of the woods, but at the sight of the flatboat stood petrified. Mario shook his head.

"If it were not so late I would take the boat farther on."

---

[1] That is, "Lake full of snags." — TRANSLATOR.

[2] The Indian village having the Mississippi probably but a few miles in its rear. — TRANSLATOR.

[Yet he went hunting with 'Tino and Gordon along the shore, leaving the father of Françoise and Suzanne lying on the deck with sick headache, Joseph fishing in the flatboat's little skiff, and the women and children on the bank, gazed at from a little distance by the sitting figures of the two strange men and the woman. Then the hunters returned, supper was prepared, and both messes ate on shore. Gordon and Mario joining freely in the conversation of the more cultivated group, and making altogether a strange Babel of English, French, Spanish, and Italian.]

After supper Joseph and Alix, followed by my sister and me, plunged into the denser part of the woods.

"Take care, comrade," we heard Mario say; "don't go far."

The last rays of the sun were in the treetops. There were flowers everywhere. Alix ran here and there, all enthusiasm. Presently Suzanne uttered a cry and recoiled with affright from a thicket of blackberries. In an instant Joseph was at her side; but she laughed aloud, returned to the assault, and drew by force from the bushes a little girl of three or four years. The child fought and cried; but Suzanne held on, drew her to the trunk of a tree, sat down, and held her on her lap by force. The poor little thing was horribly dirty, but under its rags there were pretty features and a sweetness that inspired pity. Alix sat down by my sister and stroked the child's hair, and, like Suzanne, spite of the dirt, kissed her several times; but the little creature still fought, and yelled [in English]:

" Let me alone! I want to go home! I want to go home!"

Joseph advised my sister to let the child go, and Suzanne was about to do so when she remembered having at supper filled her pocket with pecans. She quickly filled the child's hands with them and the Rubicon was passed. . . . She said that her name was Annie; that her father, mother, and brothers lived in the hut. That was all she could say. She did not know her parents' name. When Suzanne put her down she ran with all her legs towards the cabin to show Alix's gift, her pretty ribbon.

Before the sun went down the wind rose. Great clouds covered the horizon; large rain-drops began to fall. Joseph covered the head of his young wife with her mantle, and we hastened back to the camp.

" Do you fear a storm, Joseph ? " asked Alix.

" I do not know too much," he replied; " but when you are near, all dangers seem great."

We found the camp deserted; all our companions were on board the flatboat. The wind rose to fury, and now the rain fell in torrents. We descended to our rooms. Papa was asleep. We did not disturb him, though we were greatly frightened. . . . Joseph and Gordon went below to sleep. Mario and his son loosed the three bull-dogs, but first removed the planks that joined the boat to the shore. Then he hoisted a great lantern upon a mast in the bow, lighted his pipe, and sat down to keep his son awake with stories of voyages and hunts.

The storm seemed to increase in violence every minute. The rain redoubled its fury. Frightful thunders echoed each other's roars. The flatboat, tossed by the wind and waves, seemed to writhe in agony, while now and then the trunks of uprooted trees, lifted by the waves, smote it as they passed. Without a thought of the people in the hut, I made every effort to keep awake in the face of these menaces of Nature. Suzanne held my hand tightly in hers, and several times spoke to me in a low voice, fearing to wake papa, whom we could hear breathing regularly, sleeping without a suspicion of the surrounding dangers. Yet an hour had not passed ere I was sleeping profoundly. A knock on the partition awoke us and made us run to the door. Mario was waiting there.

"Quick, monsieur! Get the young ladies ready. The flatboat has probably but ten minutes to live. We must take the women and children ashore. And please, signorina," — to my sister, — "call M. and Mme. Carpentier." But Joseph had heard all, and showed himself at the door of our room.

"Ashore ?   At such a time ? "

"We have no choice.   We must go or perish."

"But where ? "

"To the hut.   We have no time to talk.   My family is ready." . . .

It took but a few minutes to obey papa's orders. We were already nearly dressed; and as sabots were worn at that time to protect the shoes from the mud and wet, we had them on in a moment. A thick shawl and a woolen hood completed our outfits. Alix was ready in a few moments.

"Save your jewels, — those you prize most, — my love," cried Carpentier, "while I dress."

Alix ran to her dressing-case, threw its combs, brushes, etc., pell-mell into the bureau, opened a lower part of the case and took out four or five jewel-boxes that glided into her pockets, and two lockets that she hid carefully in her corsage. Joseph always kept their little fortune in a leathern belt beneath his shirt. He put on his vest and over it a sort of great-coat, slung his gun by its shoulder-belt, secured his pistols, and then taking from one of his trunks a large woolen cloak he wrapped Alix in it, and lifted her like a child of eight, while she crossed her little arms about his neck and rested her head on his bosom. Then he followed us into Mario's room, where his two associates were waiting. At another time we might have laughed at Maggie, but not now. She had slipped into her belt two horse-pistols. In one hand she held in leash her bull-dog Tom, and in the other a short carbine, her own property.

IX.

MAGGIE AND THE ROBBERS.

"WE are going out of here together," said Mario; "but John and I will conduct you only to the door of the hut. Thence we shall return to the flatboat, and all that two men can do to save our fortune shall be

done. You, monsieur, have enough to do to take care of
your daughters. To you, M. Carpentier — to you, son
Celestino, I give the care of these women and children."

"I can take care of myself," said Maggie.

"You are four, well armed," continued Mario. (My
father had his gun and pistols.) "This dog is worth
two men. You have no risks to run; the danger, if
there be any, will be with the boat. Seeing us divided,
they may venture an attack; but one of you stand by
the window that faces the shore. If one of those men
in the hut leaves it, or shows a wish to do so, fire one
pistol-shot out of the window, and we shall be ready
for them; but if you are attacked, fire two shots and
we will come. Now, forward!"

We went slowly and cautiously : 'Tino first, with a
lantern; then the Irish pair and child; then Mario,
leading his two younger boys, and Celeste, with her
daughter asleep in her arms; and for rear-guard papa
with one of us on each arm, and Joseph with his
precious burden. The wind and the irregularities of
the ground made us stumble at every step. The rain
lashed us in the face and extorted from time to time
sad lamentations from the children. But, for all that,
we were in a few minutes at the door of the hovel.

"M. Carpentier," said Mario, "I give my family into
your care." Joseph made no answer but to give his
hand to the Italian. Mario strode away, followed by
Gordon.

"Knock on the door," said Joseph to 'Tino. The
boy knocked. No sound was heard inside, except the
growl of a dog.

"Knock again." The same silence. "We can't stay here in this beating rain; open and enter," cried Carpentier. 'Tino threw wide the door and we walked in.

There was but one room. A large fire burned in a clay chimney that almost filled one side of the cabin. In one corner four or five chickens showed their heads. In another, the woman was lying on a wretched pallet in all her clothes. By her slept the little creature Suzanne had found, her ribbon still on her frock. Near one wall was a big chest on which another child was sleeping. A rough table was in the middle, on it some dirty tin plates and cups, and under it half a dozen dogs and two little boys. I never saw anything else like it. On the hearth stood the pot and skillet, still half full of hominy and meat.

Kneeling by the fire was a young man molding bullets and passing them to his father, seated on a stool at a corner of the chimney, who threw them into a jar of water, taking them out again to even them with the handle of a knife. I see it still as if it was before my eyes.

The woman opened her eyes, but did not stir. The dogs rose tumultuously, but Tom showed his teeth and growled, and they went back under the table. The young man rose upon one knee, he and his father gazing stupidly at us, the firelight in their faces. We women shrank against our protectors, except Maggie, who let go a strong oath. The younger man was frightfully ugly; pale-faced, large-eyed, haggard, his long, tangled, blonde hair on his shoulders. The father's face was written all over with depravity and crime. Joseph advanced and spoke to him.

"What the devil of a language is that ?" he asked of his son in English.

"He is asking you," said Maggie, "to let us stay here till the storm is over."

"And where do you come from this way ?"

"From that flatboat tied to the bank."

"Well, the house isn't big nor pretty, but you are its masters."

Maggie went and sat by the window, ready to give the signal. Pat sank at her feet, and laying his head upon Tom went straight to sleep. Papa sat down by the fire on an inverted box and took me on one knee. With her head against his other, Suzanne crouched upon the floor. We were silent, our hearts beating hard, wishing ourselves with mamma in St. James. Joseph set Alix upon a stool beside him and removed her wrapping.

"Hello!" said the younger stranger, "I thought you were carrying a child. It's a woman!"

An hour passed. The woman in the corner seemed to sleep; Celeste, too, slumbered. When I asked Suzanne, softly, if she was asleep, she would silently shake her head. The men went on with their task, not speaking. At last they finished, divided the balls between them, put them into a leather pouch at their belt, and the father, rising, said:

"Let us go. It is time."

Maggie raised her head. The elder man went and got his gun and loaded it with two balls, and while the younger was muffling himself in an old blanket-overcoat such as we give to plantation negroes, moved towards the door and was about to pass out. But quicker than lightning Maggie had raised the window, snatched a pistol from her belt, and fired. The two men stood rooted, the elder frowning at Maggie. Tom rose and showed two rows of teeth.

"What did you fire that pistol for? What signal are you giving?"

"That is understood at the flatboat," said Maggie, tranquilly. "I was to fire if you left the house. You started, I fired, and that's all."

"——! And did you know, by yourself, what we were going to do?"

"I haven't a doubt. You were simply going to attack and rob the flatboat."

A second oath, fiercer than the first, escaped the man's lips. "You talk that way to me! Do you forget that you're in my power?"

"Ah! Do you think so?" cried Maggie, resting her fists on her hips. "Ah, ha, ha!" That was the first time I ever heard her laugh — and such a laugh! "Don't you know, my dear sir, that at one turn of my hand this dog will strangle you like a chicken? Don't you see four of us here armed to the teeth, and at another signal our comrades yonder ready to join us in an instant? And besides, this minute they are rolling a little cannon up to the bow of the boat. Go, meddle with them, you'll see." She lied, but her lie averted the attack. She quietly sat down again and paid the scoundrel not the least attention.

"And that's the way you pay us for taking you in, is it? Accuse a man of crime because he steps out of his own house to look at the weather? Well, that's all right." While the man spoke he put his gun into a corner, resumed his seat, and lighted a cob pipe. The son had leaned on his gun during the colloquy. Now he put it aside and lay down upon the floor to sleep. The awakened children slept. Maggie sat and smoked. My father, Joseph, and 'Tino talked in low tones. All at once the old ruffian took his pipe from his mouth and turned to my father.

"Where do you come from?"

"From New Orleans, sir."

"How long have you been on the way? "

"About a month."

"And where are you going," etc. Joseph, like papa, remained awake, but like him, like all of us, longed with all his soul for the end of that night of horror.

At the first crowing of the cock the denizens of the hut were astir. The father and son took their guns and went into the forest. The fire was relighted. The woman washed some hominy in a pail and seemed to have forgotten our presence; but the little girl recognized Alix, who took from her own neck a bright silk handkerchief and tied it over the child's head, put a dollar in her hand, and kissed her forehead. Then it was Suzanne's turn. She covered her with kisses. The little one laughed, and showed the turban and the silver that "the pretty lady," she said, had given her. Next, my sister dropped, one by one, upon the pallet ten dollars, amazing the child with these playthings;

and then she took off her red belt and put it about her little pet's neck.

My father handed me a handful of silver. "They are very poor, my daughter; pay them well for their hospitality." As I approached the woman I heard Joseph thank her and offer her money.

"What do you want me to do with that?" she said, pushing my hand away. "Instead of that, send me some coffee and tobacco."

That ended it; I could not pay in money. But when I looked at the poor woman's dress so ragged and torn, I took off [J'autai] my shawl, which was large and warm, and put it on her shoulders, — I had another in the boat, — and she was well content. When I got back to the flatboat I sent her some chemises, petticoats, stockings, and a pair of shoes. The shoes were papa's. Alix also sent her three skirts and two chemises, and Suzanne two old dresses and two chemises for her children, cutting down what was too large. Before quitting the hut Celeste had taken from her two lads their knitted neckerchiefs and given them to the two smaller boys, and Maggie took the old shawl that covered Pat's shoulders and threw it upon the third child, who cried out with joy. At length we returned to our vessel, which had triumphantly fought the wind and floating trees. Mario took to the cabin our gifts, to which we added sugar, biscuits, and a sack of pecans.

X.

ALIX PUTS AWAY THE PAST.

FOR two weeks more our boat continued its slow
and silent voyage among the bayous. We saw signs
of civilization, but they were still far apart. These
signs alarmed Mario. He had already chosen his
place of abode and spoke of it with his usual enthusiasm; a prairie where he had camped for two weeks
with his young hunters five years before.

"A principality — that is what I count on estab-
lishing there," he cried, pushing his hand through his
hair. "And think! — if, maybe, some one has occupied it! Oh, the thief! the robber! Let him not
fall into my hands! I'll strangle — I'll kill him!"

My father, to console him, would say that it would
be easy to find other tracts just as fine.

"Never!" replied he, rolling his eyes and bran-
dishing his arms; and his fury would grow until
Maggie cried:

"He is Satan himself! He's the devil!"

One evening the flatboat stopped a few miles only
from where is now the village of Pattersonville. The
weather was magnificent, and while papa, Gordon, and
Mario went hunting, Joseph, Alix, and we two walked
on the bank. Little by little we wandered, and, bury-
ing ourselves in the interior, we found ourselves all
at once confronting a little cottage embowered in a
grove of oranges. Alix uttered a cry of admiration

and went towards the house. We saw that it was uninhabited and must have been long abandoned. The little kitchen, the poultry-house, the dovecote, were in ruins. But the surroundings were admirable: in the rear a large court was entirely shaded with live-oaks; in front was the green belt of orange trees; farther away Bayou Teche, like a blue ribbon, marked a natural boundary, and at the bottom of the picture the great trees of the forest lifted their green-brown tops.

"Oh!" cried Alix, "if I could stay here I should be happy."

"Who knows?" replied Joseph. "The owner has left the house; he may be dead. Who knows but I may take this place?"

"Oh! I pray you, Joseph, try. Try!" At that moment my father and Mario appeared, looking for us, and Alix cried:

"Welcome, gentlemen, to my domain."

Joseph told of his wife's wish and his hope. . . . "In any case," said Mario, "count on us. If you decide to settle here we will stay two weeks — a month, if need be — to help you establish yourself."

As soon as we had breakfasted my father and Joseph set out for a plantation which they saw in the distance. They found it a rich estate. The large, well-built house was surrounded by outbuildings, stables, granaries, and gardens; fields of cane and corn extended to the limit of view. The owner, M. Gerbeau, was a young Frenchman. He led them into the house, presented them to his wife, and offered them refreshments.

[M. Gerbeau tells the travelers how he had come from the Mississippi River parish of St. Bernard to this place with all his effects in a schooner — doubtless via the mouth of the river and the bay of Atchafalaya; while Joseph is all impatience to hear of the little deserted home concerning which he has inquired. But finally he explains that its owner, a lone Swede, had died of sunstroke two years before, and M. Gerbeau's best efforts to find, through the Swedish consul at New Orleans or otherwise, a successor to the little estate had been unavailing. Joseph could take the place if he would. He ended by generously forcing upon the father of Françoise and Suzanne the free use of his traveling-carriage and " two horses, as gentle as lambs and as swift as deer," with which to make their journey up the Teche to St. Martinville,[1] the gay, not to say giddy, little capital of the royalist *émigrés.*]

My father wished to know what means of transport he could secure, on his return to this point, to take us home.

" Don't let that trouble you; I will arrange that. I already have a plan — you shall see."

The same day the work began on the Carpentier's home. The three immigrants and 'Tino fell bravely to work, and M. Gerbeau brought his carpenter and a cart-load of lumber. Two new rooms were added. The kitchen was repaired, then the stable, the dovecote, the poultry-house; the garden fences were restored;

---

[1] Now generally miscalled St. Martinville. — TRANSLATOR.

also those of the field. My father gave Joseph one of
his cows; the other was promised to Carlo. Mme.
Gerbeau was with us much, helping Alix, as were we.
We often dined with her. One Sunday M. Gerbeau
came for us very early and insisted that Mario and
Gordon should join us. Maggie, with her usual
phlegm, had declined.

At dinner our host turned the conversation upon
St. Martinville, naming again all the barons, counts,
and marquises of whom he had spoken to my father,
and descanting especially on the grandeur of the balls
and parties he had there attended.

"And we have only our camayeu skirts!" cried
Suzanne.

"Daughter," observed papa, "be content with what
you have. You are neither a duchess nor a countess,
and besides you are traveling."

"And," said M. Gerbeau, "the stores there are full
of knickknacks that would capture the desires of a
queen."

On returning to our flatboat Alix came into my
room, where I was alone, and laying her head on my
shoulder:

"Françoise," she said, "I have heard mentioned to-
day the dearest friend I ever had. That Countess de
la Houssaye of whom M. Gerbeau spoke is Madelaine
de Livilier, my companion in convent, almost my sister. We were married nearly at the same time; we
were presented at court the same day; and now here
we are, both, in Louisiana!"

"O Alix!" I cried, "I shall see her. Papa has a

letter to her husband; I shall tell her; she will come
to see you; and — "

"No, no! You must not speak of me, Françoise.
She knew and loved the Countess Alix de Morainville.
I know her; she would repel with scorn the wife of
the gardener. I am happy in my obscurity. Let
nothing remind me of other days."

Seeing that Alix said nothing of all this to Suzanne,
I imitated her example.   With all her goodness, Suzanne was so thoughtless and talkative!

XI.

ALIX PLAYS FAIRY. — PARTING TEARS.

In about fifteen days the work on the cottage was
nearly done and the moving began, Celeste, and even
Maggie, offering us their services. Alix seemed enchanted.

"Two things, only, I lack," she said — "a sofa, and
something to cover the walls."

One morning M. Gerbeau sent to Carpentier a horse,
two fine cows and their calves, and a number of sheep
and pigs. At the same time two or three negresses,
loaded down with chickens, geese, and ducks, made
their appearance. Also M. Gerbeau.

"What does all this mean?" asked Joseph.

"This is the succession of the dead Swede," replied the generous young man.

"But I have no right to his succession."

"That's a question," responded M. Gerbeau. "You have inherited the house, you must inherit all. If claimants appear — well, you will be responsible to them. You will please give me a receipt in due form; that is all."

Tears came into Carpentier's eyes. . . . As he was signing the receipt M. Gerbeau stopped him. "Wait; I forgot something. At the time of Karl's [the Swede's] death, I took from his crib fifty barrels of corn; add that."

"O sir!" cried Joseph, "that is too much — too much."

"Write!" said M. Gerbeau, laying his hand on Joseph's shoulder, "if you please. I am giving you nothing; I am relieving myself of a burden."

My dear daughter, if I have talked very much about Alix it is because talking about her is such pleasure. She has been so good to my sister and me! The memory of her is one of the brightest of my youth.

The flatboat was to go in three days. One morning, when we had passed the night with Mme. Gerbeau, Patrick came running to say that "Madame 'Lix" wished to see us at once. We hastened to the cottage. Alix met us on the gallery [veranda].

"Come in, dear girls. I have a surprise for you and a great favor to ask. I heard you say, Suzanne, you had nothing to wear — "

"But our camayeu petticoats!"

"But your camayeu petticoats." She smiled.

"And they, it seems, do not tempt your vanity. You want better?"

"Ah, indeed we do!" replied Suzanne.

"Well, let us play Cinderella. The dresses of velvet, silk, and lace, the jewels, the slippers — all are in yonder chest. Listen, my dear girls. Upon the first signs of the Revolution my frightened mother left France and crossed into England. She took with her all her wardrobe, her jewels, the pictures from her bedroom, and part of her plate. She bought, before going, a quantity of silks and ribbons. . . . When I reached England my mother was dead, and all that she had possessed was restored to me by the authorities. My poor mother loved dress, and in that chest is all her apparel. Part of it I had altered for my own use; but she was much larger than I — taller than you. I can neither use them nor consent to sell them. If each of you will accept a ball toilet, you will make me very happy." And she looked at us with her eyes full of supplication, her hands clasped.

We each snatched a hand and kissed it. Then she opened the chest, and for the first and last time in my life I saw fabrics, ornaments, and coiffures that truly seemed to have been made by the fairies. After many trials and much debate she laid aside for me a lovely dress of blue brocade glistening with large silver flowers the reflections of which seemed like rays of light. It was short in front, with a train; was very full on the sides, and was caught up with knots of ribbon. The long pointed waist was cut square and trimmed with magnificent laces that re-appeared on the half-long sleeves. The arms, to the elbow, were to be covered with white frosted gloves fastened with twelve silver buttons. To complete my toilet she gave me a blue silk fan beautifully painted, blue satin slippers with high heels and silver buckles, white silk stockings with blue clocks, a broidered white. cambric handkerchief trimmed with Brussels point lace, and, last, a lovely set of silver filigree that she assured us was of slight value, comprising the necklace, the comb, the earrings, bracelets, and a belt whose silver tassels of the same design fell down the front of the dress.

My sister's toilet was exactly like mine, save that it was rose color. Alix had us try them on. While our eyes were ravished, she, with more expert taste, decided to take up a little in one place, lower a ribbon in another, add something here, take away there, and, above all, to iron the whole with care. We staid all day helping her; and when, about 3 o'clock, all was finished, our fairy godmother said she would now dress our hair, and that we must observe closely.

"For Suzanne will have to coiffe Françoise and Françoise coiffe Suzanne," she said. She took from the chest two pasteboard boxes that she said contained the headdresses belonging to our costumes, and, making me sit facing my sister, began to dress her hair. I was all eyes. I did not lose a movement of the comb. She lifted Suzanne's hair to the middle of the head in two rosettes that she called *riquettes* and fastened them with a silver comb. Next, she made in front, or rather on the forehead, with hairpins, numberless little

knots, or whorls, and placed on each side of the head
a plume of white, rose-tipped feathers, and in front,
opposite the riquettes, placed a rose surrounded with
silver leaves. Long rose-colored, silver-frosted ribbons
falling far down on the back completed the headdress,
on which Alix dusted handfuls of silver powder. Can
you believe it, my daughter, that was the first time
my sister and I had ever seen artificial flowers? They
made very few of them, even in France, in those days.

While Suzanne admired herself in the mirror I took
her place. My headdress differed from hers in the
ends of my feathers being blue, and in the rose being
white, surrounded by pale blue violets and a few silver
leaves. And now a temptation came to all of us.
Alix spoke first:

"Now put on your ball-dresses and I will send for
our friends. What do you think?"

"Oh, that would be charming!" cried Suzanne.
"Let us hurry!" And while we dressed, Pat, always
prowling about the cottage, was sent to the flatboat
to get his parents and the Carlos, and to M. Gerbeau's
to ask my father and M. and Mme. Gerbeau to come
at once to the cottage. . . . No, I cannot tell the
cries of joy that greeted us. The children did not
know us, and Maggie had to tell Pat over and over
that these were Miss Souzie and Miss Francise. My
father's eyes filled with tears as he thanked Alix for
her goodness and generosity to us.

Alas! the happiest days, like the saddest, have an
end. On the morrow the people in the flatboat came
to say good-bye. Mario cried like a child. Celeste

carried Alix's hands to her lips and said in the midst of her tears :

"O Madame! I had got so used to you — I hoped never to leave you."

"I will come to see you, Celeste," replied Alix to the young mulattress, "I promise you."

Maggie herself seemed moved, and in taking leave of Alix put two vigorous kisses on her cheeks. As to our father, and us, too, the adieus were not final, we having promised Mario and Gordon to stop [on their journey up the shore of the bayou] as soon as we saw the flatboat.

"And we hope, my dear Carlo, to find you established in your principality."

"Amen!" responded the Italian.

Alix added to her gifts two pairs of chamois-skin gloves and a box of lovely artificial flowers. Two days after the flatboat had gone, we having spent the night with Alix, came M. Gerbeau's carriage to take us once more upon our journey. Ah! that was a terrible moment. Even Alix could scarce hold back the tears. We refused to get into the carriage, and walked, all of us together, to M. Gerbeau's, and then parted amid tears, kisses, and promises.

XII.

LITTLE PARIS.

[So the carriage rolled along the margin of Bayou Teche, with two big trunks besides Monsieur's on back and top, and a smaller one, lent by Alix, lashed underneath; but shawls, mats, and baskets were all left behind with the Carpentiers. The first stop was at the plantation and residence of Captain Patterson, who "offered his hand in the English way, saying only, 'Welcomed, young ladies.'" In 1795, the narrator stops to say, one might see in and about New Orleans some two-story houses; but along the banks of Bayou Teche, as well as on the Mississippi, they were all of one sort, — like their own; like Captain Patterson's, — a single ground floor with three rooms facing front and three back. Yet the very next stop was at a little cottage covered with roses and with its front yard full of ducks and geese, — "'A genuine German cottage,' said papa," — where a German girl, to call her father, put a great ox's horn to her lips and blew a loud blast. Almost every one was English or German till they came to where was just beginning to be the town of Franklin. One Harlman, a German, offered to exchange all his land for the silver watch that it best suited Monsieur to travel with. The exchange was made, the acts were all signed and sealed, and — when Suzanne, twenty years after, made a visit to Attakapas there was Harlman and his nu-

merous family still in peaceful possession of the place.
. . . "And I greatly fear that when some day our
grandchildren awaken from that apathy with which
I have always reproached the Creoles, I fear, my
daughter, they will have trouble to prove their titles."

But they journeyed on, Françoise ever looking out
the carriage window for the flatboat, and Suzanne
crying:

"Annie, my sister Annie, do you see nothing
coming?" And about two miles from where Franklin was to be they came upon it, greeted with joyous
laughter and cries of "Miss Souzie! O Miss Souzie!"
from the woman and the children, and from Mario:
"I have it, Signor! I have it! My principality, Miss
Souzie! It is mine, Signorina Françoise!" while he
danced, laughed, and brandished his arms. "He had
taken up enough land," says Françoise, "for five
principalities, and was already knocking the flatboat
to pieces."

She mentioned meeting Jacques and Charles Picot,
St. Domingan refugees, whose story of adventures she
says was very wonderful, but with good artistic judgment omits them. The travelers found, of course, a
charmante cordialité at the home of M. Agricole Fuselier,[1] and saw a little girl of five who afterward
became a great beauty — Uranie Fuselier. They
passed another Indian village, where Françoise per-

[1] When I used the name of Agricole Fuselier (or Agricola Fusilier, as I
have it in my novel "The Grandissimes") I fully believed it was my own
careful coinage; but on publishing it I quickly found that my supposed invention was but an unconscious reminiscence. The name still survives, I am
told, on the Teche. — TRANSLATOR.

suaded them not to stop. Its inhabitants were Cheti-
machas, more civilized than those of the village near
Plaquemine, and their sworn enemies, living in constant fear of an attack from them. At New Iberia, a
town founded by Spaniards, the voyagers saw " several
houses, some drinking-shops and other buildings," and
spent with " the pretty little Madame Dubuclet . . .
two of the pleasantest days of their lives."]

At length, one beautiful evening in July, under a
sky resplendent with stars, amid the perfume of gardens and caressed by the cool night breeze, we made
our entry into the village of St. Martinville — the
Little Paris, the oasis in the desert.

My father ordered Julien [the coachman] to stop
at the best inn. He turned two or three corners and
stopped near the bayou [Teche] just beside the
bridge, before a house of the strangest aspect possible.
There seemed first to have been built a *rez-de-chaussée*
house of ordinary size, to which had been hastily
added here a room, there a cabinet, a balcony, until
the " White Pelican " — I seem to see it now — was
like a house of cards, likely to tumble before the
first breath of wind. The host's name was Morphy.
He came forward, hat in hand, a pure-blooded American, but speaking French almost like a Frenchman.
In the house all was comfortable and shining with
cleanness. Madame Morphy took us to our room,
adjoining papa's [" tou ta côté de selle de papa "],
the two looking out, across the veranda, upon the
waters of the Teche.

After supper my father proposed a walk. Madame Morphy showed us, by its lights, in the distance, a theater!

"They are playing, this evening, 'The Barber of Seville.'"

We started on our walk, moving slowly, scanning the houses and listening to the strains of music that reached us from the distance. It seemed but a dream that at any moment might vanish. On our return to the inn, papa threw his letters upon the table and began to examine their addresses.

"To whom will you carry the first letter, papa?" I asked.

"To the Baron du Clozel," he replied. "I have already met him in New Orleans, and even had the pleasure to render him a slight service."

Mechanically Suzanne and I examined the addresses and amused ourselves reading the pompous titles.

"'Le chevalier Louis de Blanc!'" began my sister; "'L'honorable A. Déclouet'; 'Le comte Louis le Pelletrier de la Houssaye'! Ah!" she cried, throwing the packet upon the table, "the aristocrats! I am frightened, poor little plebeian that I am."

"Yes, my daughter," responded my father, "these names represent true aristocrats, as noble in virtues as in blood. My father has often told me of two uncles of the Count de la Houssaye: the first, Claude de la Pelletrier de la Houssaye, was prime minister to King Louis XV.; and the second, Barthelemy, was employed by the Minister of Finance. The count, he to whom I bear this letter, married Madelaine Victoire de Livilier. These are noble names."

Then Alix was not mistaken; it was really her friend, the Countess Madelaine, whom I was about to meet.

XIII.

THE COUNTESS MADELAINE.

EARLY the next day I saw, through the partly open door, my father finishing his toilet.

He had already fastened over his black satin breeches his garters secured with large buckles of chased silver. Similar buckles were on his shoes. His silver-buttoned vest of white piqué reached low down, and his black satin coat faced with white silk had large lappets cut square. Such dress seemed to me very warm for summer; but the fashion and etiquette allowed only silk and velvet for visits of ceremony, and though you smothered you had to obey those tyrants. At the moment when I saw him out of the corner of my eye he was sticking a cluster diamond pin into his shirt-frill and another diamond into his lace cravat. It was the first time I ever saw papa so fine, so dressed! Presently we heard him call us to arrange his queue, and although it was impossible for us to work up a club and pigeon wings like those I saw on the two young Du Clozels and on M. Neville Déclouet, we arranged a very fine queue wrapped with a black ribbon, and after smiling at himself in the glass and declaring that he thought the whole dress was in very good taste he kissed us, took his three-cornered hat and his gold-headed cane and went out. With what impatience we awaited his return!

About two hours afterward we saw papa coming back accompanied by a gentleman of a certain age, handsome, noble, elegant in his severe suit of black velvet. He had the finest black eyes in the world, and his face beamed with wit and amiability. You have guessed it was the Baron du Clozel. The baron bowed to us profoundly. He certainly knew who we were, but etiquette required him to wait until my father had presented us; but immediately then he asked papa's permission to kiss us, and you may suppose your grandfather did not refuse.

M. du Clozel had been sent by the baroness to oppose our sojourn at the inn, and to bring us back with him.

"Run, put on your hoods," said papa; "we will wait for you here."

Mr. and Mrs. Morphy were greatly disappointed to see us go, and the former declared that if these nobles kept on taking away their custom they would have to shut up shop. Papa, to appease him, paid him double what he asked. And the baron gave his arm to Suzanne, as the elder, while I followed, on papa's. Madame du Clozel and her daughter met us at the street gate. The baroness, though not young, was still pretty, and so elegant, so majestic! A few days later I could add, so good, so lovable!

Celeste du Clozel was eighteen. Her hair was black as ebony, and her eyes a beautiful blue. The young men of the village called her *Celeste la bien nommée* [Celeste the well named]; and for all her beauty, fortune, and high position she was good and simple and always ready to oblige. She was engaged, we learned afterward, to the Chevalier de Blanc, the same who in 1803 was made post-commandant of Attakapas.[1] Olivier and Charles du Clozel turned everything to our entertainment, and it was soon decided that we should all go that same evening to the theater.

Hardly was the sun down when we shut ourselves into our rooms to begin the work of dressing. Celeste put herself at our service, assuring us that she knew perfectly how to dress hair. The baroness asked us to let her lend us ornaments, ribbons — whatever we might need. We could see that she supposed two young girls who had never seen the great world, who came from a region where nearly all articles of luxury were wanting, could hardly have a choice wardrobe. We thanked them, assuring Celeste that we had always cultivated the habit of dressing each other's hair.

We put on our camayeu petticoats and our black velvet waists, adding gloves; and in our hair, sparkling with gold powder, we put, each of us, a bunch of the roses given us by Alix. We found ourselves charming, and hoped to create a sensation. But if the baroness was satisfied she showed no astonish-

[1] Ancestor of the late Judge Alcibiade de Blanc of St. Martinville, noted in Reconstruction days. — TRANSLATOR.

ment. Her hair, like her daughter's, was powdered, and both wore gloves.

Suzanne on the arm of Olivier, I on Charles's, Celeste beside her fiancé, the grandparents in front, we entered the theater of St. Martinville, and in a moment more were the observed of all observers. The play was a vaudeville, of which I remember only the name, but rarely have I seen amateurs act so well: all the prominent parts were rendered by young men. But if the French people are polite, amiable, and hospitable, we know that they are also very inquisitive. Suzanne was more annoyed than I can tell; yet we knew that our toilets were in excellent taste, even in that place full of ladies covered with costly jewels. When I asked Celeste how the merchants of St. Martinville could procure these costly goods, she explained that near by there was a place named the *Butte à la Rose* that greatly shortened the way to market.[1] They were bringing almost everything from London, owing to the Revolution. Between the acts many persons came to greet Madame du Clozel. Oh, how I longed to see the friend of Alix! But I would not ask anything; I resolved to find her by the aid of my heart alone.

Presently, as by a magnetic power, my attention was drawn to a tall and beautiful young lady dressed in white satin, with no ornaments except a set of gold and sapphires, and for headdress a *résille* the golden tassels of which touched her neck. Ah! how quickly

---

[1] By avoiding the Spanish custom-house. — TRANSLATOR.

I recognized those brown eyes faintly proud, that kind smile, that queenly bearing, that graceful step! I turned to Charles du Clozel, who sat beside me, and said:

"That is the Countess de la Houssaye, is n't it?"

"Do you know her?"

"I see her for the first time; but — I guessed it."

Several times I saw her looking at me, and once she smiled. During the last two acts she came and shook hands with us, and, caressing our hair with her gloved hand, said her husband had seen papa's letter; that it was from a dear friend, and that she came to ask Madame du Clozel to let her take us away with her. Against this the baroness cried out, and then the Countess Madelaine said to us:

"Well, you will come spend the day with me day after to-morrow, will you? I shall invite only young people. May I come for you?"

Ah, that day! how I remember it! . . . Madame de la Houssaye was fully five or six years older than Madame Carpentier, for she was the mother of four boys, the eldest of whom was fully twelve.[1] Her house was, like Madame du Clozel's, a single rez-de-chaussée surmounted by a mansard. . . . From the

---

[1] This seems to be simply a girl's thoughtless guess. She reports Alix as saying that Madelaine and she "were married nearly at the same time." But this tiny, frail, spiritual Alix, who between twenty-two and twenty-three looked scant sixteen, could hardly, even in those times, have been married under the age of fifteen, that is not before 1787–8; whereas if Madelaine had been married thirteen years she would have been married when Alix was but ten years old.

This bit of careless guessing helps to indicate the genuineness of Alix's history. For when, by the light of Françoise's own statements, we correct

drawing-room she conducted us to a room in the rear
of the house at the end of the veranda [galerie], where
. . . a low window let into a garden crossed and re-
crossed with alleys of orange and jasmine. Several
lofty magnolias filled the air with the fragrance of
their great white flowers. . . .

XIV.

"POOR LITTLE ALIX!"

HARDLY had we made a few steps into the room
when a young girl rose and advanced, supported on
the arm of a young man slightly overdressed. His
club and pigeon-wings were fastened with three or
four pins of gold, and his white-powdered queue was
wrapped with a black velvet ribbon shot with silver.
The heat was so great that he had substituted silk for
velvet, and his dress-coat, breeches, and long vest were
of pearl-gray silk, changing to silver, with large silver
buttons. On the lace frill of his embroidered shirt
shone three large diamonds, on his cravat was another,
and his fingers were covered with rings.[1] The young
girl embraced us with ceremony, while her companion

this error — totally uncorrected by any earlier hand — the correction agrees
entirely with the story of Alix as told in the separate manuscript. There
Alix is married in March, 1789, and Madelaine about a year before. In midsummer, 1795, Madelaine had been married between seven and eight years
and her infant was, likely enough, her fourth child. — TRANSLATOR.

[1] The memoirist omits to say that this person was Neville Déclouet. —
TRANSLATOR.

bowed profoundly. She could hardly have been over sixteen or seventeen. One could easily guess by her dress that the pretty creature was the slave of fashion.

"Madame du Rocher," said Charles du Clozel, throwing a wicked glance upon her.

"Madame!" I stammered.

"Impossible!" cried Suzanne.

"Don't listen to him!" interrupted the young lady, striking Charles's fingers with her fan. "He is a wretched falsifier. I am called Tonton de Blanc."

"The widow du Rocher!" cried Olivier, from the other side.

"Ah, this is too much!" she exclaimed. "If you don't stop these ridiculous jokes at once I'll make Neville call you out upon the field of battle." . . . But a little while afterward Celeste whispered in my ear that her brothers had said truly. At thirteen years Tonton, eldest daughter of Commandant Louis de Blanc and sister of Chevalier de Blanc, had been espoused to Dr. du Rocher, at least forty years older than she. He was rich, and two years later he died, leaving all his fortune to his widow. . . . One after another Madame de la Houssaye introduced to us at least twenty persons, the most of whose names, unfortunately, I have forgotten. I kept notes, but have mislaid them. . . .

A few moments before dinner the countess re-appeared among us, followed by two servants in livery bearing salvers of fruit; and while we ate she seated herself at the harpsichord and played.

"Do you sing?" she asked me.

"A little, madame."

[The two sisters sang a song together.]

"Children," she cried, "tell me, I pray you, who taught you that duet ? "

"A young French lady, one of our friends," replied Suzanne.

"But her name ! What is her name ? "

"Madame Carpentier."

The name meant nothing to her. She sighed, and asked us to sing on. . . . At dinner we met again my father and the count. After dinner the countess sent for me to come to her chamber while she was nursing her babe. After a few unimportant words she said :

"You have had your lessons from a good musician."

"Yes, madame, our friend plays beautifully on the harp."

"On the harp ! And you say her name is — "

"Madame Joseph Carpentier."

"It is strange," said Madame de la Houssaye. "The words of your duet are by me, and the music by my friend the Viscomptesse Alix de Morainville. All manner of things have happened in this terrible Revolution ; I had for a moment the hope that she had found chance to emigrate and that you had met her. Do you know M. Carpentier ? "

"Yes, madame ; he was with her. He is — in fact — a laboring gardener."

"Oh ! then there is no hope. I had the thought of a second marriage, but Alix de Morainville could never stoop so low. Poor, dear, innocent little Alix ! She must be dead — at the hand of butchers, as her father and her husband are."

When we returned to the joyous company in the garden all wanted to speak at once. The countess imposed silence, and then Tonton informed us that a grand ball was proposed in our honor, to be given in the large dining-room of Mr. Morphy's tavern, under the direction of Neville Déclouet, the following Monday — that is, in four days.

Oh, that ball! I lay my pen on the table and my head in my hands and see the bright, pretty faces of young girls and richly clad cavaliers, and hear the echoes of that music so different from what we have to-day. Alas! the larger part of that company are sleeping now in the cemetery of St. Martinville.

Wherever you went, whoever you met, the ball was the subject of all conversation. All the costumes, masculine and feminine, were prepared in profound secrecy. Each one vowed to astonish, dazzle, surpass his neighbor. My father, forgetting the presents from Alix, gave us ever so much money and begged Madame du Clozel to oversee our toilets; but what was the astonishment of the dear baroness to see us buy only some vials of perfumery and two papers of pins. We paid ten dollars for each vial and fifteen for the pins!

Celeste invited us to see her costume the moment it reached her. It certainly did great honor to the dressmaker of St. Martinville. The dress was simply made, of very fine white muslin caught up *cn paniers* on a skirt of blue satin. Her beautiful black hair

was to be fastened with a pearl comb, and to go between its riquettes she showed us two bunches of
forget-me-nots as blue as her eyes. The extremely
long-pointed waist of her dress was of the same color
as the petticoat, was decolleté, and on the front had a
drapery of white muslin held in place by a bunch of
forget-me-nots falling to the end of the point. In
the whole village she could get no white gloves. She
would have to let that pass and show her round white
arms clasped with two large bracelets of pearls. She
showed also a necklace and earrings of pearls.

Madame du Clozel, slave to the severe etiquette of
that day, did not question us, but did go so far as to
say in our presence that camayeu was never worn at
night.

"We know that, madame," replied my sister, slightly
hurt. We decided to show our dresses to our hostess.
We arranged them on the bed. When the baroness
and her daughter entered our chamber they stood
stupefied. The baroness spoke first.

"Oh, the villains! How they have fooled us!
These things are worthy of a queen. They are court
costumes."

I said to myself, "Poor, dear little Alix!"

XV.

THE DISCOVERY OF THE HAT.

"Oh!" cried Celeste, "but what will Tonton say when she sees you ? "

·" Do not let her know a thing about it, girls," said Madame du Clozel, "or, rather than yield the scepter of beauty and elegance for but one evening, she will stay in the white chapel. What! at sixteen you don't know what the white chapel is ? It is our bed."

Before the ball, came Sunday. Madame du Clozel had told us that the population of the little city — all Catholics — was very pious, that the little church could hardly contain the crowd of worshipers; and Celeste had said that there was a grand display of dress there. We thought of having new dresses made, but the dressmaker declared it impossible ; and so we were obliged to wear our camayeus a second time, adding only a lace scarf and a hat. A hat! But how could one get in that little town in the wilderness, amid a maze of lakes and bayous, hundreds of miles from New Orleans, so rare and novel a thing as a hat ? Ah, they call necessity the mother of invention, but I declare, from experience, that vanity has performed more miracles of invention, and made greater discoveries than Galileo or Columbus.

The women of St. Martinville, Tonton at their head, had revolted against fate and declared they would have hats if they had to get them at the moon. Behold, now, by what a simple accident the hat was discovered. Tonton de Blanc had one of the prettiest complexions in the world, all lily and rose, and what care she took of it! She never went into the yard or the garden without a sunbonnet and a thick veil. Yet for all that her jealous critics said she was good and sensible, and would forget every-thing, even her toilet, to succor any one in trouble. One day Tonton heard a great noise in the street be-fore her door. She was told that a child had just been crushed by a vehicle. Without stopping to ask whether the child was white or black or if it still lived, Tonton glanced around for her sun-bonnet, but, not finding it at hand, darted bareheaded into the street. At the door she met her young brother, and, as the sun was hot, she took his hat and put it on her own head. The Rubicon was crossed — Tonton had discovered the hat!

All she had heard was a false alarm. The crushed child was at play again before its mother's door. It had been startled by a galoping team, had screamed, and instantly there had been a great hubbub and crowd. But ten minutes later the little widow, the hat in her hand, entered the domicile of its maker and astonished the woman by ordering a hat for her own use, promising five dollars if the work was done to her satisfaction. The palmetto was to be split into the finest possible strips and platted into the form furnished by Madame Tonton. It was done; and on Sunday the hat, trimmed with roses and ribbons, made its appearance in the church of St. Martin, on the

prettiest head in the world. The next Sunday you
could see as many hats as the hatmaker had had time
to make, and before the end of the month all the
women in St. Martinville were wearing palmetto hats.
To-day the modistes were furnishing them at the
fabulous price of twenty-five dollars, — trimmed, you
understand, — and palmetto hats were really getting
to be a branch of the commerce of the little city; but
ours, thanks to Alix's flowers and ribbons, cost but
ten dollars.

The churĉh was crowded. The service, performed
by an old priest nearly a hundred years of age, was
listened to with interest; but what astonished me was
to see the crowd stop at the church door, the women
kissing; to hear laughter, chat, and criticism at the
door of this sacred place as if it were the public
square. I understood the discontent that knit my
father's brows and the alacrity with which he descended the church steps. Tonton saw and came to
us — so fresh, so young, she was indeed the queen of
beauty and fashion. Out of nothing Tonton could
work wonders. Her dress to-day was of camayeu the
pattern of which was bunches of strawberries — the
very same stuff as our dresses; but how had she made
it to look so different? And her hat! It was a new
marvel of her invention. She had taken a man's felt
hat and entirely covered it with the feathers of the
cardinal bird, without other ornament than a bunch of
white ribbon on the front and two long cords of white
silk falling clear to the waist. That was the first hat
of the kind I ever saw, but it was not the last. With

one turn of her little hand she could make the whole female population of St. Martinville go as she pleased. Before we left St. Martinville we had the chance to admire more than fifty hats covered with the feathers of peacocks, geese, and even guinea-fowl, and — must we confess it? — when we got home we enlisted all our hunter friends to bring us numerous innocent cardinals, and tried to make us hats; but they did not look the least like the pretty widow's.

Sunday was also the day given to visiting. Being already dressed, it was so easy to go see one's friends. . . . Among the new visitors was Saint Marc d'Arby — engaged to little Constance de Blanc, aged thirteen. He came to invite us to a picnic on the coming Wednesday.

"Ah," I cried, with regret, "the very day papa has chosen for us to leave for the town of Opelousas!" . . .

Since arriving in St. Martinville we had hardly seen papa. He left early each morning and returned late in the evening, telling of lands he had bought during the day. His wish was to go to Opelousas to register them. . . . To-day the whole town of Opelousas belongs to his heirs; but those heirs, with Creole heedlessness and afraid to spend a dollar, let strangers enjoy the possession of the beautiful lands acquired by their ancestor for so different an end. Shame on all of them !

It was decided for papa to leave us with the baroness during his visit to Opelousas.

"And be ready to depart homeward," said he, " on the following Monday."

XVI.

THE BALL.

THE evening before that of the ball gave us lively disappointment. A fine rain began to fall. But Celeste came to assure us that in St. Martinville a storm had never prevented a ball, and if one had to go by boat, still one had to go. Later the weather improved, and several young gentlemen came to visit us. . . . "Will there be a supper, chevalier ? " asked the baroness of her future son-in-law. — "Ah, good ! For me the supper is the best part of the affair."

Alas! man proposes. The next morning she was in bed suffering greatly with her throat. "Neither supper nor ball for me this evening," she said. "The Countess de la Houssaye will take care of you and Celeste this evening." . . .

At last our toilets were complete. . . .

When Madame de la Houssaye opened the door and saw us, instead of approaching, she suddenly stopped with her hands clasped convulsively, and with eyes dilated and a pallor and look of astonishment that I shall never forget. I was about to speak when she ran to Suzanne and seized her by the arm.

"Child! for pity answer me! Where did that dress — these jewels, come from ? "

"Madame ! " said my sister, quickly taking offense.

"Françoise ! " cried the countess, " you will answer me. Listen. The last time I saw the Countess

Aurélie de Morainville, six years ago, was at a reception of Queen Marie Antoinette, and she wore a dress exactly like that of Suzanne's. My child, pity my emotions and tell me where you bought that toilet." I answered, almost as deeply moved as she:

"We did not buy it, madame. These costumes were given to us by Madame Carpentier."

"Given! Do you know the price of these things?"

"Yes; and, moreover, Madame du Clozel has told us."

"And you tell me a poor woman, the wife of a gardener, made you these presents. Oh! I must see this Madame Carpentier. She must have known Alix. And who knows — oh, yes, yes! I must go myself and see her."

"And I must give her forewarning," I said to myself. But, alas! as I have just said, "Man proposes, God disposes." About six months after our return to St. James we heard of the death of the Countess de la Houssaye, which had occurred only two months after our leaving St. Martinville. . . .

Oh, how my heart beat as I saw the lights of the ball-room and heard its waves of harmony! I had already attended several dances in the neighborhood of our home, but they could not compare with this. The walls were entirely covered with green branches mingled with flowers of all colors, especially with magnolias whose odor filled the room. Hidden among the leaves were millions of fantastically colored lam-

pions seeming like so many glow-worms.[1] To me,
poor little rustic of sixteen, it seemed supernaturally
beautiful. But the prettiest part — opposite the door
had been raised a platform surmounted by a dais made
of three flags: the French, Spanish, and Prussian —
Prussia was papa's country. And under these colors,
on a pedestal that supported them, were seen, in
immense letters composed of flowers, the one German
word, *Bewillkommen!* Papa explained that the word
meant "Welcome." On the platform, attired with in-
conceivable elegance, was the master of ceremonies,
the handsome Neville Déclouet himself, waiting to
wish us welcome anew.

IT would take volumes, my daughter, to describe
the admirable toilets, masculine as well as feminine,
of that memorable night. The thing is impossible.
But I must describe that of the king of the festival,
the young Neville, that you may understand the immense difference between the toilets of 1795 and those
of 1822.

Neville had arranged his hair exactly as on the day
we first saw him. It was powdered white; his pigeon-
wings were fastened with the same pins of gold, and
his long queue was wrapped with a rose-colored ribbon. His coat was of frosted rose silk with broad
facings of black velvet. His vest came down nearly
to his knees. It also was of rose silk, but covered
with black buttons. His breeches, also rose, were

[1] Number of millions not stated. — TRANSLATOR.

fastened at the knees with black velvet ribbons escaping from diamond buckles and falling upon silk stockings shot alternately with black and rose. Diamonds sparkled again on his lace frill, at his wrists, on his cravat of rose silk, and on the buckles of his pumps.

I cast my eye around to find Tonton, but she had not come. Some one near me said, "Do you know who will escort Madame du Rocher to the ball?" And another said, "Here is Neville, so who will replace him at the side of the pretty widow?"

As we entered the room the Baron du Clozel passed his arm under papa's and conducted him to the platform, while his sons, following, drew us forward to receive the tributes prepared for us. Neville bowed low and began his address. At first he spoke with feeling and eloquence, but by and by he lost the thread. He cast a look of despair upon the crowd, which did not conceal its disposition to laugh, turned again quickly towards us, passed his hand twice across his forehead, and finished with:

"Yes, I repeat it, we are glad to see you; you are welcome among us, and — I say to you only that!"

There was a general burst of laughter. But my father pitied the young man's embarrassment. He mounted the platform, shook his hand, and thanked him, as well as all the people of St. Martinville, for his gracious welcome and their warm hospitality. Then, to our great joy, the ball opened.

It began with a minuet danced by twelve couples at once, six on each side. The minuet in vogue just then was well danced by but few persons. It had been brought to St. Martinville by émigrés who had danced it at the French court. . . . But, thanks to the lessons given us by Alix, we had the pleasure to surprise them.

Now I ought to tell you, my daughter, that these male costumes, so effeminate, extravagant, and costly, had met great opposition from part of the people of St. Martin parish. They had been brought in by the French émigrés, and many had adopted them, while others had openly revolted against them. A league had been formed against them. Among its members were the Chevalier de Blanc, the elder of the d'Arbys, the Chevalier de la Houssaye, brother of the count, Paul Briant, Adrian Dumartrait, young Morse, and many others. They had thrown off entirely the fashionable dress and had replaced it with an attire much like what men wear now. It was rumored that the pretty Tonton favored the reform of which her brother was one of the chiefs.

Just as the minuet was being finished a loud murmur ran through the hall. All eyes were turned to the door and some couples confused their steps in the dance. Tonton had come. She was received with a cry of surprise; not for her beauty, not for her exquisite toilet, but because of him who entered with her.

"Great God!" exclaimed Celeste du Clozel, "it is Tréville de Saint Julien!"—"Oh!" cried Madame de la Houssaye, "Tonton is a fool, an arch-fool. Does she want to see bloodshed this evening?"—"The Countess Madelaine is going to faint!" derisively whispered Olivier in my ear.

"Who," asked Suzanne, "is Tréville de Saint Julien?"

"He is 'the hermit of Bayou Tortue,'" responded the gentle Celeste de Blanc.

"What pretense of simplicity, look you!" said Charles du Clozel, glancing towards him disdainfully.

"But look at Madame du Rocher," cried a girl standing on a bench, "how she is dressed. What contempt of fashion and propriety! It is positively shameful."

And Tonton, indifferent to these remarks, which she heard and to which she was accustomed, and to the furious glances thrown upon her cavalier by Neville Déclouet, continued, with her arm in his, to chat and laugh with him as they walked slowly around the hall.

If I describe to you, my daughter, the toilets of Tonton and of Tréville de Saint Julien, I write it for you alone, dear child, and it seems to me it would be a theft against you if I did not. But this is the last time I shall stop to describe petticoats, gowns, and knee-breeches. Tréville was twenty-five; large, dark, of a manly, somber beauty. A great unhappiness had overtaken him in childhood and left a permanent trace on his forehead. He wore his hair slightly long, falling behind without queue or powder. In 1795 only soldiers retained their beard. Tréville de Saint Julien, despite the fashion, kept the fine black mustache on his proud lip. His shirt, without a frill, was fastened with three gold buttons. His broad-skirted coat, long vest, and breeches were of black woolen stuff. His black stockings were also of wool. His garters and shoes were without buckles. But serving him as a garter, and forming a rosette on the front of the leg, he wore a ribbon of plaided rose and black.

And Tonton. Over a dress — a real dress, such as we have nowadays — of rose satin, with long-pointed waist, was draped another, of black lace. The folds, running entirely around the skirt, were caught up by roses surrounded by their buds and leaves. The same drapery was repeated on the waist, and in front and on the shoulders re-appeared the roses. The sleeves were very short, and the arms bare and without gloves. It was simple, but prettier than you can think. Her hair was in two wide braids, without powder, forming a heart and falling low upon the neck. Among these tresses she had placed a rose like those on the skirt. For ornaments she had only a necklace and bracelets of jet to heighten the fresh whiteness of her complexion.

They had said Tonton would die of jealousy at our rich toilets. Nothing of the sort. She came to us with her habitual grace, kissed us, ignoring etiquette and the big eyes made by the Countess Madelaine. Without an allusion to our dress or seeming to see it, she sat down between us, told us persons' names, pointed out the beauty of this one, the pretty dress of that one, always admiring, never criticising. She knew well she was without a rival.

I amused myself watching Tréville and Neville out of the corner of my eyes. Tréville seemed to see but one woman in the room. He danced several times, always with her, and when he did not dance he went aside, spoke with no one, but followed with his glances her whom he seemed to adore. He made no attempt to hide his adoration; it shone from his eyes: his every movement was full of it. When she returned to her place, he came, remained before her chair, leaned towards her, listened with ravished ear, and rarely sat down by her side. It was good to watch Neville. His eyes flashed with anger, his fists fidgeted, and more than once I saw him quit the hall, no doubt to make a quarrel with his rival. Not once did he come near Tonton! Not once did he dance with her! But he danced with all the young girls in the room and pretended to be very gay. While I was dancing with him I said:

"How pretty Tonton is this evening!" And I understood the spite that made him reply:

"Ah! mademoiselle, her beauty is certainly not to be compared with yours."

After the supper, which was magnificent, the bolero was danced. Twelve couples were engaged, continually changing partners. Tonton danced with Tréville, Suzanne with Olivier, and I with Neville.

Alas, alas! all things earthly have an end, and at two in the morning the ball was over. When we reached our chamber I saw that my sister had something to tell me.

"Ah!" said she, "have patience. I will tell you after we get into bed."

[What she told was the still famous Saint Julien

feud.   Tréville and Neville were representatives of
the two sides in that, one of the darkest vendettas
known in the traditions of Louisiana.   The omission
of this episode in the present translation is the only
liberty taken with the original that probably calls for
an apology.]

XVII.

PICNIC AND FAREWELL.

THE day of the picnic rose brightly.   Oh, what a
day we passed under those grand trees, on the margin
of that clear lake full of every imaginable sort of fish!
What various games !   What pleasant companions!
All our friends were there except Tréville de Saint
Julien, and Madame Tonton gave her smiles and sweet
looks to Neville, who never left her a moment.   Oh,
how I regretted that my father was not with us !   He
had gone to Opelousas.   He had bought several plantations in St. Martin parish, and in a region called
Fausse Pointe, and in another known as the Côte
Gelée.

The days that followed were equally fête days —
a dinner here, a dance there, and everywhere the most
gracious reception.   At length came the day for us to
meet at La Fontaine — a real spring near St. Martinville, belonging to Neville Déclouet's uncle.   About five
in the afternoon we gathered on the bank of the bayou.
We never saw Tonton twice in the same dress.   To-day
she was all in blue.   Suddenly the sound of distant

music, and an open flat — not like our boat — approached, arched over with green branches and flowers. Benches stood about, and in the middle the orchestra played. In the prow stood the captain [Neville Déclouet], and during the moments of the journey the music was mingled with the laughter and songs of our joyous company. About 7 o'clock all the trees about La Fontaine were illuminated, and Neville led us to a floored place encircled by magnolia trees in bloom and by garlands running from tree to tree and mingling their perfume with the languishing odor of the magnolias. Only heaven can tell how Neville was praised and thanked.

I felt sure that Tonton's good taste had directed the details. There was something singular in this young woman. Without education save what she had taught herself, Tonton spoke with remarkable correctness, and found means to amuse every one. Her letters were curious to see, not a single word correctly spelled; yet her style was charming, and I cannot express the pleasure they gave me, for during more than a year I received them by every opportunity that presented itself.

But to return to La Fontaine. About seven the handsome Tréville de St. Julien came on a horse as black as ebony, and I saw the color mount to Suzanne's forehead. For a wonder he paid Tonton only the attentions required by politeness, and the pretty widow, while still queen of all, belonged that evening entirely to Neville.

The following Saturday my father arrived. The

next day, after mass, our friends came in a body to say adieu. And on the morrow, amid kisses, hand-shaking, regrets, tears, and waving handkerchiefs, we departed in the carriage that was to bear us far and forever from Little Paris, and the friends we shall never meet again. Suzanne and I wept like children. On the fourth day after, the carriage stopped before the door of M. Gerbeau's house. I must confess we were not over-polite to Mme. Gerbeau. We embraced her hurriedly, and, leaving my father talking about lands, started on a run for Alix's dwelling.

Oh, dear Alix! How happy she seemed to see us again! How proud to show us the innovations made in her neat little house! With what touching care had she prepared our chamber! She had wished for a sofa, and Joseph had made her one and covered it with one of the velvet robes of the Countess Aurelia de Morainville. And when we went into Alix's own room, Suzanne, whose eye nothing ever escaped, pointed out to me, half hidden behind the mosquito-net of the bed, the prettiest little cradle in the world.

"Yes," said Alix, blushing, "I am blessed. I am perfectly happy."

We told her all our adventures and pleasures. She wept when she heard that the Countess de la Houssaye had not forgotten her.

"You will see her," said Suzanne. "She will come to see you, without a doubt."

"Ah, Heaven prevent it! Our destinies are too unlike now. Me perhaps the Countess Madelaine might welcome affectionately; but Joseph? Oh, no!

My husband's lot is mine; I have no wish for any other. It is better that she and I remain strangers."

And Joseph? How he confessed his joy in seeing us!

During our absence M. Gerbeau had found means for us to return to St. James. It seems that two little boats, resembling steamboats in form, kept up a constant trade in wood — clapboards, *pieux* [split boards], shingles, even cordwood — between the lakes and the Bayou Teche plantation. M. Gerbeau had taken his skiff and two oarsmen and gone in search of one of these boats, which, as he guessed, was not far away. In fact he met it in Mexican [now Berwick's] Bay, and for two hundred dollars persuaded the captain to take us to St. James. "Yes," said M. Gerbeau to us, " you will make in a week a journey that might have taken you two months."

The following Monday the captain tied up at M. Gerbeau's landing. It was a droll affair, his boat. You must have seen on plantations what they call a horse-mill — a long pole on which a man sits, and to which a horse or mule is hitched. Such was the machinery by which we moved. The boat's cabin was all one room. The berths, one above another, ran all round the room, hung with long curtains, and men, women, and children — when there were any — were all obliged to stay in the same apartment.

We remained with Alix to the last moment. The morning we left she gave Suzanne a pretty ring, and me a locket containing her portrait. In return my sister placed upon her finger a ruby encircled with little diamonds; and I, taking off the gold medal I always wore on my neck, whispered:

"Wear it for love of me."

She smiled. [Just as we were parting she handed me the story of her life.[1]]

At an early hour my father had our trunks, baskets, and mats sent aboard the *Sirène;* and after many tears, and promises to write and to return, we took our leave. We had quitted St. James the 20th of May. We landed there once more on the 26th of September. Need I recount the joy of my mother and sisters? You understand all that.

And now, my daughter, the tale is told. Read it to your children and assure them that all is true; that there is here no exaggeration; that they can put faith in their old grandmother's story and take their part in her pleasures, her friendships, and her emotions.

[1] See "How I Got Them," page 14.

Histoire d'Alix de Morainville
écrite à la Louisiane ce 2.2. Aout
1798
pour mes chères amies Suzanne &
Francoise Bossier

—

Je vous ay promis l'histoire de
ma vie, mes trens chères &
bien bonnes amies, avec lesquelles
... en tant de plaisir à
... du chaland de voyage

ALIX DE MORAINVILLE.

1773–95.

*Written in Louisiana this 22d of August, 1795, for
my dear friends Suzanne and Françoise Bossier.*

I HAVE promised you the story of my life, my very
dear and good friends with whom I have had so much
pleasure on board the flatboat which has brought us
all to Attakapas. I now make good my promise.

And first I must speak of the place where I was
born, of the beautiful Château de Morainville, built
above the little village named Morainville in honor of
its lords. This village, situated in Normandy on the
margin of the sea, was peopled only and entirely by
fishermen, who gained a livelihood openly by sardine-
fishing, and secretly, it was said, by smuggling. The
château was built on a cliff, which it completely occupied. This cliff was formed of several terraces that
rose in a stair one above another. On the topmost one
sat the château, like an eagle in its nest. It had four
dentilated turrets, with great casements and immense
galleries, that gave it the grandest possible aspect.
On the second terrace you found yourself in the midst
of delightful gardens adorned with statues and foun-

121

tains after the fashion of the times. Then came the
avenue, entirely overshaded with trees as old as Noah,
and everywhere on the hill, forming the background
of the picture, an immense park. How my Suzanne
would have loved to hunt in that beautiful park full
of deer, hare, and all sorts of feathered game!

And yet no one inhabited that beautiful domain.
Its lord and mistress, the Count Gaston and Countess
Aurélie, my father and mother, resided in Paris, and
came to their château only during the hunting season,
their sojourn never exceeding six weeks.

Already they had been five years married. The
countess, a lady of honor to the young dauphine,
Marie Antoinette, bore the well-merited reputation of
being the most charming woman at the court of the
king, Louis the Fifteenth. Count and countess,
wealthy as they were and happy as they seemed to
be, were not overmuch so, because of their desire for
a son; for one thing, which is not seen in this country, you will not doubt, dear girls, exists in France
and other countries of Europe: it is the eldest son,
and never the daughter, who inherits the fortune and
titles of the family. And in case there were no children, the titles and fortune of the Morainvilles would
have to revert in one lump to the nephew of the count
and son of his brother, to Abner de Morainville, who
at that time was a mere babe of four years. This did
not meet the wishes of M. and Mme. de Morainville,
who wished to retain their property in their own house.

But great news comes to Morainville: the countess
is with child. The steward of the château receives

orders to celebrate the event with great rejoicings. In the avenue long tables are set covered with all sorts of inviting meats, the fiddlers are called, and the peasants dance, eat, and drink to the health of the future heir of the Morainvilles. A few months later my parents arrived bringing a great company with them; and there were feasts and balls and hunting-parties without end.

It was in the course of one of these hunts that my mother was thrown from her horse. She was hardly in her seventh month when I came into the world. She escaped death, but I was born as large as — a mouse! and with one shoulder much higher than the other.

I must have died had not the happy thought come to the woman-in-waiting to procure Catharine, the wife of the gardener, Guillaume Carpentier, to be my nurse; and it is to her care, to her rubbings, and above all to her good milk, that I owe the capability to amuse you, my dear girls and friends, with the account of my life — that life whose continuance I truly owe to my mother Catharine.

When my actual mother had recovered she returned to Paris; and as my nurse, who had four boys, could not follow her, it was decided that I should remain at the château and that my mother Catharine should stay there with me.

Her cottage was situated among the gardens. Her husband, father Guillaume, was the head gardener, and his four sons were Joseph, aged six years; next Matthieu, who was four; then Jerome, two; and my foster-brother Bastien, a big lubber of three months.

My father and mother did not at all forget me.
They sent me playthings of all sorts, sweetmeats,
silken frocks adorned with embroideries and laces,
and all sorts of presents for mother Catharine and her
children. I was happy, very happy, for I was worshiped by all who surrounded me. Mother Catharine
preferred me above her own children. Father Guillaume would go down upon his knees before me to get
a smile [risette], and Joseph often tells me he swooned
when they let him hold me in his arms. It was a
happy time, I assure you; yes, very happy.

I was two years old when my parents returned, and
as they had brought a great company with them the
true mother instructed my nurse to take me back to
her cottage and keep me there, that I might not be
disturbed by noise. Mother Catharine has often said
to me that my mother could nôt bear to look at my
crippled shoulder, and that she called me a hunch-
back. But after all it was the truth, and my nurse-
mother was wrong to lay that reproach upon my
mother Aurélie.

Seven years passed. I had lived during that time
the life of my foster-brothers, flitting everywhere
with them over the flowery grass like the veritable
lark that I was. Two or three times during that
period my parents came to see me, but without company, quite alone. They brought me a lot of beautiful
things; but really I was afraid of them, particularly
of my mother, who was so beautiful and wore a grand
air full of dignity and self-regard. She would kiss

me, but in a way very different from mother Catharine's way — squarely on the forehead, a kiss that
seemed made of ice.

One fine day she arrived at the cottage with a tall,
slender lady who wore blue spectacles on a singularly
long nose. She frightened me, especially when my
mother told me that this was my governess, and that
I must return to the château with her and live there
to learn a host of fine things of which even the names
were to me unknown; for I had never seen a book
except my picture books.

I uttered piercing cries; but my mother, without
paying any attention to my screams, lifted me cleverly,
planted two spanks behind, and passed me to the
hands of Mme. Levicq — that was the name of my
governess. The next day my mother left me and I
repeated my disturbance, crying, stamping my feet,
and calling to mother Catharine and Bastien. (To
tell the truth, Jerome and Matthieu were two big
lubbers [rougeots] very peevish and coarse-mannered,
which I could not endure.) Madame put a book into
my hands and wished to have me repeat after her; I
threw the book at her head. Then, rightly enough,
in despair she placed me where I could see the cottage
in the midst of the garden and told me that when the
lesson was ended I might go and see my mother Catharine and play with my brothers. I promptly consented,
and that is how I learned to read.

This Mme. Levicq was most certainly a woman of
good sense. She had a kind heart and much ability.
She taught me nearly all I know — first of all, French;

the harp, the guitar, drawing, embroidery; in short, I say again, all that I know.

I was fourteen years old when my mother came, and this time not alone. My cousin Abner was with her. My mother had me called into her chamber, closely examined my shoulder, loosed my hair, looked at my teeth, made me read, sing, play the harp, and when all this was ended smiled and said:

"You are beautiful, my daughter; you have profited by the training of your governess; the defect of your shoulder has not increased. I am satisfied — well satisfied; and I am going to tell you that I have brought the Viscomte Abner de Morainville because I have chosen him for your future husband. Go, join him in the avenue."

I was a little dismayed at first, but when I had seen my intended my dismay took flight — he was such a handsome fellow, dressed with so much taste, and wore his sword with so much grace and spirit. At the end of two days he loved me to distraction and I doted on him. I brought him to my nurse's cabin and told her all our plans of marriage and all my happiness, not observing the despair of poor Joseph, who had always worshiped me and who had not doubted he would have me to love. But who would have thought it — a laboring gardener lover of his lord's daughter? Ah, I would have laughed heartily then if I had known it!

On the evening before my departure — I had to leave with my mother this time — I went to say adieu to mother Catharine. She asked me if I loved Abner.

"Oh, yes, mother!" I replied, "I love him with all my soul"; and she said she was happy to hear it. Then I directed Joseph to go and request Monsieur the curé, in my name, to give him lessons in reading and writing, in order to be able to read the letters that I should write to my nurse-mother and to answer them. This order was carried out to the letter, and six months later Joseph was the correspondent of the family and read to them my letters. That was his whole happiness.

I had been quite content to leave for Paris: first, because Abner went with me, and then because I hoped to see a little of all those beautiful things of which he had spoken to me with so much charm; but how was I disappointed! My mother kept me but one day at her house, and did not even allow Abner to come to see me. During that day I must, she said, collect my thoughts preparatory to entering the convent. For it was actually to the convent of the Ursulines, of which my father's sister was the superior, that she conducted me next day.

Think of it, dear girls! I was fourteen, but not bigger than a lass of ten, used to the open air and to the caresses of mother Catharine and my brothers. It seemed to me as if I were a poor little bird shut in a great dark cage.

My aunt, the abbess, Agnes de Morainville, took me to her room, gave me bonbons and pictures, told me stories, and kissed and caressed me, but her black gown and her bonnet appalled me, and I cried with all my might:

"I want mother Catharine! I want Joseph! I want Bastien!"

My aunt, in despair, sent for three or four little pupils to amuse me; but this was labor lost, and I continued to utter the same outcries. At last, utterly spent, I fell asleep, and my aunt bore me to my little room and put me to bed, and then slowly withdrew, leaving the door ajar.

On the second floor of the convent there were large dormitories, where some hundreds of children slept; but on the first there were a number of small chambers, the sole furniture of each being a folding bed, a washstand, and a chair, and you had to pay its weight in gold for the privilege of occupying one of these cells, in order not to be mixed with the daughters of the bourgeoisie, of lawyers and merchants. My mother, who was very proud, had exacted absolutely that they give me one of these select cells.

Hardly had my aunt left me when I awoke, and fear joined itself to grief. Fancy it! I had never lain down in a room alone, and here I awoke in a corner of a room half lighted by a lamp hung from the ceiling. You can guess I began again my writhings and cries. Thereupon appeared before me in the open door the most beautiful creature imaginable. I took her for a fairy, and fell to gazing at her with my eyes full of amazement and admiration. You have seen Madelaine, and you can judge of her beauty in her early youth. It was a fabulous beauty joined to a manner fair, regal, and good.

She took me in her arms, dried my tears, and at last,

at the extremity of her resources, carried me to her
bed; and when I awoke the next day I found myself
still in the arms of Madelaine de Livilier. From that
moment began between us that great and good friendship which was everything for me during the time that
I passed in the convent. I should have died of lone-
liness and grief without Madelaine. I had neither
brothers nor sisters; she was both these to me: she
was older than I, and protected me while she loved me.

She was the niece of the rich Cardinal de Ségur,
who had sent and brought her from Louisiana. This
is why Madelaine had such large privileges at the convent. She told me she was engaged to the young
Count Louis le Pelletrier de la Houssaye, and I, with
some change of color, told her of Abner.

One day Madelaine's aunt, the Countess de Ségur,
came to take her to spend the day at her palace. My
dear friend besought her aunt with such graciousness
that she obtained permission to take me with her, and
for the first time I saw the Count Louis, Madelaine's
fiancé. He was a very handsome young man, of majestic and distinguished air. He had hair and eyes
as black as ink, red lips, and a fine mustache. He
wore in his buttonhole the cross of the royal order
of St. Louis, and on his shoulders the epaulettes of
a major. He had lately come from San Domingo
[where he had been fighting the insurgents at the
head of his regiment].[1] Yes, he was a handsome young
man, a bold cavalier; and Madelaine idolized him.

---

[1] Inserted by a later hand than the author's. — TRANSLATOR.

After that day I often accompanied my friend in her visits to the home of her aunt. Count Louis was always there to wait upon his betrothed, and Abner, apprised by him, came to join us. Ah! that was a happy time, very happy.

At the end of a year my dear Madelaine quitted the convent to be married. Ah, how I wept to see her go! I loved her so! I had neither brothers nor sisters, and Madelaine was my heart's own sister. I was very young, scarcely fifteen; yet, despite my extreme youth, Madelaine desired me to be her bridesmaid, and her aunt, the Countess de Ségur, and the Baroness de Chevigné, Count Louis's aunt, went together to find my mother and ask her to permit me to fill that office. My mother made many objections, saying that I was too young; but — between you and me — she could refuse nothing to ladies of such high station. She consented, therefore, and proceeded at once to order my costume at the dressmaker's.

It was a mass of white silk and lace with intermingled pearls. For the occasion my mother lent me her pearls, which were of great magnificence. But, finest of all, the Queen, Marie Antoinette, saw me at the church of Notre Dame, whither all the court had gathered for the occasion, — for Count Louis de la Houssaye was a great favorite, — and now the queen sent one of her lords to apprise my mother that she wished to see me, and commanded that I be presented at court — *grande rumeur!*

Mamma consented to let me remain the whole week out of the convent. Every day there was a grand dinner or breakfast and every evening a dance or a grand ball. Always it was Abner who accompanied me. I wrote of all my pleasures to my mother Catharine. Joseph read my letters to her, and, as he told me in later days, they gave him mortal pain. For the presentation my mother ordered a suit all of gold and velvet. Madelaine and I were presented the same day. The Countess de Ségur was my escort [marraine] and took me by the hand, while Mme. de Chevigné rendered the same office to Madelaine. Abner told me that day I was as pretty as an angel. If I was so to him, it was because he loved me. I knew, myself, I was too small, too pale, and ever so different from Madelaine. It was she you should have seen.

I went back to the convent, and during the year that I passed there I was lonely enough to have died. It was decided that I should be married immediately on leaving the convent, and my mother ordered for me the most beautiful wedding outfit imaginable. My father bought me jewels of every sort, and Abner did not spare of beautiful presents.

I had been about fifteen days out of the convent when terrible news caused me many tears. My dear Madelaine was about to leave me forever and return to America. The reason was this : there was much disorder in the colony of Louisiana, and the king deciding to send thither a man capable of restoring order, his choice fell upon Count Louis de la Houssaye, whose noble character he had recognized. Count Louis would have refused, for he had a great liking for France; but [he had lately witnessed the atrocities committed by the negroes of San Domingo, and [1]] something — a presentiment — warned him that the Revolution was near at hand. He was glad to bear his dear wife far from the scenes of horror that were approaching with rapid strides.

Madelaine undoubtedly experienced pleasure in thinking that she was again going to see her parents and her native land, but she regretted to leave France, where she had found so much amusement and where I must remain behind her without hope of our ever seeing each other again. She wept, oh, so much!

She had bidden me good-bye and we had wept long, and her last evening, the eve of the day when she was to take the diligence for Havre, where the vessel awaited them, was to be passed in family group at the residence of the Baroness de Chevigné. Here were present, first the young couple; the Cardinal, the Count and Countess de Ségur; then Barthelemy de la Houssaye, brother of the Count, and the old Count de [Maurepas, only a few months returned from exile and now at the pinnacle of royal favor].[1] He had said when he came that he could stay but a few hours and had ordered his coach to await him below. He was the most lovable old man in the world. All at once Madelaine said:

"Ah! if I could see Alix once more — only once more!"

The old count without a word slipped away, entered his carriage, and had himself driven to the Morainville

---

[1] Inserted by a later hand than the author's. — TRANSLATOR.

hotel, where there was that evening a grand ball. Tarrying in the ante-chamber, he had my mother called. She came with alacrity, and when she knew the object of the count's visit she sent me to get a great white burnoose, enveloped me in it, and putting my hand into the count's said to me :

"You have but to show yourself to secure the carriage." But the count promised to bring me back himself.

Oh, how glad my dear Madelaine was to see me ! With what joy she kissed me ! But she has recounted this little scene to you, as you, Françoise, have told me.

A month after the departure of the De la Houssayes, my wedding was celebrated at Notre Dame. It was a grand occasion. The king was present with all the court. As my husband was in the king's service, the queen wished me to become one of her ladies of honor.

Directly after my marriage I had Bastien come to me. I made him my confidential servant. He rode behind my carriage, waited upon me at table, and, in short, was my man of all work.

I was married the 16th of March, 1789, at the age of sixteen. Already the rumbling murmurs of the Revolution were making themselves heard like distant thunder. On the 13th of July the Bastille was taken and the head of the governor De Launay [was] carried through the streets.[1] My mother was frightened and proposed to leave the country. She came to find me and implored me to go with her to England, and

---

[1] Alix makes a mistake here of one day. The Bastille fell on the 14th. — TRANSLATOR.

asked Abner to accompany us. My husband refused
with indignation, declaring that his place was near his
king.

"And mine near my husband," said I, throwing my
arms around Abner's neck.

My father, like my husband, had refused positively to
leave the king, and it was decided that mamma should
go alone. She began by visiting the shops, and bought
stuffs, ribbons, and laces. It was I who helped her pack
her trunks, which she sent in advance to Morainville.
She did not dare go to get her diamonds, which
were locked up in the Bank of France; that would
excite suspicion, and she had to content herself with
such jewelry as she had at her residence. She left in
a coach with my father, saying as she embraced me
that her absence would be brief, for it would be easy
enough to crush the vile mob. She went down to
Morainville, and there, thanks to the devotion of
Guillaume Carpentier and of his sons, she was carried
to England in a contrabandist vessel. As she was
accustomed to luxury, she put into her trunks the
plate of the château and also several valuable pictures.
My father had given her sixty thousand francs and
charged her to be economical.

Soon I found myself in the midst of terrible scenes
that I have not the courage, my dear girls, to recount.
The memory of them makes me even to-day tremble
and turn pale. I will only tell you that one evening
a furious populace entered our palace. I saw my
husband dragged far from me by those wretches, and
just as two of the monsters were about to seize me

Bastien took me into his arms, and holding me tightly against his bosom leaped from a window and took to flight with all his speed.

Happy for us that it was night and that the monsters were busy pillaging the house. They did not pursue us at all, and my faithful Bastien took me to the home of his cousin Claudine Leroy. She was a worker in lace, whom, with my consent, he was to have married within the next fortnight. I had lost consciousness, but Claudine and Bastien cared for me so well that they brought me back to life, and I came to myself to learn that my father and my husband had been arrested and conveyed to the Conciergerie.

My despair was great, as you may well think. Claudine arranged a bed for me in a closet [cloisette] adjoining her chamber, and there I remained hidden, dying of fear and grief, as you may well suppose.

At the end of four days I heard some one come into Claudine's room, and then a deep male voice. My heart ceased to beat and I was about to faint away, when I recognized the voice of my faithful Joseph. I opened the door and threw myself upon his breast, crying over and over:

"O Joseph! dear Joseph!"

He pressed me to his bosom, giving me every sort of endearing name, and at length revealed to me the plan he had formed, to take me at once to Morainville under the name of Claudine Leroy. He went out with Claudine to obtain a passport. Thanks to God and good angels Claudine was small like me, had black hair and eyes like mine, and there was no trouble in arranging the passport. We took the diligence, and as I was clothed in peasant dress, a suit of Claudine's, I easily passed for her.

Joseph had the diligence stop beside the park gate, of which he had brought the key. He wished to avoid the village. We entered therefore by the park, and soon I was installed in the cottage of my adopted parents, and Joseph and his brothers said to every one that Claudine Leroy, appalled by the horrors being committed in Paris, had come for refuge to Morainville.

Then Joseph went back to Paris to try to save my father and my husband. Bastien had already got himself engaged as an assistant in the prison. But alas! all their efforts could effect nothing, and the only consolation that Joseph brought back to Morainville was that he had seen its lords on the fatal cart and had received my father's last smile. These frightful tidings failed to kill me; I lay a month between life and death, and Joseph, not to expose me to the recognition of the Morainville physician, went and brought one from Rouen. The good care of mother Catharine was the best medicine for me, and I was cured to weep over my fate and my cruel losses.

It was at this juncture that for the first time I suspected that Joseph loved me. His eyes followed me with a most touching expression; he paled and blushed when I spoke to him, and I divined the love which the poor fellow could not conceal. It gave me pain to see how he loved me, and increased my wish to join my mother in England. I knew she had need of me, and I had need of her.

Meanwhile a letter came to the address of father
Guillaume. It was a contrabandist vessel that brought
it and
of the first evening
other to the address
recognized the writing
set me to sobbing
all, my heart
I began   (*Torn off and gone.*)
demanded of
my father of
saying that
country well
56

added that Abner and I must come also, and that it
was nonsense to wish to remain faithful to a lost cause.
She begged my father to go and draw her diamonds
from the bank and to send them to her with at least a
hundred thousand francs. Oh! how I wept after seeing

letter ! Mother Catharine
to console me but
then to make.   Then
and said to me, Will
to make you
England, Madame
Oh ! yes, Joseph
would be so well pleased
poor fellow
the money of
family.   I

(*Torn off and gone.*)

From the way in which the cabin was built, one could see any one coming who had business there. But one day — God knows how it happened — a child of the village all at once entered the chamber where I was and knew me.

"Madame Alix!" he cried, took to his heels and went down the terrace pell-mell [quatre à quatre] to give the alarm. Ten minutes later Matthieu came at a full run and covered with sweat, to tell us that all the village was in commotion and that those people to whom I had always been so good were about to come and arrest me, to deliver me to the executioners. I ran to Joseph, beside myself with affright.

"Save me, Joseph! save me!"

"I will use all my efforts for that, Mme. la Viscomtesse."

At that moment Jerome appeared. He came to say that a representative of the people was at hand and that I was lost beyond a doubt.

"Not yet," responded Joseph. "I have foreseen this and have prepared everything to save you, Mme. la Viscomtesse, if you will but let me make myself well understood."

"Oh, all, all! Do *thou* understand, Joseph, I will do everything thou desirest."

"Then," he said, regarding me fixedly and halting at each word — "then it is necessary that you consent to take Joseph Carpentier for your spouse."

I thought I had [been] misunderstood and drew back haughtily.

"My son!" cried mother Catharine.

"Oh, you see," replied Joseph, "my mother herself accuses me, and you — you, madame, have no greater confidence in me. But that is nothing; I must save you at any price. We will go from here together; we will descend to the village; we will present ourselves at the mayoralty — "

In spite of myself I made a gesture.

"Let me speak, madame," he said. "We have not a moment to lose. Yes, we will present ourselves at the mayoralty, and there I will espouse you, not as Claudine Leroy, but as Alix de Morainville. Once my wife you have nothing to fear. Having become one of the people, the people will protect you. After the ceremony, madame, I will hand you the certificate of our marriage, and you will tear it up the moment we shall have touched the soil of England. Keep it precious till then; it is your only safeguard. Nothing prevents me from going to England to find employment, and necessarily my wife will go with me. Are you ready, madame?"

For my only response I put my hand in his; I was too deeply moved to speak. Mother Catharine threw both her arms about her son's neck and cried, "My noble child!" and we issued from the cottage guarded by Guillaume and his three other sons, armed to the teeth.

When the mayor heard the names and surnames of the wedding pair he turned to Joseph, saying:

"You are not lowering yourself, my boy."

At the door of the mayoralty we found ourselves

face to face with an immense crowd. I trembled violently and pressed against Joseph. He, never losing his presence of mind [sans perdre la carte], turned, saying:

"Allow me, my friends, to present to you my wife. The Viscomtesse de Morainville no longer exists; hurrah for the Citoyenne Carpentier." And the hurrahs and cries of triumph were enough to deafen one. Those who the moment before were ready to tear me into pieces now wanted to carry me in triumph. Arrived at the house, Joseph handed me our act of marriage.

"Keep it, madame," said he; "you can destroy it on your arrival in England."

At length one day, three weeks after our marriage, Joseph came to tell me that he had secured passage on a vessel, and that we must sail together under the name of Citoyen and Citoyenne Carpentier. I was truly sorry to leave my adopted parents and foster-brother, yet at the bottom of my heart I was rejoiced that I was going to find my mother.

But alas! when I arrived in London, at the address that she had given me, I found there only her old friend the Chevalier d'Ivoy, who told me that my mother was dead, and that what was left of her money, with her jewels and chests, was deposited in the Bank of England. I was more dead than alive; all these things paralyzed me. But my good Joseph took upon himself to do everything for me. He went and drew what had been deposited in the bank. Indeed of money there remained but twelve thousand francs; but there were plate, jewels, pictures, and many vanities in the form of gowns and every sort of attire.

Joseph rented a little house in a suburb of London, engaged an old Frenchwoman to attend me, and he, after all my husband, made himself my servant, my gardener, my factotum. He ate in the kitchen with the maid, waited upon me at table, and slept in the garret on a pallet.

"Am I not very wicked?" said I to myself every day, especially when I saw his pallor and profound sadness. They had taught me in the convent that the ties of marriage were a sacred thing and that one could not break them, no matter how they might have been made; and when my patrician pride revolted at the thought of this union with the son of my nurse my heart pleaded
and pleaded
hard the cause
of poor J
Joseph. His   (*Evidently torn before Alix*
care, his   *wrote on it, as no words*
presence, be-   *are wanting in the text.*)
came more
and more
necessary. I knew not how to do anything myself, but made him my all in all, avoiding myself every shadow of care or trouble. I must say, moreover, that since he had married me I had a kind of fear of him and was afraid that I should hear him speak to me of love; but he scarcely thought of it, poor fellow:

reverence closed his lips. Thus matters stood when
one evening Joseph
entered the room

(*Opposite page of the* where I was read-
same torn sheet. Alix ing, and stand-
has again written ing upright be-
around the rent.) fore me, his hat
in his hand, said
to me that he had something to tell me. His expression
was so unhappy that I felt the tears mount to my eyes.

"What is it, dear Joseph?" I asked; and when he
could answer nothing on account of his emotion, I
rose, crying:

"More bad news? What has happened to my
nurse-mother? Speak, speak, Joseph!"

"Nothing, Mme. la Viscomtesse," he replied. "My
mother and Bastien, I hope, are well. It is of myself
I wish to speak."

Then my heart made a sad commotion in my bosom,
for I thought he was about to speak of love. But not
at all. He began again, in a low voice:

"I am going to America, madame."

I sprung towards him. "You go away? You go
away?" I cried. "And I, Joseph?"

"You, madame?" said he. "You have money.
The Revolution will soon be over, and you can return
to your country. There you will find again your
friends, your titles, your fortune."

"Stop!" I cried. "What shall I be in France?
You well know my château, my palace are pillaged
and burned, my parents are dead."

"My mother and Bastien are in France," he responded.

"But thou — thou, Joseph; what can I do without thee ? Why have you accustomed me to your tenderness, to your protection, and now come threatening to leave me ? Hear me plainly. If you go I go with you."

He uttered a smothered cry and staggered like a drunken man.

" Alix — madame — "

"I have guessed your secret," continued I. "You seek to go because you love me — because you fear you may forget that respect which you fancy you owe me. But after all I am your wife, Joseph. I have the right to follow thee, and I am going with thee." And slowly I drew from my dressing-case the act of our marriage.

He looked at me, oh! in such a funny way, and — extended his arms. I threw myself into them, and for half an hour it was tears and kisses and words of love. For after all I loved Joseph, not as I had loved Abner, but altogether more profoundly.

The next day a Catholic priest blessed our marriage. A month later we left for Louisiana, where Joseph hoped to make a fortune for me. But alas! he was despairing of success, when he met Mr. Carlo, and — you know, dear girls, the rest.

ROLL again and slip into its ancient silken case the small, square manuscript which some one has sewed at the back with worsted of the pale tint known as "baby-blue." Blessed little word! Time justified the color. If you doubt it go to the Teche; ask any of the De la Houssayes — or count, yourself, the Carpentiers and Charpentiers. You will be more apt to quit because you are tired than because you have finished.

And while there ask, over on the Attakapas side, for any trace that any one may be able to give of Dorothea Müller. She too was from France: at least, not from Normandy or Paris, like Alix, but, like Françoise's young aunt with the white hair, a German of Alsace, from a village near Strasbourg; like her, an emigrant, and, like Françoise, a voyager with father and sister by flatboat from old New Orleans up the Mississippi, down the Atchafalaya, and into the land of Attakapas. You may ask, you may seek; but if you find the faintest trace you will have done what no one else has succeeded in doing. We shall never know her fate. Her sister's we can tell; and we shall now see how different from the stories of Alix and Françoise is that of poor Salome Müller, even in the same land and almost in the same times.

SALOME MÜLLER,

THE WHITE SLAVE.

1818–45.

I.

SALOME AND HER KINDRED.

SHE may be living yet, in 1889. For when she came to Louisiana, in 1818, she was too young for the voyage to fix itself in her memory. She could not, to-day, be more than seventy-five.

In Alsace, France, on the frontier of the Department of Lower Rhine, about twenty English miles from Strasburg, there was in those days, as I suppose there still is, a village called Langensoultz. The region was one of hills and valleys and of broad, flat meadows yearly overflowed by the Rhine. It was noted for its fertility; a land of wheat and wine, hop-fields, flax-fields, hay-stacks, and orchards.

It had been three hundred and seventy years under French rule, yet the people were still, in speech and traditions, German. Those were not the times to make them French. The land swept by Napoleon's wars, their firesides robbed of fathers and sons by the conscription, the awful mortality of the Russian cam-

paign, the emperor's waning star, Waterloo — these
were not the things or conditions to give them comfort
in French domination.   There was a widespread longing among them to seek another land where men and
women and children were not doomed to feed the
ambition of European princes.

In the summer of 1817 there lay at the Dutch port
of Helder — for the great ship-canal that now lets the
largest vessels out from Amsterdam was not yet con-
structed — a big, foul, old Russian ship which a certain man had bought purposing to crowd it full of
emigrants to America.

These he had expected to find up the Rhine, and
he was not disappointed.   Hundreds responded from
Alsace; some in Strasburg itself, and many from the
surrounding villages, grain-fields, and vineyards.   They
presently numbered nine hundred, husbands, wives,
and children.   There was one family named Thomas,
with a survivor of which I conversed in 1884.   And
there was Eva Kropp, *née* Hillsler, and her husband,
with their daughter of fifteen, named for her mother.
Also Eva Kropp's sister Margaret and her husband,
whose name does not appear.· And there were Koelhoffer and his wife, and Frau Schultzheimer.   There
is no need to remember exact relationships.   All these
except the Thomases were of Langensoultz.

As they passed through another village some three
miles away they were joined by a family of name not
given, but the mother of which we shall know by and
by, under a second husband's name, as Madame Fleikener.   And there too was one Wagner, two genera-

tions of whose descendants were to furnish each a
noted journalist to New Orleans. I knew the younger
of these in my boyhood as a man of, say, fifty. And
there was young Frank Schuber, a good, strong-hearted,
merry fellow who two years after became the husband
of the younger Eva Kropp; he hailed from Strasburg;
I have talked with his grandson. And lastly there
were among the Langensoultz group two families
named Müller.

The young brothers Henry and Daniel Müller were
by birth Bavarians. They had married, in the Hillsler
family, two sisters of Eva and Margaret. They had
been known in the village as lockmaker Müller and
shoemaker Müller. The wife of Daniel, the shoemaker, was Dorothea. Henry, the locksmith, and his
wife had two sons, the elder ten years of age and
named for his uncle Daniel, the shoemaker. Daniel
and Dorothea had four children. The eldest was a
little boy of eight years, the youngest was an infant,
and between these were two little daughters, Dorothea
and Salome.

And so the villagers were all bound closely together,
as villagers are apt to be. Eva Kropp's young daughter
Eva was godmother to Salome. Frau Koelhoffer had
lived on a farm about an hour's walk from the Müllers
and had not known them; but Frau Schultzheimer
was a close friend, and had been a schoolmate and
neighbor of Salome's mother. The husband of her
who was afterward Madame Fleikener was a nephew
of the Müller brothers, Frank Schuber was her cousin,
and so on.

II.

SIX MONTHS AT ANCHOR.

SETTING out thus by whole families and with brothers' and sisters' families on the right and on the left, we may safely say that, once the last kisses were given to those left behind and the last look taken of childhood's scenes, they pressed forward brightly, filled with courage and hope. They were poor, but they were bound for a land where no soldier was going to snatch the beads and cross from the neck of a little child, as one of Napoleon's had attempted to do to one of the Thomas children. They were on their way to golden America; through Philadelphia to the virgin lands of the great West. Early in August they reached Amsterdam. There they paid their passage in advance, and were carried out to the Helder, where, having laid in their provisions, they embarked and were ready to set sail.

But no sail was set. Word came instead that the person who had sold the ship had not been paid its price and had seized the vessel; the delays of the law threatened, when time was a matter of fortune or of ruin.

And soon came far worse tidings. The emigrants refused to believe them as long as there was room for doubt. Henry and Daniel Müller — for locksmith Müller, said Wagner twenty-seven years afterwards on the witness-stand, "was a brave man and was foremost in doing everything necessary to be done for the passengers " — went back to Amsterdam to see if such news could be true, and returned only to confirm despair. The man to whom the passage money of the two hundred families — nine hundred souls — had been paid had absconded.

They could go neither forward nor back. Days, weeks, months passed, and there still lay the great hulk teeming with its population and swinging idly at anchor; fathers gazing wistfully over the high bulwarks, mothers nursing their babes, and the children, Eva, Daniel, Henry, Andrew, Dorothea, Salome, and all the rest, by hundreds.

Salome was a pretty child, dark, as both her parents were, and looking much like her mother; having especially her black hair and eyes and her chin. Playing around with her was one little cousin, a girl of her own age, — that is, somewhere between three and five, — whose face was strikingly like Salome's. It was she who in later life became Madame Karl Rouff, or, more familiarly, Madame Karl.

Provisions began to diminish, grew scanty, and at length were gone. The emigrants' summer was turned into winter; it was now December. So pitiful did their case become that it forced the attention of the Dutch Government. Under its direction they were brought back to Amsterdam, where many of them, without goods, money, or even shelter, and strangers to the place and to the language, were reduced to beg for bread.

But by and by there came a word of great relief.

The Government offered a reward of thirty thousand gilders — about twelve thousand dollars — to any merchant or captain of a vessel who would take them to America, and a certain Grandsteiner accepted the task. For a time he quartered them in Amsterdam, but by and by, with hearts revived, they began to go again on shipboard. This time there were three ships in place of the one; or two ships, and one of those old Dutch, flattish-bottomed, round-sided, two-masted crafts they called galiots. The number of ships was trebled — that was well; but the number of souls was doubled, and eighteen hundred wanderers from home were stowed in the three vessels.

III.

FAMINE AT SEA.

These changes made new farewells and separations. Common aims, losses, and sufferings had knit together in friendship many who had never seen each other until they met on the deck of the big Russian ship, and now not a few of these must part.

The first vessel to sail was one of the two ships, the *Johanna Maria*. Her decks were black with people: there were over six hundred of them. Among the number, waving farewell to the Kropps, the Koelhoffers, the Schultzheimers, to Frank Schuber and to the Müllers, stood the Thomases, Madame Fleikener, as we have to call her, and one whom we have not yet named, the jungfrau Hemin, of Würtemberg, just turning nineteen, of whom the little Salome and her mother had made a new, fast friend on the old Russian ship.

A week later the *Captain Grone* — that is, the galiot — hoisted the Dutch flag as the *Johanna Maria* had done, and started after her with other hundreds on her own deck, I know not how many, but making eleven hundred in the two, and including, for one, young Wagner. Then after two weeks more the remaining ship, the *Johanna*, followed, with Grandsteiner as supercargo, and seven hundred emigrants. Here were the Müllers and most of their relatives and fellow-villagers. Frank Schuber was among them, and was chosen steward for the whole shipful.

At last they were all off. But instead of a summer's they were now to encounter a winter's sea, and to meet it weakened and wasted by sickness and destitution. The first company had been out but a week when, on New Year's night, a furious storm burst upon the crowded ship. With hatches battened down over their heads they heard and felt the great buffetings of the tempest, and by and by one great crash above all other noises as the mainmast went by the board. The ship survived; but when the storm was over and the people swarmed up once more into the pure ocean atmosphere and saw the western sun set clear, it set astern of the ship. Her captain had put her about and was steering for Amsterdam.

" She is too old," the travelers gave him credit for saying, when long afterwards they testified in court;

"too old, too crowded, too short of provisions, and too crippled, to go on such a voyage; I don't want to lose my soul that way." And he took them back.

They sailed again; but whether in another ship, or in the same with another captain, I have not discovered. Their sufferings were terrible. The vessel was foul. Fevers broke out among them. Provisions became scarce. There was nothing fit for the sick, who daily grew more numerous. Storms tossed them hither and yon. Water became so scarce that the sick died for want of it.

One of the Thomas children, a little girl of eight years, whose father lay burning with fever and moaning for water, found down in the dark at the back of one of the water-casks a place where once in a long time a drop of water fell from it. She placed there a small vial, and twice a day bore it, filled with water-drops, to the sick man. It saved his life. Of the three ship-loads only two families reached America whole, and one of these was the Thomases. A younger sister told me in 1884 that though the child lived to old age on the banks of the Mississippi River, she could never see water wasted and hide her anger.

The vessels were not bound for Philadelphia, as the Russian ship had been. Either from choice or of necessity the destination had been changed before sailing, and they were on their way to New Orleans.

That city was just then — the war of 1812–15 being so lately over — coming boldly into notice as commercially a strategic point of boundless promise. Steam navigation had hardly two years before won its first victory against the powerful current of the Mississippi, but it was complete. The population was thirty-three thousand; exports, thirteen million dollars. Capital and labor were crowding in, and legal, medical, and commercial talent were hurrying to the new field.

Scarcely at any time since has the New Orleans bar, in proportion to its numbers, had so many brilliant lights. Edward Livingston, of world-wide fame, was there in his prime. John R. Grymes, who died a few years before the opening of the late civil war, was the most successful man with juries who ever plead in Louisiana courts. We must meet him in the court-room by and by, and may as well make his acquaintance now. He was emphatically a man of the world. Many anecdotes of him remain, illustrative rather of intrepid shrewdness than of chivalry. He had been counsel for the pirate brothers Lafitte in their entanglements with the custom-house and courts, and was believed to have received a hundred thousand dollars from them as fees. Only old men remember him now. They say he never lifted his voice, but in tones that grew softer and lower the more the thought behind them grew intense would hang a glamour of truth over the veriest sophistries that intellectual ingenuity could frame. It is well to remember that this is only tradition, which can sometimes be as unjust as daily gossip. It is sure that he could entertain most showily. The young Duke of Saxe-Weimar-

Eisenach was once his guest. In his book of travels in America (1825–26) he says:

> My first excursion [in New Orleans] was to visit Mr. Grymes, who here inhabits a large, massive, and splendidly furnished house. . . . In the evening we paid our visit to the governor of the State. . . . After this we went to several coffee-houses where the lower classes amuse themselves. . . . Mr. Grymes took me to the masked ball, which is held every evening during the carnival at the French theater. . . . The dress of the ladies I observed to be very elegant, but understood that most of those dancing did not belong to the better class of society. . . . At a dinner, which Mr. Grymes gave me with the greatest display of magnificence, . . . we withdrew from the first table, and seated ourselves at the second, in the same order in which we had partaken of the first. As the variety of wines began to set the tongues of the guests at liberty, the ladies rose, retired to another apartment, and resorted to music. Some of the gentlemen remained with the bottle, while others, among whom I was one, followed the ladies. . . . We had waltzing until 10 o'clock, when we went to the masquerade in the theater in St. Philip street. . . . The female company at the theater consisted of quadroons, who, however, were masked.

Such is one aspect given us by history of the New Orleans towards which that company of emigrants, first of the three that had left the other side, were toiling across the waters.

IV.

SOLD INTO BONDAGE.

THEY were fever-struck and famine-wasted. But February was near its end, and they were in the Gulf of Mexico. At that time of year its storms have lulled and its airs are the perfection of spring; March is a kind of May. And March came.

They saw other ships now every day; many of them going their way. The sight cheered them; the passage had been lonely as well as stormy. Their own vessels, of course, — the other two, — they had not expected to see, and had not seen. They did not know whether they were on the sea or under it.

At length pilot-boats began to appear. One came to them and put a pilot on board. Then the blue water turned green, and by and by yellow. A fringe of low land was almost right ahead. Other vessels were making for the same lighthouse towards which they were headed, and so drew constantly nearer to one another. The emigrants line the bulwarks, watching the nearest sails. One ship is so close that some can see the play of waters about her bows. And now it is plain that her bulwarks, too, are lined with emigrants who gaze across at them. She glides nearer, and just as the cry of recognition bursts from this whole company the other one yonder suddenly waves caps and kerchiefs and sends up a cheer. Their ship is the *Johanna*.

Do we dare draw upon fancy? We must not. The companies did meet on the water, near the Mississippi's mouth, though whether first inside or outside the stream I do not certainly gather. But they met; not the two vessels only, but the three. They were towed up the river side by side, the *Johanna* here, the *Captain Grone* there, and the other ship between them. Wagner, who had sailed on the galiot, was still alive. Many years afterwards he testified:

"We all arrived at the Balize [the river's mouth] the same day. The ships were so close we could speak to each other from on board our respective ships. We inquired of one another of those who had died and of those who still remained."

Madame Fleikener said the same:

"We hailed each other from the ships and asked who lived and who had died. The father and mother of Madame Schuber [Kropp and his wife] told me Daniel Müller and family were on board."

But they had suffered loss. Of the *Johanna's* 700 souls only 430 were left alive. Henry Müller's wife was dead. Daniel Müller's wife, Dorothea, had been sick almost from the start; she was gone, with the babe at her bosom. Henry was left with his two boys, and Daniel with his one and his little Dorothea and Salome. Grandsteiner, the supercargo, had lived; but of 1800 homeless poor whom the Dutch king's gilders had paid him to bring to America, foul ships and lack of food and water had buried 1200 in the sea.

The vessels reached port and the passengers pre-

pared to step ashore, when to their amazement and
dismay Grandsteiner laid the hand of the law upon
them and told them they were "redemptioners." A
redemptioner was an emigrant whose services for a
certain period were liable to be sold to the highest
bidder for the payment of his passage to America.
It seems that in fact a large number of those on
board the *Johanna* had in some way really become
so liable; but it is equally certain that of others,
the Kropps, the Schultzheimers, the Koelhoffers, the
Müllers, and so on, the transportation had been paid
for in advance, once by themselves and again by the
Government of Holland.   Yet Daniel Müller and
his children were among those held for their passage money.

Some influential German residents heard of these
troubles and came to the rescue.   Suits were brought
against Grandsteiner, the emigrants remaining meanwhile on the ships.   Mr. Grymes was secured as
counsel in their cause; but on some account not now
remembered by survivors scarce a week had passed
before they were being sold as redemptioners.   At
least many were, including Daniel Müller and his
children.

Then the dispersion began.   The people were bound
out before notaries and justices of the peace, singly
and in groups, some to one, some to two years' service,
according to age.   "They were scattered," — so testified Frank Schuber twenty-five years afterwards, —
"scattered about like young birds leaving a nest, without knowing anything of each other."   They were

"taken from the ships," says the jungfrau Hemin, "and went here and there so that one scarcely knew where the other went."

Many went no farther than New Orleans or its suburbs, but settled, some in and about the old rue Chartres — the Thomas family, for example; others in the then new faubourg Marigny, where Eva Kropp's daughter, Salome's young cousin Eva, for one, seems to have gone into domestic service. Others, again, were taken out to plantations near the city; Madame Fleikener to the well-known estate of Maunsell White, Madame Schultzheimer to the locally famous Hopkins plantation, and so on.

But others were carried far away; some, it is said, even to Alabama. Madame Hemin was taken a hundred miles up the river, to Baton Rouge, and Henry Müller and his two little boys went on to Bayou Sara, and so up beyond the State's border and a short way into Mississippi.

When all his relatives were gone Daniel Müller was still in the ship with his little son and daughters. Certainly he was not a very salable redemptioner with his three little motherless children about his knees. But at length, some fifteen days after the arrival of the ships, Frank Schuber met him on the old custom-house wharf with his little ones and was told by him that he, Müller, was going to Attakapas. About the same time, or a little later, Müller came to the house where young Eva Kropp, afterwards Schuber's wife, dwelt, to tell her good-bye. She begged to be allowed to keep Salome. During the sickness of the little

one's mother and after the mother's death she had
taken constant maternal care of the pretty, black-eyed,
olive-skinned godchild. But Müller would not leave
her behind.

V.

THE LOST ORPHANS.

THE prospective journey was the same that we saw
Suzanne and Françoise, Joseph and Alix, take with
toil and danger, yet with so much pleasure, in 1795.
The early company went in a flatboat; these went in
a round-bottom boat. The journey of the latter was
probably the shorter. Its adventures have never been
told, save one line. When several weeks afterwards
the boat returned, it brought word that Daniel Müller
had one day dropped dead on the deck and that his
little son had fallen overboard and was drowned. The
little girls had presumably been taken on to their
destination by whoever had been showing the way;
but that person's name and residence, if any of those
left in New Orleans had known them, were forgotten.
Only the wide and almost trackless region of Attakapas was remembered, and by people to whom every
day brought a struggle for their own existence.
Besides, the children's kindred were bound as redemptioners.

Those were days of rapid change in New Orleans.
The redemptioners worked their way out of bondage
into liberty. At the end of a year or two those who had

been taken to plantations near by returned to the city. The town was growing, but the upper part of the river front in faubourg Ste. Marie, now in the heart of the city, was still lined with brick-yards, and thitherward cheap houses and opportunities for market gardening drew the emigrants. They did not colonize, however, but merged into the community about them, and only now and then, casually, met one another. Young Schuber was an exception; he throve as a butcher in the old French market, and courted and married the young Eva Kropp. When the fellow-emigrants occasionally met, their talk was often of poor shoemaker Müller and his lost children.

No clear tidings of them came. Once the children of some Germans who had driven cattle from Attakapas to sell them in the shambles at New Orleans corroborated to Frank Schuber the death of the father; but where Salome and Dorothea were they could not say, except that they were in Attakapas.

Frank and Eva were specially diligent inquirers after Eva's lost godchild; as also was Henry Müller up in or near Woodville, Mississippi. He and his boys were, in their small German way, prospering. He made such effort as he could to find the lost children. One day in the winter of 1820–21 he somehow heard that there were two orphan children named Miller — the Müllers were commonly called Miller — in the town of Natchez, some thirty-five miles away on the Mississippi. He bought a horse and wagon, and, leaving his own children, set out to rescue those of his dead brother. About midway on

the road from Woodville to Natchez the Homochitto
Creek runs through a swamp which in winter it over-
flows. In here Müller lost his horse. But, nothing
daunted, he pressed on, only to find in Natchez the
trail totally disappear.

Again, in the early spring of 1824, a man driving
cattle from Attakapas to Bayou Sara told him of two
little girls named Miller living in Attakapas. He
was planning another and bolder journey in search of
them, when he fell ill; and at length, without telling
his sons, if he knew, where to find their lost cousins,
he too died.

Years passed away. Once at least in nearly every
year young Daniel Miller — the "u" was dropped —
of Woodville came down to New Orleans. At such
times he would seek out his relatives and his father's
and uncle's old friends and inquire for tidings of the
lost children. But all in vain. Frank and Eva Schuber
too kept up the inquiry in his absence, but no breath
of tidings came. On the city's south side sprung up
the new city of Lafayette, now the Fourth District of
New Orleans, and many of the aforetime redemptioners moved thither. Its streets near the river became almost a German quarter. Other German immigrants, hundreds and hundreds, landed among them,
and in the earlier years many of these were redemptioners. Among them one whose name will always be
inseparable from the history of New Orleans has a
permanent place in this story.

VI.

CHRISTIAN ROSELIUS.

ONE morning many years ago, when some business had brought me into a corridor of one of the old court buildings facing the Place d'Armes, a loud voice from within one of the court-rooms arrested my own and the general ear. At once from all directions men came with decorous haste towards the spot whence it proceeded. I pushed in through a green door into a closely crowded room and found the Supreme Court of the State in session. A short, broad, big-browed man of an iron sort, with silver hair close shorn from a Roman head, had just begun his argument in the final trial of a great case that had been before the court for many years, and the privileged seats were filled with the highest legal talent, sitting to hear him. It was a famous will case,[1] and I remember that he was quoting from "King Lear" as I entered.

"Who is that?" I asked of a man packed against me in the press.

"Roselius," he whispered; and the name confirmed my conjecture: the speaker looked like all I had once heard about him. Christian Roselius came from Brunswick, Germany, a youth of seventeen, something more than two years later than Salome Müller and her friends. Like them he came an emigrant under the Dutch flag, and like them his passage was paid in New

---

[1] The will of R. D. Shepherd.

Orleans by his sale as a redemptioner. A printer bought his services for two years and a half. His story is the good old one of courage, self-imposed privations, and rapid development of talents. From printing he rose to journalism, and from journalism passed to the bar. By 1836, at thirty-three years of age, he stood in the front rank of that brilliant group where Grymes was still at his best. Before he was forty he had been made attorney-general of the State. Punctuality, application, energy, temperance, probity, bounty, were the strong features of his character. It was a common thing for him to give his best services free in the cause of the weak against the strong. As an adversary he was decorous and amiable, but thunderous, heavy-handed, derisive if need be, and inexorable. A time came for these weapons to be drawn in defense of Salome Müller.

VII.

MILLER *versus* BELMONTI.

In 1843 Frank and Eva Schuber had moved to a house on the corner of Jackson and Annunciation streets.[1] They had brought up sons, two at least, who were now old enough to be their father's mainstay in his enlarged business of "farming" (leasing and subletting) the Poydras market. The father and mother and their kindred and companions in long past misfortunes and sorrows had grown to wealth and stand-

---

[1] Long since burned down.

ing among the German-Americans of New Orleans and Lafayette. The little girl cousin of Salome Müller, who as a child of the same age had been her playmate on shipboard at the Helder and in crossing the Atlantic, and who looked so much like Salome, was a woman of thirty, the wife of Karl Rouff.

One summer day she was on some account down near the lower limits of New Orleans on or near the river front, where the population was almost wholly a lower class of Spanish people. Passing an open door her eye was suddenly arrested by a woman of about her own age engaged in some humble service within with her face towards the door.

Madame Karl paused in astonishment. The place was a small drinking-house, a mere *cabaret;* but the woman! It was as if her aunt Dorothea, who had died on the ship twenty-five years before, stood face to face with her alive and well. There were her black hair and eyes, her olive skin, and the old, familiar expression of countenance that belonged so distinctly to all the Hillsler family. Madame Karl went in.

" My name," the woman replied to her question, "is Mary." And to another question, "No; I am a yellow girl. I belong to Mr. Louis Belmonti, who keeps this 'coffee-house.' He has owned me for four or five years. Before that? Before that, I belonged to Mr. John Fitz Miller, who has the saw-mill down here by the convent. I always belonged to him." Her accent was the one common to English-speaking slaves.

But Madame Karl was not satisfied. " You are not rightly a slave. Your name is Müller. You are of pure German blood. I knew your mother. I know you. We came to this country together on the same ship, twenty-five years ago."

"No," said the other; "you must be mistaking me for some one else that I look like."

But Madame Karl: "Come with me. Come up into Lafayette and see if I do not show you to others who will know you the moment they look at you."

The woman enjoyed much liberty in her place and was able to accept this invitation. Madame Karl took her to the home of Frank and Eva Schuber.

Their front door steps were on the street. As Madame Karl came up to them Eva stood in the open door much occupied with her approach, for she had not seen her for two years. Another woman, a stranger, was with Madame Karl. As they reached the threshold and the two old-time friends exchanged greetings, Eva said:

"Why, it is two years since last I saw you. Is that a German woman? — I know her!"

"Well," said Madame Karl, "if you know her, who is she?"

"My God!" cried Eva, — "the long-lost Salome Müller!"

"I needed nothing more to convince me," she afterwards testified in court. "I could recognize her among a hundred thousand persons."

Frank Schuber came in, having heard nothing. He glanced at the stranger, and turning to his wife asked:

"Is not that one of the girls who was lost?"

"It is," replied Eva; "it is. It is Salome Müller!"

On that same day, as it seems, for the news had not

reached them, Madame Fleikener and her daughter —
they had all become madams in Creole America — had
occasion to go to see her kinswoman, Eva Schuber.
She saw the stranger and instantly recognized her,
" because of her resemblance to her mother."

They were all overjoyed. For twenty-five years
dragged in the mire of African slavery, the mother
of quadroon children and ignorant of her own identity, they nevertheless welcomed her back to their
embrace, not fearing, but hoping, she was their long-
lost Salome.

But another confirmation was possible, far more con-
clusive than mere recognition of the countenance. Eva
knew this. For weeks together she had bathed and
dressed the little Salome every day. She and her mother
and all Henry Müller's family had known, and had made
it their common saying, that it might be difficult to iden-
tify the lost Dorothea were she found; but if ever Salome
were found they could prove she was Salome beyond the
shadow of a doubt. It was the remembrance of this
that moved Eva Schuber to say to the woman:

" Come with me into this other room." They went,
leaving Madame Karl, Madame Fleikener, her daughter,
and Frank Schuber behind. And when they returned
the slave was convinced, with them all, that she was
the younger daughter of Daniel and Dorothea Müller.
We shall presently see what fixed this conviction.

The next step was to claim her freedom. She appears to have gone back to Belmonti, but within a very
few days, if not immediately, Madame Schuber and
a certain Mrs. White — who does not become prom-

inent — followed down to the cabaret. Mrs. White went out somewhere on the premises, found Salome at work, and remained with her, while Madame Schuber confronted Belmonti, and, revealing Salome's identity and its proofs, demanded her instant release.

Belmonti refused to let her go. But while doing so he admitted his belief that she might be of pure white blood and of right entitled to freedom. He confessed having gone back to John F. Miller [1] soon after buying her and proposing to set her free; but Miller, he said, had replied that in such a case the law required her to leave the country. Thereupon Belmonti had demanded that the sale be rescinded, saying: "I have paid you my money for her."

"But," said Miller, "I did not sell her to you as a slave. She is as white as you or I, and neither of us can hold her if she chooses to go away."

Such at least was Belmonti's confession, yet he was as far from consenting to let his captive go after this confession was made as he had been before. He seems actually to have kept her for a while; but at length she went boldly to Schuber's house, became one of his household, and with his advice and aid asserted her intention to establish her freedom by an appeal to law. Belmonti replied with threats of public imprisonment, the chain-gang, and the auctioneer's block.

Salome, or Sally, for that seems to be the nickname by which her kindred remembered her, was never to be sold again; but not many months were to

[1] The similarity in the surnames of Salome and her master is odd, but is accidental and without significance.

pass before she was to find herself, on her own petition and bond of $500, a prisoner, by the only choice
the laws allowed her, in the famous calaboose, not as
a criminal, but as sequestered goods in a sort of sheriff's warehouse. Says her petition: "Your petitioner
has good reason to believe that the said Belmonti in-
tends to remove her out of the jurisdiction of the
court during the pendency of the suit"; wherefore
not *he* but *she* went to jail. Here she remained for
six days and was then allowed to go at large, but
only upon *giving still another bond and security,* and
in a much larger sum than she had ever been sold for.

The original writ of sequestration lies before me as
I write, indorsed as follows:

No. 23,041.

SALLY MILLER	Sequestration.
vs.	Sigur, Caperton
LOUIS BELMONTI.	and Bonford.

Received 24th January, 1844, and on the 26th of the same
month sequestered the body of the plaintiff and committed her
to prison for safe keeping; but on the 1st February, 1844, she
was released from custody, having entered bond in the sum of
one thousand dollars with Francis Schuber as the security con-
ditioned according to law, and which bond is herewith returned
this 3d February, 1844.

B. F. LEWIS, d'y sh'ff.

Inside is the bond with the signatures, Frantz
Schuber in German script, and above in English,

THE COURT PAPERS.

Sally her + mark *Miller*

Also the writ, ending in words of strange and solemn irony: "In the year of our Lord one thousand eight hundred and forty-four and in the sixty-eighth year of the Independence of the United States."

We need not follow the history at the slow gait of court proceedings. At Belmonti's petition John F. Miller was called in warranty; that is, made the responsible party in Belmonti's stead. There were "prayers" and rules, writs and answers, as the cause slowly gathered shape for final contest. Here are papers of date February 24 and 29 — it was leap year — and April 1, 2, 8, and 27. On the 7th of May Frank Schuber asked leave, and on the 14th was allowed, to substitute another bondsman in his place in order that he himself might qualify as a witness; and on the 23d of May the case came to trial.

VIII.

THE TRIAL.

It had already become famous. Early in April the press of the city, though in those days unused to giving local affairs more than the feeblest attention, had spoken of this suit as destined, if well founded, to

develop a case of "unparalleled hardship, cruelty,
and oppression." The German people especially were
aroused and incensed. A certain newspaper spoke of
the matter as the case "that had for several days
created so much excitement throughout the city."
The public sympathy was with Salome.

But by how slender a tenure was it held! It rested
not on the "hardship, cruelty, and oppression" she
had suffered for twenty years, but only on the fact,
which she might yet fail to prove, that she had suffered these things without having that tincture of
African race which, be it ever so faint, would entirely
justify, alike in the law and in the popular mind,
treatment otherwise counted hard, cruel, oppressive,
and worthy of the public indignation.

And now to prove the fact. In a newspaper of
that date appears the following:

HON. A. M. BUCHANAN, *Judge.*

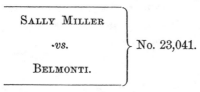

SALLY MILLER

·vs.   } No. 23,041.

BELMONTI.

This cause came on to-day for trial before the court, Roselius
and Upton for plaintiff, Canon for defendant, Grymes and
Micou for warrantor; when after hearing evidence the same is
continued until to-morrow morning at 11 o'clock.

Salome's battle had begun. Besides the counsel
already named, there were on the slave's side a second

Upton and a Bonford, and on the master's side a Sigur, a Caperton, and a Lockett. The redemptioners had made the cause their own and prepared to sustain it with a common purse.

Neither party had asked for a trial by jury; the decision was to come from the bench.

The soldier, in the tableaux of Judge Buchanan's life, had not dissolved perfectly into the justice, and old lawyers of New Orleans remember him rather for unimpeachable integrity than for fine discrimination, a man of almost austere dignity, somewhat quick in temper.

Before him now gathered the numerous counsel, most of whose portraits have long since been veiled and need not now be uncovered. At the head of one group stood Roselius, at the head of the other, Grymes. And for this there were good reasons. Roselius, who had just ceased to be the State's attorney-general, was already looked upon as one of the readiest of all champions of the unfortunate. He was in his early prime, the first full spread of his powers, but he had not forgotten the little Dutch brig *Jupiter*, or the days when he was himself a redemptioner. Grymes, on the other side, had had to do — as we have seen — with these same redemptioners before. The uncle and the father of this same Sally Miller, so called, had been chief witnesses in the suit for their liberty and hers, which he had — blamelessly, we need not doubt — lost some twenty-five years before. Directly in consequence of that loss Salome had gone into slavery and disappeared. And now the loser of that suit was here to maintain that slavery over a woman who, even if she should turn out not to be the lost child, was enough like to be mistaken for her. True, causes must have attorneys, and such things may happen to any lawyer; but here was a cause which in our lights to-day, at least, had on the defendant's side no moral right to come into court.

One other person, and only one, need we mention. Many a New York City lawyer will recall in his reminiscences of thirty years ago a small, handsome, gold-spectacled man with brown hair and eyes, noted for scholarship and literary culture; a brilliant pleader at the bar, and author of two books that became authorities, one on trade-marks, the other on prize law. Even some who do not recollect him by this description may recall how the gifted Frank Upton — for it is of him I write — was one day in 1863 or 1864 struck down by apoplexy while pleading in the well-known Peterhoff case. Or they may remember subsequently his constant, pathetic effort to maintain his old courtly mien against his resultant paralysis. This was the young man of about thirty, of uncommon masculine beauty and refinement, who sat beside Christian Roselius as an associate in the cause of Sally Miller *versus* Louis Belmonti.

IX.

THE EVIDENCE.

We need not linger over the details of the trial. The witnesses for the prosecution were called. First came a Creole woman, so old that she did not know her own age, but was a grown-up girl in the days of the Spanish governor-general Galvez, sixty-five years before. She recognized in the plaintiff the same person whom she had known as a child in John F. Miller's domestic service with the mien, eyes, and color of a white person and with a German accent. Next came Madame Hemin, who had not known the Müllers till she met them on the Russian ship and had not seen Salome since parting from them at Amsterdam, yet who instantly identified her "when she herself came into the court-room just now." "Witness says," continues the record, "she perceived the family likeness in plaintiff's face when she came in the door."

The next day came Eva and told her story; and others followed, whose testimony, like hers, we have anticipated. Again and again was the plaintiff recognized, both as Salome and as the girl Mary, or Mary Bridget, who for twenty years and upward had been owned in slavery, first by John F. Miller, then by his mother, Mrs. Canby, and at length by the cabaret keeper Louis Belmonti. If the two persons were but one, then for twenty years at least she had lived a slave within five miles, and part of the time within two, of her kindred and of freedom.

That the two persons were one it seemed scarcely possible to doubt. Not only did every one who remembered Salome on shipboard recognize the plaintiff as she, but others, who had quite forgotten her appearance then, recognized in her the strong family likeness of the Müllers. This likeness even witnesses for the defense had to admit. So, on Salome's side, testified Madame Koelhoffer, Madame Schultzheimer, and young Daniel Miller (Müller) from Mississippi. She was easily pointed out in the throng of the crowded court-room.

And then, as we have already said, there was another means of identification which it seemed ought alone to have carried with it overwhelming conviction. But this we still hold in reserve until we have heard the explanation offered by John F. Miller both in court and at the same time in the daily press in reply to its utterances which were giving voice to the public sympathy for Salome.

It seems that John Fitz Miller was a citizen of New Orleans in high standing, a man of property, money, enterprises, and slaves. John Lawson Lewis, commanding-general of the State militia, testified in the case to Mr. Miller's generous and social disposition, his easy circumstances, his kindness to his eighty slaves, his habit of entertaining, and the exceptional fineness of his equipage. Another witness testified that complaints were sometimes made by Miller's neighbors of his too great indulgence of his slaves.

Others, ladies as well as gentlemen, corroborated these good reports, and had even kinder and higher praises for his mother, Mrs. Canby. They stated with alacrity, not intending the slightest imputation against the gentleman's character, that he had other slaves even fairer of skin than this Mary Bridget, who nevertheless, "when she was young," they said, "looked like a white girl." One thing they certainly made plain — that Mr. Miller had never taken the Müller family or any part of them to Attakapas or knowingly bought a redemptioner.

He accounted for his possession of the plaintiff thus: In August, 1822, one Anthony Williams, being or pretending to be a negro-trader and from Mobile, somehow came into contact with Mr. John Fitz Miller in New Orleans. He represented that he had sold all his stock of slaves except one girl, Mary Bridget, ostensibly twelve years old, and must return at once to Mobile. He left this girl with Mr. Miller to be sold for him for his (Williams's) account under a formal power of attorney so to do, Mr. Miller handing him one hundred dollars as an advance on her prospective sale. In January, 1823, Williams had not yet been heard from, nor had the girl been sold; and on the 1st of February Mr. Miller sold her to his own mother, with whom he lived — in other words, *to himself,* as we shall see. In this sale her price was three hundred and fifty dollars and her age was still represented as about twelve. "From that time she remained in the house of my mother," wrote Miller to the newspapers, "as a domestic servant" until 1838, when "she was sold to Belmonti."

Mr. Miller's public statement was not as full and candid as it looked.   How, if the girl was sold to Mrs. Canby, his mother — how is it that Belmonti bought her of Miller himself?   The answer is that while Williams never re-appeared, the girl, in February, 1835, "the girl Bridget," now the mother of three children, was with these children bought back again by that same Mr. Miller from the entirely passive Mrs. Canby, for the same three hundred and fifty dollars; the same price for the four which he had got, or had seemed to get, for the mother alone when she was but a child of twelve years.   Thus had Mr. Miller become the owner of the woman, her two sons, and her daughter, had had her service for the keeping, and had never paid but one hundred dollars.   This point he prudently overlooked in his public statement.   Nor did he count it necessary to emphasize the further fact that when this slave-mother was about twenty-eight years old and her little daughter had died, he sold her alone, away from her two half-grown sons, for ten times what he had paid for her, to be the bond-woman of the wifeless keeper of a dram-shop.

But these were not the only omissions.   Why had Williams never come back either for the slave or for the proceeds of her sale?   Mr. Miller omitted to state, what he knew well enough, that the girl was so evidently white that Williams could not get rid of her, even to him, by an open sale.   When months and years passed without a word from Williams, the presumption was strong that Williams knew the girl was not of African tincture, at least within the definition of the law, and was content to count the provisional transfer to Miller equivalent to a sale.

Miller, then, was — heedless enough, let us call it — to hold in African bondage for twenty years a woman who, his own witnesses testified, had every appearance of being a white person, without ever having seen the shadow of a title for any one to own her, and with everything to indicate that there was none. Whether he had any better right to own the several other slaves whiter than this one whom those same witnesses of his were forward to state he owned and had owned, no one seems to have inquired. Such were the times; and it really was not then remarkable that this particular case should involve a lady noted for her good works and a gentleman who drove "the finest equipage in New Orleans."

One point, in view of current beliefs of to-day, compels attention. One of Miller's witnesses was being cross-examined. Being asked if, should he see the slave woman among white ladies, he would not think her white, he replied:

"I cannot say. There are in New Orleans many white persons of dark complexion and many colored persons of light complexion." The question followed:

"What is there in the features of a colored person that designates them to be such?"

"I cannot say. Persons who live in countries where there are many colored persons acquire an instinctive means of judging that cannot be well explained."

And yet neither this man's "instinct" nor that of any one else, either during the whole trial or during

twenty years' previous knowledge of the plaintiff, was
of the least value to determine whether this poor slave
was entirely white or of mixed blood. It was more
utterly worthless than her memory. For as to that
she had, according to one of Miller's own witnesses,
in her childhood confessed a remembrance of having
been brought "across the lake"; but whether that
had been from Germany, or only from Mobile, must
be shown in another way. That way was very simple,
and we hold it no longer in suspense.

X.

THE CROWNING PROOF.

"IF ever our little Salome is found," Eva Kropp had
been accustomed to say, "we shall know her by two
hair moles about the size of a coffee-bean, one on the
inside of each thigh, about midway up from the knee.
Nobody can make those, or take them away without
leaving the tell-tale scars." And lo! when Madame
Karl brought Mary Bridget to Frank Schuber's house,
and Eva Schuber, who every day for weeks had bathed
and dressed her godchild on the ship, took this stranger
into another room apart and alone, there were the
birth-marks of the lost Salome.

This incontestable evidence the friends of Salome
were able to furnish, but the defense called in question the genuineness of the marks.

The verdict of science was demanded, and an order

of the court issued to two noted physicians, one chosen
by each side, to examine these marks and report "the
nature, appearance, and cause of the same." The
kindred of Salome chose Warren Stone, probably the
greatest physician and surgeon in one that New Orleans
has ever known. Mr. Grymes's client chose a Creole
gentleman almost equally famed, Dr. Armand Mercier.

Dr. Stone died many years ago; Dr. Mercier, if I
remember aright, in 1885. When I called upon Dr.
Mercier in his office in Girod street in the summer of
1883, to appeal to his remembrance of this long-for-
gotten matter, I found a very noble-looking, fair old
gentleman whose abundant waving hair had gone all
to a white silken floss with age. He sat at his desk
in persistent silence with his strong blue eyes fixed
steadfastly upon me while I slowly and carefully
recounted the story. Two or three times I paused
inquiringly; but he faintly shook his head in the
negative, a slight frown of mental effort gathering for
a moment between the eyes that never left mine. But
suddenly he leaned forward and drew his breath as if
to speak. I ceased, and he said:

"My sister, the wife of Pierre Soulé, refused to
become the owner of that woman and her three children because they were so white!" He pressed me
eagerly with an enlargement of his statement, and
when he paused I said nothing or very little; for, sad
to say, he had only made it perfectly plain that it was
not the girl Mary Bridget whom he was recollecting,
but *another case.*

He did finally, though dimly, call to mind having

served with Dr. Stone in such a matter as I had described. But later I was made independent of his
powers of recollection, when the original documents
of the court were laid before me. There was the certificate of the two physicians. And there, over their
signatures, "Mercier d.m.p." standing first, in a bold
heavy hand underscored by a single broad quill-
stroke, was this "Conclusion":

"1. These marks ought to be considered as *nœvi
materni.*

"2. They are congenital; or, in other words, the
person was born with them.

"3. There is no process by means of which artificial
spots bearing all the character of the marks can be
produced."

*3: There is no process by means of which artificial spots bearing
all the character of these marks, can be produced.*

New Orleans, 4th of June 1844 —

Mercier

F. Stone d.m.p. M.D.

XI.

JUDGMENT.

On the 11th of June the case of Sally Miller *versus*
Louis Belmonti was called up again and the report of
the medical experts received. Could anything be

offered by Mr. Grymes and his associates to offset that? Yes; they had one last strong card, and now they played it.

It was, first, a certificate of baptism of a certain Mary's child John, offered in evidence to prove that this child was born at a time when Salome Müller, according to the testimony of her own kindred, was too young by a year or two to become a mother; and secondly, the testimony of a free woman of color, that to her knowledge that Mary was this Bridget or Sally, and the child John this woman's eldest son Lafayette. And hereupon the court announced that on the morrow it would hear the argument of counsel.

Salome's counsel besought the court for a temporary postponement on two accounts: first, that her age might be known beyond a peradventure by procuring a copy of her own birth record from the official register of her native Langensoultz, and also to procure in New Orleans the testimony of one who was professionally present at the birth of her son, and who would swear that it occurred some years later than the date of the baptismal record just accepted as evidence.

"We are taken by surprise," exclaimed in effect Roselius and his coadjutors, "in the production of testimony by the opposing counsel openly at variance with earlier evidence accepted from them and on record. The act of the sale of this woman and her children from Sarah Canby to John Fitz Miller in 1835, her son Lafayette being therein described as but five years of age, fixes his birth by irresistible infer-

ence in 1830, in which year by the recorded testimony
of her kindred Salome Müller was fifteen years old."

But the combined efforts of Roselius, Upton, and
others were unavailing, and the newspapers of the
following day reported: "This cause, continued from
yesterday, came on again to-day, when, after hearing
arguments of counsel, the court took the same under
consideration."

It must be a dull fancy that will not draw for itself
the picture, when a fortnight later the frequenters
of the court-room hear the word of judgment. It is
near the end of the hot far-southern June. The judge
begins to read aloud. His hearers wait languidly
through the prolonged recital of the history of the
case. It is as we have given it here: no use has been
made here of any testimony discredited in the judge's
reasons for his decision. At length the evidence is
summed up and every one attends to catch the next
word. The judge reads:

"The supposed identity is based upon two circumstances: first, a striking resemblance of plaintiff to
the child above mentioned and to the family of that
child. Second, two certain marks or moles on the
inside of the thighs [one on each thigh], which marks
are similar in the child and in the woman. This resemblance and these marks are proved by several
witnesses. Are they sufficient to justify me in declaring the plaintiff to be identical with the German
child in question? I answer this question in the
negative."

What stir there was in the room when these words

were heard the silent records lying before me do not tell, or whether all was silent while the judge read on; but by and by his words were these:

" I must admit that the relatives of the said family of redemptioners seem to be very firmly convinced of the identity which the plaintiff claims. . . . As, however, it is quite out of the question to take away a man's property upon grounds of this sort, I would suggest that the friends of the plaintiff, if honestly convinced of the justice of her pretensions, should make some effort to settle *à l'aimable* with the defendant, who has honestly and fairly paid his money for her. They would doubtless find him well disposed to part on reasonable terms with a slave from whom he can scarcely expect any service after what has passed. Judgment dismissing the suit with costs."

The white slave was still a slave. We are left to imagine the quiet air of dispatch with which as many of the counsel as were present gathered up any papers they may have had, exchanged a few murmurous words with their clients, and, hats in hand, hurried off and out to other business. Also the silent, slow dejection of Salome, Eva, Frank, and their neighbors and kin — if so be that they were there — as they rose and left the hall where a man's property was more sacred than a woman's freedom. But the attorney had given them ground of hope. Application would be made for a new trial; and if this was refused, as it probably would be, then appeal would be made to the Supreme Court of the State.

So it happened. Only two days later the plaintiff,

through one of her counsel, the brother of Frank
Upton, applied for a new trial. She stated that important evidence not earlier obtainable had come to
light; that she could produce a witness to prove that
John F. Miller had repeatedly said she was white;
and that one of Miller's own late witnesses, his own
brother-in-law, would make deposition of the fact, rec-
ollected only since he gave testimony, that the girl
Bridget brought into Miller's household in 1822 was
much darker than the plaintiff and died a few years
afterwards. And this witness did actually make such
deposition. In the six months through which the
suit had dragged since Salome had made her first
petition to the court and signed it with her mark she
had learned to write. The application for a new trial
is signed —

The new trial was refused. Roselius took an appeal. The judge "allowed" it, fixing the amount of
Salome's bond at $2000. Frank Schuber gave the
bond and the case went up to the Supreme Court.

In that court no witnesses were likely to be examined. New testimony was not admissible; all
testimony taken in the inferior courts "went up" by
the request of either party as part of the record, and
to it no addition could ordinarily be made. The case
would be ready for argument almost at once.

XII.

BEFORE THE SUPREME COURT.

ONCE more it was May, when in the populous but silent court-room the clerk announced the case of Miller *versus* Louis Belmonti, and John F. Miller, warrantor. Well-nigh a year had gone by since the appeal was taken. Two full years had passed since Madame Karl had found Salome in Belmonti's cabaret. It was now 1845; Grymes was still at the head of one group of counsel, and Roselius of the other. There again were Eva and Salome, looking like an elder and a younger sister. On the bench sat at the right two and at the left two associate judges, and between them in the middle the learned and aged historian of the State, Chief-Justice Martin.

The attorneys had known from the first that the final contest would be here, and had saved their forces for this; and when on the 19th of May the deep, rugged voice of Roselius resounded through the old Cabildo, a nine-days' contest of learning, eloquence, and legal tactics had begun. Roselius may have filed a brief, but I have sought it in vain, and his words in Salome's behalf are lost. Yet we know one part in the defense which he must have retained to himself; for Francis Upton was waiting in reserve to close the argument on the last day of the trial, and so important a matter as this that we shall mention would hardly have been trusted in any but the strongest hands. It was this: Roselius, in the middle of his argument upon the evidence, proposed to read a certain certified copy of a registry of birth. Grymes and his colleagues instantly objected. It was their own best gun captured and turned upon them. They could not tolerate it. It was no part of the record, they stoutly maintained, and must not be introduced nor read nor commented upon. The point was vigorously argued on both sides; but when Roselius appealed to an earlier decision of the same court the bench decided that, as then, so now, "in suits for freedom, and *in favorem libertatis,* they would notice facts which come credibly before them, even though they be *dehors* the record."[1] And so Roselius thundered it out. The consul for Baden at New Orleans had gone to Europe some time before, and was now newly returned. He had brought an official copy, from the records of the prefect of Salome's native village, of the registered date of her birth. This is what was now heard, and by it Salome and her friends knew to their joy, and Belmonti to his chagrin, that she was two years older than her kinsfolk had thought her to be.

Who followed Roselius is not known, but by and by men were bending the ear to the soft persuasive tones and finished subtleties of the polished and courted Grymes. He left, we are told, no point unguarded, no weapon unused, no vantage-ground unoccupied. The high social standing and reputation of his client were set forth at their best. Every slen-

---

[1] Marie Louise *vs.* Marot, 8 La. R.

derest discrepancy of statement between Salome's witnesses was ingeniously expanded. By learned citation and adroit appliance of the old Spanish laws concerning slaves, he sought to ward off as with a Toledo blade the heavy blows by which Roselius and his colleagues endeavored to lay upon the defendants the burden of proof which the lower court had laid upon Salome. He admitted generously the entire sincerity of Salome's kinspeople in believing plaintiff to be the lost child; but reminded the court of the credulity of ill-trained minds, the contagiousness of fanciful delusions, and especially of what he somehow found room to call the inflammable imagination of the German temperament. He appealed to history; to the scholarship of the bench; citing the stories of Martin Guerre, the Russian Demetrius, Perkin Warbeck, and all the other wonderful cases of mistaken or counterfeited identity. Thus he and his associates pleaded for the continuance in bondage of a woman whom their own fellow-citizens were willing to take into their houses after twenty years of degradation and infamy, make their oath to her identity, and pledge their fortunes to her protection as their kinswoman.

Day after day the argument continued. At length the Sabbath broke its continuity, but on Monday it was resumed, and on Tuesday Francis Upton rose to make the closing argument for the plaintiff. His daughter, Miss Upton, now of Washington, once did me the honor to lend me a miniature of him made about the time of Salome's suit for freedom. It is a pleasing evidence of his modesty in the domestic circle — where masculine modesty is rarest — that his daughter had never heard him tell the story of this case, in which, it is said, he put the first strong luster on his fame. In the picture he is a very David — "ruddy and of a fair countenance"; a countenance at once gentle and valiant, vigorous and pure. Lifting this face upon the wrinkled chief-justice and associate judges, he began to set forth the points of law, in an argument which, we are told, "was regarded by those who heard it as one of the happiest forensic efforts ever made before the court."

He set his reliance mainly upon two points: one, that, it being obvious and admitted that plaintiff was not entirely of African race, the presumption of law was in favor of liberty and with the plaintiff, and therefore that the whole burden of proof was upon the defendants, Belmonti and Miller; and the other point, that the presumption of freedom in such a case could be rebutted only by proof that she was descended from a slave mother. These points the young attorney had to maintain as best he could without precedents fortifying them beyond attack; but "Adele *versus* Beauregard" he insisted firmly established the first point and implied the court's assent to the second, while as legal doctrines "Wheeler on Slavery" upheld them both. When he was done Salome's fate was in the hands of her judges.

Almost a month goes by before their judgment is rendered. But at length, on the 21st of June, the gathering with which our imagination has become

familiar appears for the last time. The chief-justice is to read the decision from which there can be
no appeal. As the judges take their places one seat
is left void; it is by reason of sickness. Order is
called, silence falls, and all eyes are on the chief-justice.

He reads. To one holding the court's official copy
of judgment in hand, as I do at this moment, following down the lines as the justice's eyes once followed
them, passing from paragraph to paragraph, and turning the leaves as his hand that day turned them, the
scene lifts itself before the mind's eye despite every
effort to hold it to the cold letter of the time-stained
files of the court. In a single clear, well-compacted
paragraph the court states Salome's claim and Belmonti's denial; in another, the warrantor Miller's
denial and defense; and in two lines more, the decision of the lower court. And now —

"The first inquiry," so reads the chief-justice —
"the first inquiry that engages our attention is, What
is the color of the plaintiff?"

But this is far from bringing dismay to Salome and
her friends. For hear what follows:

"Persons of color" — meaning of mixed blood, not
pure negro — "are presumed to be free. . . . The
burden of proof is upon him who claims the colored
person as a slave. . . . In the highest courts of the
State of Virginia . . . a person of the complexion of
the plaintiff, without evidence of descent from a slave
mother, would be released even on *habeas corpus*. . . .
Not only is there no evidence of her [plaintiff] being

descended from a slave mother, or even a mother of the African race, but no witness has ventured a positive opinion that she is of that race."

Glad words for Salome and her kindred. The reading proceeds: "The presumption is clearly in favor of the plaintiff." But suspense returns, for — "It is next proper," the reading still goes on, "to inquire how far that presumption has been weakened or justified or repelled by the testimony of numerous witnesses in the record. . . . If a number of witnesses had sworn" — here the justice turns the fourth page; now he is in the middle of it, yet all goes well; he is making a comparison of testimony for and against, unfavorable to that which is against. And now — "But the proof does not stop at mere family resemblance." He is coming to the matter of the birth-marks. He calls them "evidence which is not impeached."

He turns the page again, and begins at the top to meet the argument of Grymes from the old Spanish Partidas. But as his utterance follows his eye down the page he sets that argument aside as not good to establish such a title as that by which Miller received the plaintiff. He *exonerates* Miller, but accuses the absent Williams of imposture and fraud. One may well fear the verdict after that. But now he turns a page which every one can see is the last:

"It has been said that the German witnesses are imaginative and enthusiastic, and their confidence ought to be distrusted. That kind of enthusiasm is at least of a quiet sort, evidently the result of profound conviction and certainly free from any taint of worldly interest, and is by no means incompatible with the most perfect conscientiousness. If they are mistaken as to the identity of the plaintiff; if there be in truth two persons about the same age bearing a strong resemblance to the family of Miller [Müller] and having the same identical marks from their birth, and the plaintiff is not the real lost child who arrived here with hundreds of others in 1818, it is certainly one of the most extraordinary things in history. If she be not, then nobody has told who she is. After the most mature consideration of the case, we are of opinion the plaintiff is free, and it is our duty to declare her so.

"It is therefore ordered, adjudged, and decreed, that the judgment of the District Court be reversed; and ours is that the plaintiff be released from the bonds of slavery, that the defendants pay the costs of the appeal, and that the case be remanded for further proceedings as between the defendant and his warrantor."

So ends the record of the court. "The question of damage," says the "Law Reporter," "is the subject-matter of another suit now pending against Jno. F. Miller and Mrs. Canby." But I have it verbally from Salome's relatives that the claim was lightly and early dismissed. Salome being free, her sons were, by law, free also. But they could only be free mulattoes, went to Tennessee and Kentucky, were heard of once or twice as stable-boys to famous horses, and disappeared. A Mississippi River pilot, John Given by name, met Salome among her relatives, and courted and married her. As might readily be supposed, this alliance was only another misfortune to Salome, and the pair separated. Salome went to California. Her cousin, Henry Schuber, tells me he saw her in 1855 in Sacramento City, living at last a respected and comfortable life.

THE "HAUNTED HOUSE" IN
ROYAL STREET.

1831–82.

I.

AS IT STANDS NOW.

WHEN you and —— make that much-talked-of visit to New Orleans, by all means see early whatever evidences of progress and aggrandizement her hospitable citizens wish to show you; New Orleans belongs to the living present, and has serious practical relations with these United States and this great living world and age. And yet I want the first morning walk that you two take together and alone to be in the old French Quarter. Go down Royal street.

You shall not have taken many steps in it when, far down on the right-hand side, where the narrow street almost shuts its converging lines together in the distance, there will begin to rise above the extravagant confusion of intervening roofs and to stand out against the dazzling sky a square, latticed remnant of a belvedere. You can see that the house it surmounts is a large, solid, rectangular pile, and that it stands directly on the street at what residents call

192

the "upper, river corner," though the river is several
squares away on the right. There are fifty people in
this old rue Royale who can tell you their wild ver-
sions of this house's strange true story against any
one who can do this present writer the honor to point
out the former residence of 'Sieur George, Madame
Délicieuse, or Doctor Mossy, or the unrecognizably
restored dwelling of Madame Delphine.

I fancy you already there. The neighborhood is
very still. The streets are almost empty of life, and
the cleanness of their stone pavements is largely the
cleanness of disuse. The house you are looking at is
of brick, covered with stucco, which somebody may
be lime-washing white, or painting yellow or brown,
while I am saying it is gray. An uncovered balcony
as wide as the sidewalk makes a deep arcade around
its two street sides. The last time I saw it it was for
rent, and looked as if it had been so for a long time ;
but that proves nothing. Every one of its big window-
shutters was closed, and by the very intensity of their
rusty silence spoke a hostile impenetrability. Just
now it is occupied.

They say that Louis Philippe, afterwards king of
the French, once slept in one of its chambers. That
would have been in 1798 ; but in 1798 they were not
building such tall buildings as this in New Orleans —
did not believe the soil would uphold them. As late
as 1806, when 'Sieur George's house, upon the St.
Peter street corner, was begun, people shook their
heads ; and this house is taller than 'Sieur George's.
I should like to know if the rumor is true. Lafayette,

too, they say, occupied the same room. Maybe so.
That would have been in 1824–25. But we know he
had elegant apartments, fitted up for him at the city's
charge, in the old Cabildo. Still —

It was, they say, in those, its bright, early days, the
property of the Pontalbas, a noble Franco-Spanish
family; and I have mentioned these points, which
have no close bearing upon our present story, mainly
to clear the field of all mere they-says, and leave the
ground for what we know to be authenticated fact,
however strange.

The entrance, under the balcony, is in Royal street.
Within a deep, white portal, the walls and ceiling of
which are covered with ornamentations, two or three
steps, shut off from the sidewalk by a pair of great
gates of open, ornamental iron-work with gilded tops,
rise to the white door. This also is loaded with a
raised work of urns and flowers, birds and fonts, and
Phœbus in his chariot. Inside, from a marble floor,
an iron-railed, winding stair ("said the spider to the
fly") leads to the drawing-rooms on the floor even
with the balcony. These are very large. The various
doors that let into them, and the folding door between
them, have carved panels. A deep frieze covered
with raised work — white angels with palm branches
and folded wings, stars, and wreaths — runs all around,
interrupted only by high, wide windows that let out
between fluted Corinthian pilasters upon the broad
open balcony. The lofty ceilings, too, are beautiful
with raised garlandry.

Measure one of the windows — eight feet across.

THE ENTRANCE OF THE HAUNTED HOUSE.

[*From a Photograph.*]

Each of its shutters is four feet wide. Look at those old crystal chandeliers. And already here is something uncanny — at the bottom of one of these rooms, a little door in the wall. It is barely a woman's height, yet big hinges jut out from the jamb, and when you open it and look in you see only a small dark place without steps or anything to let you down to its floor below, a leap of several feet. It is hardly noteworthy; only neither you nor —— can make out what it ever was for.

The house is very still. As you stand a moment in the middle of the drawing-room looking at each other you hear the walls and floors saying those soft nothings to one another that they so often say when left to themselves. While you are looking straight at one of the large doors that lead into the hall its lock gives a whispered click and the door slowly swings open. No cat, no draft, you and —— exchange a silent smile and rather like the mystery; but do you know? That is an old trick of those doors, and has made many an emotional girl smile less instead of more; although I doubt not any carpenter could explain it.

I assume, you see, that you visit the house when it is vacant. It is only at such times that you are likely to get in. A friend wrote me lately: "Miss —— and I tried to get permission to see the interior. Madame said the landlord had requested her not to allow visitors; that over three hundred had called last winter, and had been refused for that reason. I thought of the three thousand who would call if they knew its story." Another writes: "The landlord's orders are positive that no photographer of any kind shall come into his house."

The house has three stories and an attic. The windows farthest from the street are masked by long, green latticed balconies or "galleries," one to each story, which communicate with one another by staircases behind the lattices and partly overhang a small, damp, paved court which is quite hidden from outer view save from one or two neighboring windows. On your right as you look down into this court a long, narrow wing stands out at right angles from the main house, four stories high, with the latticed galleries continuing along the entire length of each floor. It bounds this court on the southern side. Each story is a row of small square rooms, and each room has a single high window in the southern wall and a single door on the hither side opening upon the latticed gallery of that floor. Wings of that sort were once very common in New Orleans in the residences of the rich; they were the house's slave quarters. But certainly some of the features you see here never were common — locks seven inches across; several windows without sashes, but with sturdy iron gratings and solid iron shutters. On the fourth floor the doorway communicating with the main house is entirely closed twice over, by *two pairs* of full length batten shutters held in on the side of the main house by iron hooks eighteen inches long, two to each shutter. And yet it was through this doorway that the ghosts — figuratively speaking, of course, for we are dealing with plain fact and history — got into this house.

Will you go to the belvedere ?   I went there once.
Unless the cramped stair that reaches it has been
repaired you will find it something rickety.   The
newspapers, writing fifty-five years ago in the heat
and haste of the moment, must have erred as to heavy
pieces of furniture being carried up this last cramped
flight of steps to be cast out of the windows into the
street far below.   Besides, the third-story windows
are high enough for the most thorough smashing of
anything dropped from them for that purpose.

The attic is cut up into little closets.   Lying in one
of them close up under the roof maybe you will still
find, as I did, all the big iron keys of those big iron
locks down-stairs.   The day I stepped up into this
belvedere it was shaking visibly in a squall of wind.
An electric storm was coming out of the north and
west.   Yet overhead the sun still shone vehemently
through the rolling white clouds.   It was grand to
watch these.   They were sailing majestically hither
and thither southward across the blue, leaning now
this way and now that like a fleet of great ships of the
line manœuvring for position against the dark northern enemy's already flashing and thundering onset.
I was much above any neighboring roof.   Far to the
south and south-west the newer New Orleans spread
away over the flat land.   North-eastward, but near at
hand, were the masts of ships and steamers, with
glimpses here and there of the water, and farther
away the open breadth of the great yellow river
sweeping around Slaughterhouse Point under an air
heavy with the falling black smoke and white steam

of hurrying tugs. Closer by, there was a strange confusion of roofs, trees, walls, vines, tiled roofs, brown
and pink, and stuccoed walls, pink, white, yellow, red,
and every sort of gray. The old convent of the Ursulines stood in the midst, and against it the old chapel
of St. Mary with a great sycamore on one side and
a willow on the other. Almost under me I noticed
some of the semicircular arches of rotten red brick
that were once a part of the Spanish barracks. In
the north the "Old Third" (third city district) lay,
as though I looked down upon it from a cliff — a
tempestuous gray sea of slate roofs dotted with toss-
ing green tree-tops. Beyond it, not far away, the deep
green, ragged line of cypress swamp half encircled it
and gleamed weirdly under a sky packed with dark
clouds that flashed and growled and boomed and
growled again. You could see rain falling from one
cloud over Lake Pontchartrain; the strong gale
brought the sweet smell of it. Westward, yonder,
you may still descry the old calaboose just peeping
over the tops of some lofty trees; and that bunch a
little at the left is Congo Square; but the *old*, old
calaboose — the one to which this house was once
strangely related — is hiding behind the cathedral
here on the south. The street that crosses Royal
here and makes the corner on which the house stands
is Hospital street; and yonder, westward, where it
bends a little to the right and runs away so bright,
clean, and empty between two long lines of groves
and flower gardens, it is the old Bayou Road to the
lake. It was down that road that the mistress of this

house fled in her carriage from its door with the howl-
ing mob at her heels. Before you descend from the
belvedere turn and note how the roof drops away in
eight different slopes; and think — from whichever
one of these slopes it was — of the little fluttering,
befrocked lump of terrified childhood that leaped from
there and fell clean to the paved yard below. A last
word while we are still here: there are other reasons
— one, at least, besides tragedy and crime — that
make people believe this place is haunted. This particular spot is hardly one where a person would prefer
to see a ghost, even if one knew it was but an optical
illusion; but one evening, some years ago, when a
bright moon was mounting high and swinging well
around to the south, a young girl who lived near by
and who had a proper skepticism for the marvels of
the gossips passed this house. She was approaching
it from an opposite sidewalk, when, glancing up at
this belvedere outlined so loftily on the night sky,
she saw with startling clearness, although pale and
misty in the deep shadow of the cupola, — "It made
me shudder," she says, "until I reasoned the matter
out," — a single, silent, motionless object; the figure
of a woman leaning against its lattice. By careful
scrutiny she made it out to be only a sorcery of moon-
beams that fell aslant from tho farther oido through
the skylight of the belvedere's roof and sifted through
the lattice. Would that there were no more reality
to the story before us.

II.

MADAME LALAURIE.

On the 30th of August, 1831, before Octave de Armas, notary, one E. Soniat Dufossat sold this property to a Madame Lalaurie. She may have dwelt in the house earlier than this, but here is where its tragic history begins. Madame Lalaurie was still a beautiful and most attractive lady, though bearing the name of a third husband. Her surname had been first McCarty, — a genuine Spanish-Creole name, although of Irish origin, of course, — then Lopez, or maybe first Lopez and then McCarty, and then Blanque. She had two daughters, the elder, at least, the issue of her first marriage.

The house is known to this day as Madame Blanque's house, — which, you notice, it never was, — so distinctly was she the notable figure in the household. Her husband was younger than she. There is strong sign of his lesser importance in the fact that he was sometimes, and only sometimes, called doctor — Dr. Louis Lalaurie. The graces and graciousness of their accomplished and entertaining mother quite outshone his step-daughters as well as him. To the frequent and numerous guests at her sumptuous board these young girls seemed comparatively unanimated, if not actually unhappy. Not so with their mother. To do her full share in the upper circles of good society, to dispense the pleasures of drawing-room and dining-room with generous frequency and captivating amiability, was the eager pursuit of a lady who nevertheless kept the management of her money affairs, real estate, and slaves mainly in her own hands. Of slaves she had ten, and housed most of them in the tall narrow wing that we have already noticed.

We need not recount again the state of society about her at that time. The description of it given by the young German duke whom we quoted without date in the story of "Salome Müller" belongs exactly to this period. Grymes stood at the top and front of things. John Slidell was already shining beside him. They were co-members of the Elkin Club, then in its glory. It was trying energetically to see what incredible quantities of Madeira it could drink. Judge Mazereau was "avocat-général" and was being lampooned by the imbecile wit of the singers and dancers of the calinda in Congo Square. The tree-planted levee was still populous on summer evenings with promenaders and loungers. The quadroon caste was in its dying splendor, still threatening the moral destruction of private society, and hated — as only woman can hate enemies of the hearthstone — by the proud, fair ladies of the Creole pure-blood, among whom Madame Lalaurie shone brilliantly. Her elegant house, filled with "furniture of the most costly description," — says the "New Orleans Bee" of a date which we shall come to, — stood central in the swirl of "downtown" gayety, public and private. From Royal into Hospital street, across Circus street — rue de la Cirque — that was a good way to get into Bayou Road, white, almost

as snow, with its smooth, silent pavement of powdered
shells. This road followed the slow, clear meander-.
ings of Bayou St. Jean, from red-roofed and embowered
suburb St. Jean to the lake, the swamp of giant, grizzly
bearded cypresses hugging it all the way, and the
whole five miles teeming with gay, swift carriages,
some filled with smokers, others with ladies and
children, the finest equipage of all being, as you may
recollect, that of John Fitz Miller. He was at that
very time master of Salome Müller, and of "several others fairer than Salome." He belongs in
the present story only here in this landscape, and
here not as a typical, but only as an easily possible, slaveholder. For that matter, Madame Lalaurie, let it be plainly understood, was only another
possibility, not a type. The two stories teach the
same truth: that a public practice is answerable for
whatever can happen easier with it than without it,
no matter whether it must, or only may, happen.
However, let the moral wait or skip it entirely if
you choose: a regular feature of that bright afternoon throng was Madame Lalaurie's coach with the
ever-so-pleasant Madame Lalaurie inside and her
sleek black coachman on the box.

"Think," some friend would say, as he returned her
courteous bow — "think of casting upon that woman
the suspicion of starving and maltreating her own
house-servants! Look at that driver; his skin shines
with good keeping. The truth is those jealous
Americans " —

There was intense jealousy between the Americans

and the Creoles. The Americans were just beginning
in public matters to hold the odds. In private society
the Creoles still held power, but it was slipping from
them even there. Madame Lalaurie was a Creole.
Whether Louisiana or St. Domingo born was no
matter; she should not be criticised by American
envy ! Nor would the Creoles themselves go nosing
into the secretest privacy of her house.

"Why, look you, it is her common practice, even
before her guests, to leave a little wine in her glass and
hand it, with some word of kindness, to the slave waiting at her back. Thin and hollow-chested — the slaves ?
Yes, to be sure; but how about your rich uncle, or
my dear old mother; are they not hollow-chested ?
Well ! "

But this kind of logic did not satisfy everybody, not
even every Creole; and particularly not all her neighbors. The common populace too had unflattering
beliefs.

"Do you see this splendid house ? Do you see
those attic windows ? There are slaves up there confined in chains and darkness and kept at the point of
starvation."

A Creole gentleman, M. Montreuil, who seems to
have been a neighbor, made several attempts to bring
the matter to light, but in vain. Yet rumors and
suspicious indications grew so rank that at length
another prominent citizen, an "American" lawyer,
who had a young Creole studying law in his office,
ventured to send him to the house to point out to
Madame Lalaurie certain laws of the State. For

instance there was Article XX. of the old Black
Code : " Slaves who shall not be properly fed, clad,
and provided for by their masters, may give information thereof to the attorney-general or the
Superior Council, or to all the other officers of justice of an inferior jurisdiction, and may put the
written exposition of their wrongs into their hands;
upon which information, and even ex officio, should
the information come from another quarter, the
attorney-general shall prosecute said masters," etc.
But the young law student on making his visit was
captivated by the sweetness of the lady whom he had
been sent to warn against committing unlawful mis-
demeanors, and withdrew filled with indignation
against any one who could suspect her of the slightest unkindness to the humblest living thing.

III.

A TERRIBLE REVELATION.

The house that joined Madame Lalaurie's premises
on the eastern side had a staircase window that looked
down into her little courtyard.   One day all by chance
the lady of that adjoining house was going up those
stairs just when the keen scream of a terrified child
resounded from the next yard.   She sprung to the
window, and, looking down, saw a little negro girl
about eight years old run wildly across the yard
and into the house, with Madame Lalaurie, a cow-

hide whip in her hand, following swiftly and close upon her.

They disappeared; but by glimpses through the dark lattices and by the sound of the tumult, the lady knew that the child was flying up stairway after stairway, from gallery to gallery, hard pressed by her furious mistress. Soon she heard them rise into the belvedere and the next instant they darted out upon the roof. Down into its valleys and up over its ridges the little fugitive slid and scrambled. She reached the sheer edge, the lady at the window hid her face in her hands, there came a dull, jarring thud in the paved court beneath, and the lady, looking down, saw the child lifted from the ground and borne out of sight, limp, silent, dead.

She kept her place at the window. Hours passed, the day waned, darkness settled down. Then she saw a torch brought, a shallow hole was dug, — as it seemed to her; but in fact a condemned well of slight depth, a mere pit, was uncovered, — and the little broken form was buried. She informed the officers of justice. From what came to light at a later season, it is hard to think that in this earlier case the investigation was more than superficial. Yet an investigation was made, and some legal action was taken against Madame Lalaurie for cruelty to her slaves. They were taken from her and — liberated? Ah! no. They were sold by the sheriff, bid in by her relatives, and by them sold back to her. Let us believe that this is what occurred, or at least was shammed; for unless we do we must accept the implication of a newspaper statement of two or three years afterwards, and the confident impression of an aged Creole gentleman and notary still living who was an eye-witness to much of this story, that all Madame Lalaurie ever suffered for this part of her hideous misdeeds was a fine. Lawyers will doubtless remind us that Madame Lalaurie was not legally chargeable with the child's death. The lady at the window was not the only witness who might have been brought. A woman still living, who after the civil war was for years a domestic in this "haunted house," says her husband, now long dead, then a lad, was passing the place when the child ran out on the roof, and he saw her scrambling about on it seeking to escape. But he did not see the catastrophe that followed. No one saw more than what the law knows as assault; and the child was a slave.

Miss Martineau, in her short account of the matter, which she heard in New Orleans and from eye-witnesses only a few years after it had occurred, conjectures that Madame Lalaurie's object in buying back these slaves was simply to renew her cruelties upon them. But a much easier, and even kinder, guess would be that they knew things about her that had not been and must not be told, if she could possibly prevent it. A high temper, let us say, had led her into a slough of misdoing to a depth beyond all her expectation, and the only way out was on the farther side.

Yet bring to bear all the generous conjecture one can, and still the fact stands that she did starve, whip, and otherwise torture these poor victims. She even mistreated her daughters for conveying to them food which she had withheld. Was she not insane? One would hope so; but we cannot hurry to believe just what is most comfortable or kindest. That would be itself a kind of "emotional insanity." If she was insane, how about her husband? For Miss Martineau, who was told that he was no party to her crimes, was misinformed; he was as deep in the same mire as passive complicity could carry him. If she was insane her insanity stopped abruptly at her plump, well-fed coachman. He was her spy against all others. And if she was insane, then why did not her frequent guests at table suspect it?

All that society knew was that she had carried her domestic discipline to excess, had paid dearly for it, and no doubt was desisting and would henceforth desist from that kind of thing. Enough allowance can hardly be made in our day for the delicacy society felt about prying into one of its own gentleman or lady member's treatment of his or her own servants. Who was going to begin such an inquiry — John Fitz Miller?

And so time passed, and the beautiful and ever sweet and charming Madame Lalaurie — whether sane or insane we leave to the doctors, except Dr. Lalaurie — continued to drive daily, yearly, on the gay Bayou Road, to manage her business affairs, and to gather bright groups around her tempting board, without their suspicion that she kept her cook in the kitchen by means of a twenty-four-foot chain fastened to her person and to the wall or floor.

And yet let this be said to the people's credit, that public suspicion and indignation steadily grew. But they were still only growing when one day, the 10th of April, 1834, the aged cook, — she was seventy, — chained as she was, purposely set the house on fire. It is only tradition that, having in a dream the night before seen the drawing-room window curtains on fire, she seized the happy thought and made the dream a reality. But it is in the printed record of the day that she confessed the deed to the mayor of the city.

The desperate stratagem succeeds. The alarm of fire spreads to the street and a hundred men rush in, while a crowd throngs the streets. Some are neighbors, some friends, some strangers. One is M. Montreuil, the gentleman who has so long been watching his chance to bring the law upon the house and its mistress. Young D——, a notary's clerk, is another. And another is Judge Cononge — Aha! And there are others of good and well-known name!

The fire has got a good start; the kitchen is in flames; the upper stories are filling with smoke. Strangers run to the place whence it all comes and fall to fighting the fire. Friends rally to the aid of Monsieur and Madame Lalaurie. The pretty lady has not lost one wit — is at her very best. Her husband is as passive as ever.

"This way," she cries; "this way! Take this — go, now, and hurry back, if you please. This way!" And in a moment they are busy carrying out, and to places of safety, plate, jewels, robes, and the lighter and costlier pieces of furniture. "This way, please, gentlemen; that is only the servants' quarters."

The servants' quarters — but where are the servants?

Madame's answers are witty but evasive. "Never mind them now — save the valuables!"

Somebody touches Judge Canonge — "Those servants are chained and locked up and liable to perish."

"Where?"

"In the garret rooms."

He hurries towards them but fails to reach them, and returns, driven back and nearly suffocated by the smoke. He looks around him — this is no sketch of the fancy; we have his deposition sworn before a magistrate next day — and sees some friends of the family. He speaks to them:

"I am told" — so and so — "can it be? Will you speak to Monsieur or to Madame?" But the friends repulse him coldly.

He turns and makes fresh inquiries of others. He notices two gentlemen near him whom he knows. One is Montreuil. "Here, Montreuil, and you, Fernandez, will you go to the garret and search? I am blind and half smothered." Another — he thinks it was Felix Lefebre — goes in another direction, most likely towards the double door between the attics of the house and wing. Montreuil and Fernandez come back saying they have searched thoroughly and found nothing. Madame Lalaurie begs them, with all her sweetness, to come other ways and consider other things. But here is Lefebre. He cries, "I have found some of them! I have broken some bars, but the doors are locked!"

Judge Canonge hastens through the smoke. They reach the spot.

"Break the doors down!" Down come the doors. The room they push into is a "den." They bring out two negresses. One has a large heavy iron collar at the neck and heavy irons on her feet. The fire is subdued now, they say, but the search goes on. Here is M. Guillotte; he has found another victim in another room. They push aside a mosquito-net and see a negro woman, aged, helpless, and with a deep wound in the head.

Some of the young men lift her and carry her out.

Judge Canonge confronts Doctor Lalaurie again:

"Are there slaves still in your garret, Monsieur?" And the doctor "replies with insulting tone that 'There are persons who would do much better by remaining at home than visiting others to dictate to them laws in the quality of officious friends.'"

The search went on. The victims were led or carried out. The sight that met the public eye made the crowd literally groan with horror and shout with indignation. "We saw," wrote the editor of the "Advertiser" next day, "one of these miserable beings. The sight was so horrible that we could scarce look upon it. The most savage heart could not have witnessed the spectacle unmoved. He had a large hole in his head; his body from head to foot was covered with scars and filled with worms! The sight inspired us with so much horror that even at the moment of writing this article we shudder from its effects. Those who have seen the others represent them to be in a similar condition." One after another, seven dark human forms were brought forth, gaunt and wild-eyed with famine and loaded with irons, having been found chained and tied in attitudes in which they had been kept so long that they were crippled for life.

It must have been in the first rush of the inside throng to follow these sufferers into the open air and sunlight that the quick-witted Madame Lalaurie clapped to the doors of her house with only herself and her daughters — possibly the coachman also — inside, and nothing but locks and bars to defend her from the rage of the populace. The streets under her windows — Royal street here, Hospital yonder — and the yard were thronged. Something by and by put some one in mind to look for buried bodies. There had been nine slaves besides the coachman; where were the other two ? A little digging brought their skeletons to light — an adult's out of the soil, and the little child's out of the "condemned well"; there they lay. But the living seven — the indiscreet crowd brought them food and drink in fatal abundance, and before the day was done two more were dead. The others were tenderly carried — shall we say it ? — to prison; — to the calaboose. Thither "at least two thousand people" flocked that day to see, if they might, these wretched sufferers.

A quiet fell upon the scene of the morning's fire. The household and its near friends busied themselves in getting back the jewelry, plate, furniture, and the like, the idle crowd looking on in apathy and trusting, it may be, to see arrests made. But the restoration was finished and the house remained close barred; no arrest was made. As for Dr. Lalaurie, he does not appear in this scene. Then the crowd, along in the afternoon, began to grow again; then to show anger and by and by to hoot and groan, and cry for satis-faction.

IV.

THE LADY'S FLIGHT.

THE old Bayou Road saw a strange sight that after-noon. Down at its farther end lay a little settlement of fishermen and Spanish moss gatherers, pot-hunters, and shrimpers, around a custom-house station, a light-house, and a little fort. There the people who drove out in carriages were in the habit of alighting and taking the cool air of the lake, and sipping lemonades, wines, and ices before they turned homeward again along the crowded way that they had come. In after years the place fell into utter neglect. The customs station was removed, the fort was dismantled, the gay carriage people drove on the "New Shell Road" and its tributaries, Bienville and Canal streets, Washing-ton and Carrollton avenues, and sipped and smoked in the twilights and starlights of Carrollton Gardens and the "New Lake End." The older haunt, once so bright with fashionable pleasure-making, was left to the sole illumination of "St. John Light" and the mongrel life of a bunch of cabins branded Crabtown, and became, in popular superstition at least, the yearly rendezvous of the voodoos. Then all at once in latter days it bloomed out in electrical, horticultural, festal, pyrotechnical splendor as "Spanish Fort," and the carriages all came rolling back.

So, whenever you and —— visit Spanish Fort and stroll along the bayou's edge on the fort side, and watch the broad schooners glide out through the bayou's mouth and into the open water, you may say: "Somewhere just along this bank, within the few paces between here and yonder, must be where *that* schooner lay, moored and ready to sail for Mandeville the afternoon that Madame Lalaurie, fleeing from the mob," etc.

For on that afternoon, when the people surrounded the house, crying for vengeance, she never lost, it seems, her cunning. She and her sleek black coachman took counsel together, and his plan of escape was adopted. The early afternoon dinner-hour of those times came and passed and the crowd still filled the street, but as yet had done nothing. Presently, right in the midst of the throng, her carriage came to the door according to its well-known daily habit at that hour, and at the same moment the charming Madame Lalaurie, in all her pretty manners and sweetness of mien, stepped quickly across the sidewalk and entered the vehicle.

The crowd was taken all aback. When it gathered its wits the coach-door had shut and the horses were starting. Then her audacity was understood.

"She is getting away!" was the cry, and the multitude rushed upon her. "Seize the horses!" they shouted, and dashed at the bits and reins. The black driver gave the word to his beasts, and with his coach whip lashed the faces of those who sprung forward. The horses reared and plunged, the harness held, and the equipage was off. The crowd went with it.

"Turn the coach over!" they cry, and attempt it, but fail. "Drag her out!"

They try to do it, again and again, but in vain; away it rattles! Away it flashes! down Hospital street, past Bourbon, Dauphine, Burgundy, and the Rampart, with the crowd following, yelling, but fast growing thin and thinner.

"Stop her! Stop her! Stop that carriage! Stop that *carriage!*"

In vain! On it spins! Out upon the Bayou Road come the pattering hoofs and humming wheels — not wildly driven, but just at their most telling speed — into the whole whirling retinue of fashionable New Orleans out for its afternoon airing. Past this equipage; past that one; past half a dozen; a dozen; a score! Their inmates sit chatting in every sort of mood over the day's sensation, when — what is this? A rush from behind, a whirl of white dust, and — "As I live, there she goes now, on her regular drive! What scandalous speed! and — see here! they are after her!" Past fifty gigs and coaches; past a hundred; around this long bend in the road; around that one. Good-bye, pursuers! Never a chance to cut her off, the swamp forever on the right, the bayou on the left; she is getting away, getting away! the crowd is miles behind!

The lake is reached. The road ends. What next? The coach dashes up to the bayou's edge and stops. Why just here? Ah! because just here so near the bayou's mouth a schooner lies against the bank. Is Dr. Lalaurie's hand in this? The coachman parleys a moment with the schooner-master and hands him down a purse of gold. The coach-door is opened, the lady alights, and is presently on the vessel's deck. The lines are cast off, the great sails go up, the few lookers-on are there without reference to her and offer no interruption; a little pushing with poles lets the wind fill the canvas, and first slowly and silently, and then swiftly and with a grateful creaking of cordage and spars, the vessel glides out past the lighthouse, through the narrow opening, and stands away towards the northern horizon, below which, some thirty miles away, lies the little watering-place of Mandeville with roads leading as far away northward as one may choose to fly. Madame Lalaurie is gone!

The brave coachman — one cannot help admiring the villain's intrepidity — turned and drove back towards the city. What his plan was is not further known. No wonder if he thought he could lash and dash through the same mob again. But he mistook. He had not reached town again when the crowd met him. This time they were more successful. They stopped the horses — killed them. What they did with the driver is not told; but one can guess. They broke the carriage into bits. Then they returned to the house.

They reached it about 8 o'clock in the evening. The two daughters had just escaped by a window. The whole house was locked and barred; "hermetically sealed," says "L'Abeille" of the next morning. The human tempest fell upon it, and "in a few minutes," says "The Courier," "the doors and windows were broken open, the crowd rushed in, and the work of destruction began." "Those who rush in are of all classes and *colors*," continues "The Courier" of next day; but "No, no!" says a survivor of to-day who was there and took part; "we would n't have allowed that!" In a single hour everything movable disappeared or perished. The place was rifled of jewelry and plate; china was smashed; the very stair-balusters were pulled piece from piece; hangings, bedding and table linen were tossed into the streets; and the elegant furniture, bedsteads, wardrobes, buffets, tables, chairs, pictures, "pianos," says the newspaper, were taken with pains to the third-story windows, hurled out and broken — "smashed into a thousand pieces" — upon the ground below. The very basements were emptied, and the floors, wainscots, and iron balconies damaged as far as at the moment they could be. The sudden southern nightfall descended, and torches danced in the streets and through the ruined house. The débris was gathered into hot bonfires, feather-beds were cut open, and the pavements covered with a thick snow of feathers. The night wore on, but the mob persisted. They mounted and battered the roof; they defaced the inner walls. Morning found them still at their senseless mischief, and they were "in the act of pulling down the walls when the sheriff and several citizens interfered and put an end to their work."

It was proposed to go at once to the houses of others long suspected of like cruelties to their slaves. But against this the highest gentility of the city alertly and diligently opposed themselves. Not at all because of sympathy with such cruelties. The single reason has its parallel in our own day. It was the fear that the negroes would be thereby encouraged to seek by violence those rights which their masters thought it not expedient to give them. The movement was suppressed, and the odious parties were merely warned that they were watched.

Madame Lalaurie, we know by notarial records, was in Mandeville ten days after, when she executed a power of attorney in favor of her New Orleans business agent, in which act she was "authorized and assisted by her husband, Louis Lalaurie." So he disappears.

His wife made her way to Mobile — some say to the North — and thence to Paris. Being recognized and confronted there, she again fled. The rest of her story is tradition, but comes very directly. A domestic in a Creole family that knew Madame Lalaurie — and slave women used to enjoy great confidence and familiarity in the Creole households at times — tells that one day a letter from France to one of the family informed them that Madame Lalaurie, while spending a season at Pau, had engaged with a party of fashionable people in a boar-hunt, and somehow meeting the boar while apart from her companions had been set upon by the infuriated beast, and too quickly for any one to come to her rescue had been torn and killed. If this occurred after 1836 or 1837 it has no disagreement with Harriet Martineau's account, that at the latter date Madame Lalaurie was supposed to be still "skulking about some French province under a false name."

The house remained untouched for at least three years, "ornamented with various writings expressive of indignation and just punishment." The volume of "L'Abeille" containing this account seems to have been abstracted from the city archives. It was in the last week of April or the first week of May, 1836, that Miss Martineau saw the house. It "stands," she wrote about a year later, "and is meant to stand, in its ruined state. It was the strange sight of its gaping windows and empty walls, in the midst of a busy street, which excited my wonder, and was the cause of my being told the story the first time. I gathered other particulars afterwards from eye-witnesses."

So the place came to be looked upon as haunted. In March, 1837, Madame Lalaurie's agent sold the house to a man who held it but a little over three months and then sold it at the same price that he had paid — only fourteen thousand dollars. The notary who made the earlier act of sale must have found it interesting. He was one of those who had helped find and carry out Madame Lalaurie's victims. It did not change hands again for twenty-five years. And then — in what state of repair I know not — it was sold at an advance equal to a yearly increase of but six-sevenths of one per cent. on the purchase price of the gaping ruin sold in 1837. There is a certain poetry in notarial records. But we will not delve for it now. Idle talk of strange sights and sounds crowded out of notice any true history the house may have had in those twenty-five years, or until war had destroyed that slavery to whose horridest possibilities the gloomy pile, even when restored and renovated, stood a ghost-ridden monument. Yet its days of dark romance were by no means ended.

V.

A NEW USE.

THE era of political reconstruction came. The victorious national power decreed that they who had once been master and slave should enter into political partnership on terms of civil equality. The slaves grasped the boon; but the masters, trained for generations in the conviction that public safety and private purity were possible only by the subjection of the black race under the white, loathed civil equality as but another name for private companionship, and spurned, as dishonor and destruction in one, the restoration of their sovereignty at the price of political copartnership with the groveling race they had bought and sold and subjected easily to the leash and lash.

What followed took every one by surprise. The negro came at once into a larger share of power than it was ever intended he should or expected he would attain. His master, related to him long and only under the imagined necessities of plantation government, vowed the issue must and should be, not How shall the two races share public self-government in prosperous amity? but, Which race shall exclusively rule the other, race by race?

The necessities of national authority tipped the scale, and the powers of legislation and government and the spoils of office tumbled, all together, into the freedman's ragged lap. Thereupon there fell upon New Orleans, never well governed at the best, a volcanic shower of corruption and misrule.

And yet when history's calm summing-up and final judgment comes, there must this be pointed out, which was very hard to see through the dust and smoke of those days: that while plunder and fraud ran riot, yet no serious attempt was ever made by the freedman or his allies to establish any un-American principle of government, and for nothing else was he more fiercely, bloodily opposed than for measures approved by the world's best thought and in full harmony with the national scheme of order. We shall see now what these things have to do with our strange true story.

In New Orleans the American public school system, which recognizes free public instruction as a profitable investment of the public funds for the common public safety, had already long been established. The negro adopted and enlarged it. He recognized the fact that the relation of pupils in the public schools is as distinctly a public and not a private relation as that of the sidewalk, the market, the public park, or the street-car. But recognizing also the impracticabilities of place and time, he established separate schools for whites and blacks. In one instance, however, owing mainly to smallness of numbers, it seemed more feasible to allow a common enjoyment of the civil right of public instruction without separation by race than to maintain two separate schools, one at least of which would be very feeble for lack of numbers. Now, it being so decided, of all the buildings in New Orleans which one was chosen for this experiment but the "haunted house" in Royal street!

I shall never forget the day — although marked by no startling incident — when I sat in its lofty drawing-rooms and heard its classes in their annual examination. It was June, and the teachers and pupils were clad in recognition of the special occasion and in the light fabrics fitted to the season. The rooms were adorned with wreaths, garlands, and bouquets. Among the scholars many faces were beautiful, and all were fresh and young. Much Gallic blood asserted itself in complexion and feature, generally of undoubted, unadulterated "Caucasian" purity, but sometimes of visible and now and then of preponderating African tincture. Only two or three, unless I have forgotten, were of pure negro blood. There, in the rooms that had once resounded with the screams of Madame Lalaurie's little slave fleeing to her death, and with the hootings and maledictions of the enraged mob, was being tried the experiment of a common enjoyment of public benefits by the daughters of two widely divergent races, without the enforcement of private social companionship.

From such enforcement the school was as free as any school is or ought to be. The daily discipline did not require any two pupils to be social, but only every one to be civil, and civil to all. These pages are written, however, to tell a strange true story, and not to plead one cause or another. Whatever the story itself pleads, let it plead. Outside the "haunted house," far and near, the whole community was divided into two fiercely hostile parties, often at actual war with each other, the one striving to maintain government upon a co-citizenship regardless of race in all public relations, the other sworn to make race the supreme, sufficient, inexorable condition of supremacy on the one part and subjection on the other. Yet for all this the school prospered.

Nevertheless, it suffered much internal unrest. Many a word was spoken that struck like a club, many a smile stung like a whip-lash, many a glance stabbed like a knife; even in the midst of recitations a wounded one would sometimes break into sobs or silent tears while the aggressor crimsoned and palpitated with the proud indignation of the master caste. The teachers met all such by-play with prompt, impartial repression and concentration upon the appointed duties of the hour.

Sometimes another thing restored order. Few indeed of the pupils, of whatever racial purity or preponderance, but held more or less in awe the ghostly traditions of the house; and at times it chanced to be just in the midst of one of these ebullitions of scorn, grief, and resentful tears that noiselessly and majestically the great doors of the reception-rooms, untouched by visible hands, would slowly swing open, and the hushed girls would call to mind Madame Lalaurie.

Not all who bore the tincture of the despised race suffered alike. Some were fierce and sturdy, and played a savage tit-for-tat. Some were insensible. A few bore themselves inflexibly by dint of sheer nerve; while many, generally much more white than black, quivered and winced continually under the contumely that fell, they felt, with peculiar injustice and cruelty upon them.

Odd things happened from time to time to remind one of the house's early history. One day a deep hidden well that no one had suspected the existence of was found in the basement of the main house. Another time — But we must be brief.

Matters went on thus for years. But at length there was a sudden and violent change.

VI.

EVICTIONS.

THE "Radical" party in Louisiana, gorged with private spoils and loathed and hated by the all but unbroken ranks of well-to-do society, though it held a *creed* as righteous and reasonable as any political party

ever held, was going to pieces by the sheer weakness
of its own political corruption. It was made mainly
of the poor and weak elements of the people. Had
it been ever so pure it could not have made headway
against the strongest ranks of society concentrating
against it with revolutionary intent, when deserted
by the power which had called it to responsibility
and — Come! this history of a house must not run
into the history of a government. It is a fact in our
story, however, that in the " Conservative " party there
sprung up the " White League," purposing to wrest
the State government from the " Radicals " by force
of arms.

On the 14th of September, 1874, the White League
met and defeated the Metropolitan Police in a hot and
bloody engagement of infantry and artillery on the
broad steamboat landing in the very middle of New
Orleans. But the Federal authority interfered. The
" Radical " government resumed control. But the
White League survived and grew in power. In
November elections were held, and the State legisla-
ture was found to be Republican by a majority of
only two.

One bright, spring-like day in December, such as a
northern March might give in its best mood, the school
had gathered in the " haunted house" as usual, but
the hour of duty had not yet struck. Two teachers
sat in an upper class-room talking over the history of
the house. The older of the two had lately heard of
an odd new incident connected with it, and was telling
of it. A distinguished foreign visitor, she said, guest

at a dinner-party in the city the previous season, turned unexpectedly to his hostess, the talk being of quaint old New Orleans houses, and asked how to find "the house where that celebrated tyrant had lived who was driven from the city by a mob for maltreating her slaves." The rest of the company sat aghast, while the hostess silenced him by the severe coldness with which she replied that she "knew nothing about it." One of Madame Lalaurie's daughters was sitting there, a guest at the table.

When the teacher's story was told her companion made no comment. She had noticed a singular sound that was increasing in volume. It was out-of-doors — seemed far away; but it was drawing nearer. She started up, for she recognized it now as a clamor of human voices, and remembered that the iron gates had not yet been locked for the day. They hurried to the window, looked down, and saw the narrow street full from wall to wall for a hundred yards with men coming towards them. The front of the crowd had already reached the place and was turning towards the iron gates.

The two women went quickly to the hall, and, looking down the spiral staircase to the marble pavement of the entrance three stories below, saw the men swarming in through the wide gateway and doorway by dozens. While they still leaned over the balustrade, Marguerite, one of their pupils, a blue-eyed blonde girl of lovely complexion, with red, voluptuous lips, and beautiful hair held by a carven shell comb, came and bent over the balustrade with them. Sud-

denly her comb slipped from its hold, flashed downward, and striking the marble pavement flew into
pieces at the feet of the men who were about to ascend.
Several of them looked quickly up.

"It was my mother's comb!" said Marguerite, turned
ashy pale, and sunk down in hysterics. The two
teachers carried her to a remote room, the bed-chamber of the janitress, and then obeyed an order of the
principal calling her associates to the second floor.
A band of men were coming up the winding stair with
measured, military tread towards the landing, where
the principal, with her assistants gathered around her,
stood to confront them.

She was young, beautiful, and of calm temper. Her
skin, says one who was present, was of dazzling clearness, her abundant hair was golden auburn, and in
happy hours her eyes were as "soft as velvet." But
when the leader of the band of men reached the stair-
landing, threw his coat open, and showed the badge of
the White League, her face had blanched and hardened
to marble, and her eyes darkened to black as they
glowed with indignation.

"We have come," said the White Leaguer, "to
remove the colored pupils. You will call your school
to order." To which the principal replied :

"You will permit me first to confer with my corps
of associates." He was a trifle disconcerted.

"Oh, certainly."

The teachers gathered in the principal's private
room. Some were dumb, one broke into tears, another
pleaded devotion to the principal, and one was just

advising that the *onus* of all action be thrown upon the intruders, when the door was pushed open and the White Leaguer said:

"Ladies, we are waiting. Assemble the school; we are going to clean it out."

The pupils, many of them trembling, weeping, and terrified, were with difficulty brought to order in the assembly room. This place had once been Madame Lalaurie's dining-hall. A frieze of angels ran round its four walls, and, oddly, for some special past occasion, a legend in crimson and gold on the western side bore the words, "The Eye of God is on us."

"Gentlemen, the school is assembled," said the principal.

"Call the roll," was the reply, "and we will challenge each name."

It was done. As each name was called its young bearer rose and confronted her inquisitors. And the inquisitors began to blunder. Accusations of the fatal taint were met with denials and withdrawn with apologies. Sometimes it was truth, and sometimes pure arrogance and falsehood, that triumphed over these champions of instinctive racial antagonism. One dark girl shot up haughtily at the call of her name—

"I am of Indian blood, and can prove it!"

"You will not be disturbed."

"Coralie——," the principal next called. A thin girl of mixed blood and freckled face rose and said:

"My mother is white."

"Step aside!" commanded the White Leaguer.

"But by the law the color follows the mother, and so *I* am white."

"Step aside!" cried the man, in a fury. (In truth there was no such law.)

"Octavie ——."

A pretty, Oriental looking girl rises, silent, pale, but self-controlled.

"Are you colored?"

"Yes; I am colored." She moves aside.

"Marie O——."

A girl very fair, but with crinkling hair and other signs of negro extraction, stands up and says:

"I am the sister of the Hon. ——," naming a high Democratic official, "and I shall not leave this school."

"You may remain; your case will be investigated."

"Eugénie ——."

A modest girl, visibly of mixed race, rises, weeping silently.

"Step aside."

"Marcelline V——."

A bold-eyed girl of much African blood stands up and answers:

"I am not colored! We are Spanish, and *my brother will call on you and prove it.*" She is allowed to stay.

At length the roll-call is done. "Now, madam, you will dismiss these pupils that we have set aside, at once. We will go down and wait to see that they come out." The men tramped out of the room, went down-stairs, and rejoined the impatient crowd that was clamoring in the street.

Then followed a wild scene within the old house.

Restraint was lost. Terror ruled. The girls who had
been ordered into the street sobbed and shrieked and
begged:

"Oh, save us! We cannot go out there; the mob
will kill us! What shall we do?"

One girl of grand and noble air, as dark and handsome as an East Indian princess, and standing first in
her class for scholarship, threw herself at her teacher's
feet, crying, "Have pity on me, Miss —— !"

"My poor Léontine," replied the teacher, "what
can I do? There are good 'colored' schools in the
city; would it not have been wiser for your father to
send you to one of them?"

But the girl rose up and answered:

"Must I go to school with my own servants to
escape an unmerited disdain?" And the teacher was
silent, while the confusion increased.

" The shame of it will kill me!" cried gentle Eugénie
L——. And thereupon, at last, a teacher, commonly
one of the sternest in discipline, exclaimed:

"If Eugénie goes, Marcelline shall go, if I have to
put her out myself! Spanish, indeed! And Eugénie
a pearl by the side of her!"

Just then Eugénie's father came. He had forced
his way through the press in the street, and now stood
bidding his child have courage and return with him
the way he had come.

"Tie your veil close, Eugénie," said the teacher,
"and they will not know you." And so they went,
the father and the daughter. But they went alone.
None followed. This roused the crowd to noisy anger.

"Why don't the rest come?" it howled. But the teachers tried in vain to inspire the panic-stricken girls with courage to face the mob, and were in despair, when a school official arrived, and with calm and confident authority bade the expelled girls gather in ranks and follow him through the crowd. So they went out through the iron gates, the great leaves of which closed after them with a rasping of their key and shooting of their bolts, while a teacher said:

"Come; the reporters will soon be here. Let us go and see after Marguerite."

They found her in the room of the janitress, shut in and fast asleep.

"Do you think," one asked of the janitress, "that mere fright and the loss of that comb made this strong girl ill?"

"No. I think she must have guessed those men's errand, and her eye met the eye of some one who knew her."

"But what of that?"

"She is 'colored.'"

"Impossible!"

"I tell you, yes!"

"Why, I thought her as pure German as her name."

"No, the mixture is there; though the only trace of it is on her lips. Her mother — she is dead now — was a beautiful quadroon. A German sea-captain loved her. The law stood between them. He opened a vein in his arm, forced in some of her blood, went to court, swore he had African blood, got his license, and married her. Marguerite is engaged to be married to a white man, a gentleman who does not know this. It was like life and death, so to speak, for her not to let those men turn her out of here."

The teacher turned away, pondering.

The eviction did not, at that time, hold good. The political struggle went on, fierce and bitter. The "Radical" government was doomed, but not dead. A few weeks after the scene just described the evicted girls were reinstated. A long term of suspense followed. The new year became the old and went out. Twice this happened. In 1877 there were two governors and two governments in Louisiana. In sight from the belvedere of the "haunted house," eight squares away up Royal street, in the State House, the *de facto* government was shut up under close military siege by the *de jure* government, and the Girls' High School in Madame Lalaurie's old house, continuing faithfully their daily sessions, knew with as little certainty to which of the two they belonged as though New Orleans had been some Italian city of the fifteenth century. But to guess the White League, was not far from right, and in April the Radical government expired.

A Democratic school-board came in. June brought Commencement day, and some of the same girls who had been evicted in 1874 were graduated by the new Board in 1877. During the summer the schools and school-laws were overhauled, and in September or October the high school was removed to another place, where each pupil suspected of mixed blood was examined officially behind closed doors and only those who

could prove white or *Indian* ancestry were allowed to
stay. A "colored" high school was opened in Madame
Lalaurie's house with a few pupils. It lasted one session, maybe two, and then perished.

In 1882 the "haunted house" had become a Con-
servatory of Music. Chamber concerts were frequent
in Madame Lalaurie's old dining-hall. On a certain
sweet evening in the spring of that year there sat
among those who had gathered to hear the haunted
place filled with a deluge of sweet sounds one who
had been a teacher there when the house had been, as
some one — Conservative or Radical, who can tell
which ? — said on the spot, "for the second time
purged of its iniquities." The scene was "much
changed," says the auditor; but the ghosts were all
there, walking on the waves of harmony. And thick-
est and fastest they trooped in and out when a passionate song thrilled the air with the promise that

"Some day — some day
Eyes clearer grown the truth may see."

ATTALIE BROUILLARD.

1855.

I.

The strange true stories we have thus far told have all been matter of public or of private record. Pages of history and travel, law reports, documents of court, the testimony of eye-witnesses, old manuscripts and letters, have insured to them the full force and charm of their reality. But now we must have it clearly and mutually understood that here is one the verity of which is vouched for stoutly, but only by tradition. It is very much as if we had nearly finished a strong, solid stone house and would now ask permission of our underwriters to add to it at the rear a small frame lean-to.

It is a mere bit of lawyers' table-talk, a piece of after-dinner property. It originally belonged, they say, to Judge Collins of New Orleans, as I believe we have already mentioned; his by right of personal knowledge. I might have got it straight from him had I heard of it but a few years sooner. His small, iron-gray head, dark, keen eyes, and nervous face and

form are in my mind's eye now, as I saw him one day
on the bench interrupting a lawyer at the bar and
telling him in ten words what the lawyer was trying
to tell in two hundred and fifty.

That the judge's right to this story was that of discovery, not of invention, is well attested; and if he
or any one else allowed fictitious embellishments to
gather upon it by oft telling of it in merry hours, the
story had certainly lost all such superfluities the day
it came to me, as completely as if some one had stolen
its clothes while it was in swimming. The best I can
say is that it came unmutilated, and that I have done
only what any humane person would have done —
given it drapery enough to cover its nakedness.

To speak yet plainer, I do not, even now, put aside,
abridge, or alter a single *fact;* only, at most, restore
one or two to spaces that indicate just what has
dropped out. If a dentist may lawfully supply the
place of a lost tooth, or an old beau comb his hair
skillfully over a bald spot, then am I guiltless. I
make the tale not less, and only just a trifle more,
true; not more, but only a trifle less, strange. And
this is it:

In 1855 this Attalie Brouillard — so called, mark
you, for present convenience only — lived in the French
quarter of New Orleans; I think they say in Bienville
street, but that is no matter; somewhere in the *vieux
carré* of Bienville's original town. She was a worthy
woman; youngish, honest, rather handsome, with a
little money — just a little; of attractive dress, with
good manners, too; alone in the world, and — a quad-

roon. She kept furnished rooms to rent — as a matter of course; what would she do?

Hence she was not so utterly alone in the world as she might have been. She even did what Stevenson says is so good, but not so easy, to do, "to keep a few friends, but these without capitulation." For instance there was Camille Ducour. That was not his name; but as we have called the woman A. B., let the man be represented as C. D.

He, too, was a quadroon; an f. m. c.[1] His personal appearance has not been described to us, but he must have had one. Fancy a small figure, thin, let us say, narrow-chested, round-shouldered, his complexion a dull clay color spattered with large red freckles, his eyes small, gray, and close together, his hair not long or bushy, but dense, crinkled, and hesitating between a dull yellow and a hot red; his clothes his own and his linen last week's.

He is said to have been a shrewd fellow; had picked up much practical knowledge of the law, especially of notarial business, and drove a smart trade giving private advice on points of law to people of his caste. From many a trap had he saved his poor clients of an hour. Out of many a danger of their own making had he safely drawn them, all unseen by, though not unknown to, the legitimate guild of judges, lawyers, and notaries out of whose professional garbage barrel he enjoyed a sort of stray dog's privilege of feeding.

[1] Free man of color.

His meetings with Attalie Brouillard were almost always on the street and by accident. Yet such meetings were invariably turned into pleasant visits in the middle of the sidewalk, after the time-honored Southern fashion. Hopes, ailments, the hardness of the times, the health of each one's "folks," and the condition of their own souls, could not be told all in a breath. He never failed, when he could detain her no longer, to bid her feel free to call on him whenever she found herself in dire need of a wise friend's counsel. There was always in his words the hint that, though he never had quite enough cash for one, he never failed of knowledge and wisdom enough for two. And the gentle Attalie believed both clauses of his avowal.

Attalie had another friend, a white man.

II.

JOHN BULL.

THIS other friend was a big, burly Englishman, forty-something years old, but looking older; a big pink cabbage-rose of a man who had for many years been Attalie's principal lodger. He, too, was alone in the world.

And yet neither was he so utterly alone as he might have been. For he was a cotton buyer. In 1855 there was no business like the cotton business. Everything else was subservient to that. The cotton buyer's part, in particular, was a "pretty business." The cotton *factor* was harassingly responsible to a whole swarm of planter patrons, of whose feelings he had to be all the more careful when they were in his debt. The cotton *broker* could be bullied by his buyer. But the *buyer* was answerable only to some big commercial house away off in Havre or Hamburg or Liverpool, that had to leave all but a few of the largest and most vital matters to his discretion. Commendations and criticisms alike had to come by mail across the Atlantic.

Now, if a cotton buyer of this sort happened to be a bachelor, with no taste for society, was any one likely to care what he substituted, out of business hours, for the conventional relations of domestic life? No one answers. Cotton buyers of that sort were apt to have very comfortable furnished rooms in the old French quarter. This one in Attalie's house had the two main rooms on the first floor above the street.

Honestly, for all our winking and tittering, we know nothing whatever against this person's private character except the sad fact that he was a man and a bachelor. At forty-odd, it is fair to suppose, one who knows the world well enough to be the trusted agent of others, thousands of miles across the ocean, has bid farewell to all mere innocence and has made choice between virtue and vice. But we have no proof whatever that Attalie's cotton buyer had not solemnly chosen virtue and stuck to his choice as an Englishman can.

All we know as to this, really, is that for many years here he had roomed, and that, moved by some sentiment, we know not certainly what, he had again and again assured Attalie that she should never want while

he had anything, and that in his will, whenever he
should make it, she would find herself his sole legatee.
On neither side of the water, said he, had he any one
to whom the law obliged him to leave his property
nor, indeed, any large wealth; only a little money in
bank — a very indefinite statement.   In 1855 the will
was still unwritten.

There is little room to doubt that this state of affairs
did much interest Camille Ducour—at a distance.
The Englishman may have known him by sight.   The
kind of acquaintance he might have had with the
quadroon was not likely to vary much from an
acquaintance with some unknown neighbor's cat on
which he mildly hoped to bestow a pitcher of water if
ever he caught him under his window.

Camille mentioned the Englishman approvingly to
three other friends of Attalie, when, with what they
thought was adroitness, they turned conversation upon
her pecuniary welfare.   They were Jean d'Eau, a
slumberous butcher; Richard Reau, an embarrassed
baker; and one —— Ecswyzee, an illiterate but prosperous candlestick-maker.   These names may sound
inexact, but *can you prove* that these were not their
names and occupations?   We shall proceed.

These three simple souls were bound to Attalie by
the strong yet tender bonds of debit and credit.   She
was not distressingly but only interestingly "behind"
on their well-greased books, where Camille's account,
too, was longer on the left-hand side.   When they
alluded inquiringly to her bill, he mentioned the Englishman vaguely and assured them it was "good paper

to hold," once or twice growing so extravagant as to add that his (Camille's) own was hardly better !

The tradesmen replied that they had n't a shadow of doubt. In fact, they said, their mention of the matter was mere jest, etc.

III.

DUCOUR'S MEDITATIONS.

THERE were a few points in this case upon which Camille wished he could bring to bear those purely intellectual — not magical — powers of divination which he modestly told his clients were the secret of all his sagacious advice. He wished he could determine conclusively and exactly what was the mutual relation of Attalie and her lodger. Out of the minutest corner of one eye he had watched her for years.

A quadroon woman's lot was a hard one; any true woman would say that, even while approving the laws and popular notions of necessity that made that lot what it was. The law, popular sentiment, public policy, always looked at Attalie's sort with their right eye shut. And according to all the demands of the other eye Camille knew that Attalie was honest, faithful. But was that all; or did she stand above and beyond the demands of law and popular sentiment ? In a word, to whom was she honest, faithful; to the Englishman merely, or actually to herself ? If to herself actually, then in case of his early death, —

for Camille had got a notion of that, and had got it
from Attalie, who had got it from the Englishman,
— what then? Would she get his money, or any of
it? No, not if Camille knew men — especially white
men. For a quadroon woman to be true to herself and
to her God was not the kind of thing that white men
— if he knew them — rewarded. But if the case was
not of that sort, and the relation was what he *hoped*
it was, and according to his ideas of higher law it had
a right to be, why, then, she might reasonably hope
for a good fat slice — if there should turn out, after
all, to be any fat to slice.

Thence arose the other question — had the Englishman any money? And if so, was it much, or was it
so little as to make it hardly worth while for the Englishman to die early at all? You can't tell just by
looking at a man or his clothes. In fact, is it not astonishing how quietly a man — of the quiet kind —
can either save great shining stacks of money, or get
rid of all he makes as fast as he makes it? Is n't it
astonishing? Being a cotton buyer did not answer
the question. He might be getting very large pay
or very small; or even none. Some men had got
rich without ever charging anything for their services.
The cotton business those days was a perfectly lovely
business — so many shady by-paths and circuitous
labyrinths. Even in the law — why, sometimes even
he, Camille Ducour, did not charge anything. But
that was not often.

Only one thing was clear — there ought to be a
written will. For Attalie Brouillard, f. w. c., could

by no means be or become the Englishman's legal heir. The law mumbled something about "one-tenth," but for the rest answered in the negative and with a black frown. Her only chance — but we shall come to that.

All in a tremor one day a messenger, Attalie's black slave girl, came to Camille to say that her mistress was in trouble! in distress! in deeper distress than he could possibly imagine, and in instant need of that wise counsel which Camille Ducour had so frequently offered to give.

"I am busy," he said, in the Creole-negro *patois*, "but — has anybody — has anything happened to — to anybody in Madame Brouillard's house?"

"Yes," the messenger feared that "*ce Michié qui poté soulié jaune* — that gentleman who wears yellow shoes — is ill. Madame Brouillard is hurrying to and fro and crying."

"Very loud?"

"No, silently; yet as though her heart were breaking."

"And the doctor?" asks Camille, as he and the messenger are hurrying side by side out of Exchange alley into Bienville street.

"—— was there yesterday and the day before."

They reach the house. Attalie meets her counselor alone at the top of the stairs. "*Li bien malade,*" she whispers, weeping; "he is very ill."

"—— wants to make his will?" asks Camille. All their talk is in their bad French.

Attalie nods, answers inaudibly, and weeps afresh. Presently she manages to tell how the sick man had tried to write, and failed, and had fallen back exclaiming, " Attalie — Attalie — I want to leave it all to you — what little — " and did not finish, but presently gasped out, "Bring a notary."

" And the doctor ? "

" —— has not come to-day. Michié told the doctor if he came again he would kick him downstairs. Yes, and the doctor says whenever a patient of his says that he stops coming."

They reach the door of the sick man's bed-chamber. Attalie pushes it softly, looks into the darkened chamber and draws back, whispering, " He has dropped asleep."

Camille changes places with her and looks in. Then he moves a step across the threshold, leans forward peeringly, and then turns about, lifts his ill-kept forefinger, and murmurs while he fixes his little eyes on hers :

"If you make a noise, or in any way let any one know what has happened, it will cost you all he is worth. I will leave you alone with him just ten minutes." He makes as if to pass by her towards the stair, but she seizes him by the wrist.

" What do you mean ? " she asks, with alarm.

" Hush ! you speak too loud. He is dead."

The woman leaps by him, slamming him against the banisters, and disappears within the room. Camille hears her loud, long moan as she reaches the bedside. He takes three or four audible steps away from the door and towards the stairs, then turns, and darting with the swift silence of a cat surprises her on her knees by the bed, disheveled, unheeding, all moans and tears, and covering with passionate kisses the dead man's — hands only !

To impute moral sublimity to a white man and a quadroon woman at one and the same time and in one and the same affair was something beyond the powers of Camille's small soul. But he gave Attalie, on the instant, full credit, over credit it may be, and felt a momentary thrill of spiritual contagion that he had scarcely known before in all his days. He uttered not a sound; but for all that he said within himself, drawing his breath in through his clenched teeth, and tightening his fists till they trembled, " Oho-o ! — Aha ! — No wonder you postponed the writing of your will day by day, month by month, year in and year out! But you shall see, my fine Michié White man — dead as you are, you shall see — you'll see if you shan't ! — she shall have the money, little or much! Unless there are heirs she shall have every picayune of it ! " Almost as quickly as it had flashed up, the faint flicker of moral feeling died out; yet the resolution remained. He was going to "beat" a dead white man.

IV.

PROXY.

CAMILLE glided to the woman's side and laid a gentle yet commanding touch upon her.

" Come, there is not a moment to lose."

"What do you want?" asked Attalie. She neither rose nor turned her head, nor even let go the dead man's hand.

"I must make haste to fulfill the oft-repeated request of my friend here."

" *Your* friend!" She still knelt, and held the hand, but turned her face, full of pained resentment, upon the speaker behind her. He was calm.

" Our friend; yes, this man here. You did not know that I was his secret confidential adviser? Well, that was all right; I told him to tell no one. But now I must carry out his instructions. Madame Brouillard, this man wished to leave you every cent he had in the world."

Attalie slowly laid her lips on the big cold hand lying in her two hot ones and let the silent tears wet all three. Camille spoke on to her averted form:

"He may never have told you so till to-day, but he has often told me. 'I tell you, Camille,' he used to say, 'because I can trust you: I can't trust a white man in a matter like this.' He told you? Yes; then you know that I speak the truth. But one thing you did not know; that this intention of his was the result of my earnest advice. — Stop! Madame Brouillard — if you please — we have no time for amazement or questions now; and less than none for expressions of gratitude. Listen to me. You know he was always afraid he would die some day suddenly? Yes, of course; everybody knew that. One night — our meetings were invariably at night — he said to me, 'Camille, my dear friend, if I should go all of a sudden some day before I write that will, *you know what to do.'* Those were his exact words : ' Camille, my dear friend, *you know what to do.'* " All this was said to the back of Attalie's head and neck ; but now the speaker touched her with one finger : " Madame, are your lodgers all up town ? "

She nodded.

" Good. And you have but the one servant. Go tell her that our dear friend has been in great suffering but is now much better, quite free from pain, in fact, and wants to attend to some business. Send her to Exchange alley, to the office of Eugene Favre. He is a notary public " — He murmured some further description. " Understand ? "

Attalie, still kneeling, kept her eyes on his in silence, but she understood ; he saw that.

" She must tell him," he continued, " to come at once. But before she goes there she must stop on the way and tell three persons to come and witness a notarial act. Now whom shall they be ? For they must be white male residents of the parish, and they must not be insane, deaf, dumb, blind, nor disqualified by crime. I will tell you : let them be Jean d'Eau — at the French market. He will still be there ; it is his turn to scrub the market to-day. Get him, get Richard Reau, and old man Ecswyzee. And on no account must the doctor be allowed to come. Do that, Madame Brouillard, as quickly as you can. I will wait here."

But the kneeling figure hesitated, with intense distress in her upturned face : " What are you going to do, Michié Ducour ? "

"We are going to make you sole legatee."

"I do not want it! How are you going to do it? How?"

"In a way which he knows about and approves."

Attalie hid her shapely forehead again on the dead hand. "I cannot leave him. Do what you please, only let me stay here. Oh! let me stay here."

"I see," said Camille, with cold severity, "like all women, you count the foolish sentiments of the living of more value than the reasonable wish of the dead." He waited a moment for these words to take effect upon her motionless form, and then, seeing that — again like a woman — she was waiting and wishing for compulsion, he lifted her by one arm. "Come. Go. And make haste to get back again; we are losing priceless time."

She went. But just outside the door she seemed to halt. Camille put out his freckled face and turtle neck. "Well?"

"O Michié Ducour!" the trembling woman whispered, "those three witnesses will never do. I am in debt to every one of them!"

"Madame Brouillard, the one you owe the most to will be the best witness. Well? What next?"

"O my dear friend! what is this going to cost? — in money, I mean. I am so afraid of lawyers' accounts! I have nothing, and if it turns out that he has very, very little — It is true that I sent for you, but — I did not think you — what must you charge?"

"Nothing!" whispered Camille. "Madame Brouillard, whether he leaves you little or much, this must be for me a labor of love to him who was secretly my friend, or I will not touch it. He certainly had something, however, or he would not have tried to write a will. But, my dear madame, if you do not right here, now, stop looking scared, as if you were about to steal something instead of saving something from being stolen, it will cost us a great deal. Go. Make haste! That's right! — Ts-s-st! Hold on! Which is your own bedroom, upstairs? — Never mind why I ask; tell me. Yes; all right! Now, go! — Ts-s-st! Bring my hat up as you return."

She went downstairs. Camille tiptoed quickly back into the death chamber, whipped off his shoes, ran to a small writing-table, then to the bureau, then to the armoire, trying their drawers. They were locked, every one. He ran to the bed and searched swiftly under pillows and mattresses — no keys. Never mind. He wrapped a single sheet about the dead man's form, stepped lightly to the door, looked out, listened, heard nothing, and tripped back again.

And then with all his poor strength he lifted the bulk, still limp, in his arms, and with only two or three halts in the toilsome journey, to dash the streaming sweat from his brows and to better his hold so that the heels should not drag on the steps, carried it up to Attalie's small room and laid it, decently composed, on her bed.

Then he glided downstairs again and had just slipped into his shoes when Attalie came up hastily from below. She was pale and seemed both awe-struck and suspicious. As she met him outside the door grief and dismay were struggling in her eyes with mistrust, and as he coolly handed her the key of her room indignation joined the strife. She reddened and flashed:

"My God! you have not, yourself, already?"

"I could not wait, Madame Brouillard. We must run up now, and do for him whatever cannot be put off; and then you must let me come back, leaving my hat and shoes and coat up there, and — you understand?"

Yes; the whole thing was heartless and horrible, but — she understood. They went up.

V.

THE NUNCUPATIVE WILL.

In their sad task upstairs Attalie held command. Camille went and came on short errands to and from the door of her room, and was let in only once or twice when, for lifting or some such thing, four hands were indispensable. Soon both he and she came down to the door of the vacated room again together. He was in his shirt sleeves and without his shoes; but he had resumed command.

"And now, Madame Brouillard, to do this thing in the very best way I ought to say to you at once that our dear friend — did he ever tell you what he was worth?" The speaker leaned against the door-post and seemed to concern himself languidly with his black-rimmed finger-nails, while in fact he was watching Attalie from head to foot with all his senses and wits. She looked grief-stricken and thoroughly wretched.

"No," she said, very quietly, then suddenly burst into noiseless fresh tears, sank into a chair, buried her face in her wet handkerchief, and cried, "Ah! no, no, no! that was none of my business. He was going to leave it all to me. I never asked if it was little or much."

While she spoke Camille was reckoning with all his might and speed : " She has at least some notion as to whether he is rich or poor. She seemed a few minutes ago to fear he is poor, but I must try her again. Let me see : if he is poor and I say he is rich she will hope I know better than she, and will be silent. But if he is rich and she knows it, and I say he is poor, she will suspect fraud and will out with the actual fact indignantly on the spot." By this time she had ceased, and he spoke out :

"Well, Madame Brouillard, the plain fact is he was — as you may say — poor."

She looked up quickly from her soaking handkerchief, dropped her hands into her lap, and gazing at Camille through her tears said, "Alas! I feared it. That is what I feared. But ah! since it makes no difference to him now, it makes little to me. I feared it. That accounts for his leaving it to me, poor *milatraise*."

"But would you have imagined, madame, that all he had was barely three thousand dollars ? "

"Ah! three thousand — ah! Michié Ducour," she said between a sob and a moan, "that is not so little.

Three thousand ! In Paris, where my brother lives, that would be fifteen thousand francs. Ah ! Michié Ducour, I never guessed half that much, Michié Ducour, I tell you — he was too good to be rich." Her eyes stood full.

Camille started busily from his leaning posture and they began again to be active. But, as I have said, their relations were reversed once more. He gave directions from within the room, and she did short errands to and from the door.

The witnesses came : first Jean d'Eau, then Richard Reau, and almost at the same moment the aged Ecswyzee. The black maid led them up from below, and Attalie, tearless now, but meek and red-eyed, and speaking low through the slightly opened door from within the Englishman's bed-chamber, thanked them, explained that a will was to be made, and was just asking them to find seats in the adjoining front room, when the notary, aged, bent, dark-goggled, and as insensible as a machine, arrived. Attalie's offers to explain were murmurously waved away by his wrinkled hand, and the four men followed her into the bed-chamber. The black maid-of-all-work also entered.

The room was heavily darkened. There was a rich aroma of fine brandy on its air. The Englishman's little desk had been drawn up near the bedside. Two candles were on it, unlighted, in small, old silver candle-sticks. Attalie, grief-worn, distressed, visibly agitated, moved close to the bedside. Her sad figure suited the place with poetic fitness. The notary stood by the chair at the desk. The three witnesses edged along the wall where the curtained windows glimmered, took seats there, and held their hats in their hands. All looked at one object.

It was a man reclining on the bed under a light covering, deep in pillows, his head and shoulders much bundled up in wrappings. He moaned faintly and showed every sign of utmost weakness. His eyes opened only now and then, but when they did so they shone intelligently, though with a restless intensity apparently from both pain and anxiety.

He gasped a faint word. Attalie hung over him for an instant, and then turning quickly to her maid, who was lighting the candles for the notary and placing them so they should not shine into the eyes of the man in bed, said:

"His feet — another hot-water bottle."

The maid went to get it. While she was gone the notary asked the butcher, then the baker, and then the candlestick-maker, if they could speak and understand English, and where they resided. Their answers were satisfactory. Then he sat down, bent low to the desk, and wrote on a blank form the preamble of a nuncupative will. By the time he had finished, the maid had got back and the hot bottle had been properly placed. The notary turned his goggles upon the reclining figure and asked in English, with a strong Creole accent:

"What is your name?"

The words of the man in the bed were an inaudible gasp. But Attalie bent her ear quickly, caught them, and turning repeated:

"More brandy."

The black girl brought a decanter from the floor behind the bureau, and a wine-glass from the washstand. Attalie poured, the patient drank, and the maid replaced glass and decanter. The eyes of the butcher and the baker followed the sparkling vessel till it disappeared, and the maker of candlesticks made a dry swallow and faintly licked his lips. The notary remarked that there must be no intervention of speakers between himself and the person making the will, nor any turning aside to other matters; but that merely stopping a moment to satisfy thirst without leaving the room was not a vitiative turning aside and would not be, even if done by others besides the party making the will. But here the patient moaned and said audibly, "Let us go on." And they went on. The notary asked the patient's name, the place and date of his birth, etc., and the patient's answers were in every case whatever the Englishman's would have been. Presently the point was reached where the patient should express his wishes unprompted by suggestion or inquiry. He said faintly, "I will and bequeath"—

The servant girl, seeing her mistress bury her face in her handkerchief, did the same. The patient gasped audibly and said again, but more faintly:

"I will and bequeath — some more brandy."

The decanter was brought. He drank again. He let Attalie hand it back to the maid and the maid get nearly to the bureau when he said in a low tone of distinct reproof:

"Pass it 'round." The four visitors drank.

Then the patient resumed with stronger voice. " I will and bequeath to my friend Camille Ducour " —

Attalie started from her chair with a half-uttered cry of amazement and protest, but dropped back again at the notary's gesture for silence, and the patient spoke straight on without hesitation — " to my friend Camille Ducour, the sum of fifteen hundred dollars in cash."

Attalie and her handmaiden looked at each other with a dumb show of lamentation; but her butcher and her baker turned slowly upon her candlestick-maker, and he upon them, a look of quiet but profound approval. The notary wrote, and the patient spoke again :

" I will everything else which I may leave at my death, both real and personal property, to Madame Attalie Brouillard."

" Ah ! " exclaimed Attalie, in the manner of one largely, but not entirely, propitiated. The maid suited her silent movement to the utterance, and the three witnesses exchanged slow looks of grave satisfaction. Mistress and maid, since the will seemed to them so manifestly and entirely finished, began to whisper together, although the patient and the notary were still perfecting some concluding formalities. But presently the notary began to read aloud the instrument he had prepared, keeping his face buried in the paper and running his nose and purblind eyes about it nervously, like a new-born thing hunting the warm fountain of life. All gave close heed. We need not give the document in its full length, nor its Creole accent in its entire breadth. This is only something like it:

" Dthee State of Louisiana," etc. "Be h-it known dthat on dthees h-eighth day of dthee month of May, One thousan' h-eight hawndred and fifty-five, dthat I, Eugene Favre, a not-arie pewblic een and for dthe State of Louisiana, parrish of Orleans, duly commission-ed and qualeefi-ed, was sue-mon-ed to dthe domee-ceel of Mr. [the Englishman's name], Number [so-and-so] Bienville street; . . . dthat I found sayed Mr. [Eng-lishman] lyingue in heez bade in dthee rear room of dthee second floor h-of dthee sayed house . . . at about two o'clawk in dthee h-afternoon, and beingue inform-ed by dthee sayed Mr. [Englishman] dthat he *diz*-i-red too make heez weel, I, sayed not-arie, sue-mon-ed into sayed bedchamber of dthe sayed Mr. [Englishman] dthe following nam-ed wit*nes*ses of lawfool h-age and residents of dthe sayed cittie, parrish, and State, to wit: Mr. Jean d'Eau, Mr. Richard Reau, and Mr. V. Deblieux Ecswyzee. That there *up*-on sayed Mr. [Englishman] being seek in bodie but of soun' mine, which was *hap*parent to me not-arie and dthe sayed wit*nes*ses by heez lang-uage and h-actions then and there in dthe presence of sayed wit*nes*ses *dic*tated to me not-arie dthe following as heez laz weel and tes-*tam*ent, wheech was written by me sayed not-arie as *dic*tated by the sayed Mr. [Englishman], to wit:

" 'My name ees [John Bull]. I was born in,' etc. 'My father and mother are dade. I have no chil'ren. I have never had annie brawther or seester. I have never been marri-ed. Thees is my laz weel. I have never made a weel befo'. I weel and *bick*weath to my fran' Camille Ducour dthe sawm of fifteen hawndred dollars in cash. I weel h-everything h-else wheech I may leave at my daith, both real and personal property, to Madame Attalie Brouillard, leevingue at Number,' etc. 'I appoint my sayed fran' Camille Ducour as my testamentary exe*cu*tor, weeth-out bon', and grant heem dthe seizin' of my h-estate, h-and I dir-ect heem to pay h-all my juz debts.'

"Thees weel and tes*tam*ent as thus *dic*tated too me by sayed *tes*tator and wheech was wreeten by me not-arie by my h-own han' jus' as *dic*tated, was thane by me not-arie rade to sayed Mr. [Englishman] in an au*dib*le voice and in the presence of dthe aforesayed three wit*nes*ses, and dthe sayed Mr. [Englishman] *dic*lar-ed that he well awnder-stood me not-arie and per*sev*er-ed een *dic*laring the same too be his laz weel; all of wheech was don' at one time and place weethout in*ter*'uption and weethout turningue aside to other acts.

"Thus done and pass-ed," etc.

The notary rose, a wet pen in one hand and the will — with his portfolio under it for a tablet — in the other. Attalie hurried to the bedside and stood ready to assist. The patient took the pen with a trembling hand. The writing was laid before him, and Attalie with a knee on the bed thrust her arm under the pillows behind him to make a firmer support.

The patient seemed to summon all his power to poise and steady the pen, but his hand shook, his fingers loosened, and it fell upon the document, making two or three blots there and another on the bed-cover-ing, whither it rolled. He groped faintly for it, moaned, and then relaxed.

"He cannot sign!" whispered Attalie, piteously.

"Yes," gasped the patient.

The notary once more handed him the pen, but the same thing happened again.

The butcher cleared his throat in a way to draw at-tention. Attalie looked towards him and he drawled, half rising from his chair:

"I t'ink — a li'l more cognac" —

"Yass," murmured the baker. The candlestick-maker did not speak, but unconsciously wet his lips with his tongue and wiped them with the back of his forefinger. But every eye turned to the patient, who said:

"I cannot write — my hand — shakes so."

The notary asked a formal question or two, to which the patient answered "yes" and "no." The official sat again at the desk, wrote a proper statement of the patient's incapacity to make his signature, and then read it aloud. The patient gave assent, and the three witnesses stepped forward and signed. Then the no-tary signed.

As the four men approached the door to depart the baker said, lingeringly, to Attalie, smiling diffidently as he spoke:

"Dat settin' still make a man mighty dry, yass."

"Yass, da's true," said Attalie.

"Yass," he added, "same time he dawn't better drink much *water* dat hot weader, no." The butcher turned and smiled concurrence; but Attalie, though she again said "yass," only added good-day, and the maid led them and the notary down stairs and let them out.

VI.

MEN CAN BE BETTER THAN THEIR LAWS.

An hour later, when the black maid returned from an errand, she found her mistress at the head of the stairs near the Englishman's door, talking in suppressed tones to Camille Ducour, who, hat in hand, seemed to have just dropped in and to be just going out again. He went, and Attalie said to her maid that he was "so good" and was going to come and sit up all night with the sick man.

The next morning the maid — and the neighborhood — was startled to hear that the cotton buyer had died in the night. The physician called and gave a certificate of death without going up to the death chamber.

The funeral procession was short. There was first the carriage with the priest and the acolytes; then the hearse; then a carriage in which sat the cotton buyer's clerk, — he had had but one, — his broker, and two mon of that singular sort that make it a point to go to everybody's funeral; then a carriage occupied by Attalie's other lodgers, and then, in a carriage bringing up the rear, were Camille Ducour and Madame Brouillard. She alone wept, and, for all we have seen, we yet need not doubt her tears were genuine. Such was the cortége. Oh! also, in his private vehicle, driven by himself, was a very comfortable and genteel-looking man, whom neither Camille nor Attalie knew, but whom every other attendant at the funeral seemed to regard with deference. While the tomb was being sealed Camille sidled up to the broker and made bold to ask who the stranger was. Attalie did not see the movement, and Camille did not tell her what the broker said.

Late in the next afternoon but one Camille again received word from Attalie to call and see her in all haste. He found her in the Englishman's front room. Five white men were sitting there with her. They not only looked amused, but plainly could have looked more so but for the restraints of rank and station. Attalie was quite as visibly frightened. Camille's knees weakened and a sickness came over him as he glanced around the group. For in the midst sat the stranger who had been at the funeral, while on his right sat two, and on his left two, men, the terror of whose presence we shall understand in a moment.

"Mr. Ducour," said the one who had been at the funeral, "as friends of Mr. [Englishman] we desire to express our satisfaction at the terms of his last will and testament. We have had a long talk with Madame Brouillard; but for myself, I already know his wish that she should have whatever he might leave. But a wish is one thing; a will, even a nuncupative will by public act, is another and an infinitely better and more effective thing. But we wish also to express our determination to see that you are not hindered in the

execution of any of the terms of this will, whose genuineness we, of course, do not for a moment question."
He looked about upon his companions. Three of
them shook their heads gravely; but the fourth, in
his over-zeal, attempted to say "No," and burst into
a laugh; whereupon they all broadly smiled, while
Camille looked ghastly. The speaker resumed.

"I am the custodian of all Mr. [Englishman's]
accounts and assets. This gentleman is a judge, this
one is a lawyer, — I believe you know them all by
sight, — this one is a banker, and this one — a — in
fact, a detective. We wish you to feel at all times
free to call upon any or all of us for advice, and to
bear in mind that our eyes are ever on you with a
positively solicitous interest. You are a busy man,
Mr. Ducour, living largely by your wits, and we must
not detain you longer. We are glad that you are
yourself to receive fifteen hundred dollars. We doubt
not you have determined to settle the affairs of the
estate without other remuneration, and we not merely
approve but distinctly recommend that decision. The
task will involve an outlay of your time and labor,
for which fifteen hundred dollars will be a generous, a handsome, but not an excessive remuneration. You will be glad to know there will still be
something left for Madame Brouillard. And now,
Mr. Ducour," — he arose and approached the pallid
scamp, smiling benevolently, — "*remember* us as your
friends, who will *watch* you" — he smote him on the
shoulder with all the weight of his open palm —
"with no *ordinary* interest. Be assured you shall get

your fifteen hundred, and Attalie shall have the rest, which — as Attalie tells me she has well known for years — will be about thirty thousand dollars. Gentlemen, our dinner at the lake will be waiting. Goodday, Mr. Ducour. Good-day, Madame Brouillard. Have no fear. Mr. Ducour is going to render you full justice, — without unnecessary delay, — in solid cash."

And he did.

WAR DIARY OF A UNION WOMAN
IN THE SOUTH.

1860–63.

[THE following diary was originally written in lead pencil and in a book the leaves of which were too soft to take ink legibly. I have it direct from the hands of its writer, a lady whom I have had the honor to know for nearly thirty years. For good reasons the author's name is omitted, and the initials of people and the names of places are sometimes fictitiously given. Many of the persons mentioned were my own acquaintances and friends. When some twenty years afterwards she first resolved to publish it, she brought me a clear, complete copy in ink. It had cost much trouble, she said, for much of the pencil writing had been made under such disadvantages and was so faint that at times she could decipher it only under direct sunlight. She had succeeded, however, in making a copy, *verbatim* except for occasional improvement in the grammatical form of a sentence, or now and then the omission, for brevity's sake, of something unessential. The narrative has since been severely abridged to bring it within the limits of this volume.

In reading this diary one is much charmed with its constant understatement of romantic and perilous incidents and conditions. But the original penciled pages show that, even in copying, the strong bent of the writer to be brief has often led to the exclusion of facts that enhance the interest of exciting situations, and sometimes the omission robs her own heroism of due emphasis. I have restored one example of this in the short paragraph following her account of the night she spent fanning her sick husband on their perilous voyage down the Mississippi.]

G. W. C.

I.

SECESSION.

New Orleans, Dec. 1, 1860. — I understand it now. Keeping journals is for those who can not, or dare not, speak out. So I shall set up a journal, being only a rather lonely young girl in a very small and hated minority. On my return here in November, after a foreign voyage and absence of many months, I found myself behind in knowledge of the political conflict, but heard the dread sounds of disunion and war muttered in threatening tones. Surely no native-born woman loves her country better than I love America. The blood of one of its revolutionary patriots flows in my veins, and it is the Union for which he pledged his "life, fortune, and sacred honor" that I love, not any divided or special section of it. So I have been reading attentively and seeking light from foreigners and natives on all questions at issue. Liv-

ing from birth in slave coun‍
American, and passing throug‍
in early childhood, the saddes‍
est features of slavery have
South goes to war for slaver‍
this country. To say so is lik‍ ‍ ‍ ‍ ‍ ‍ ‍ ‍ ‍ ‍ ‍ ‍
a roaring torrent. This is a good time to follow St.
Paul's advice that women should refrain from speaking, but they are speaking more than usual and forcing others to speak against their will.

Sunday, Dec. —, 1860. — In this season for peace I
had hoped for a lull in the excitement, yet this day
has been full of bitterness. "Come, G.," said Mrs. F.
at breakfast, "leave *your* church for to-day and come
with us to hear Dr. —— on the situation. He will
convince you." "It is good to be convinced," I said;
"I will go." The church was crowded to suffocation
with the élite of New Orleans. The preacher's text
was, "Shall we have fellowship with the stool of
iniquity which frameth mischief as a law?" . . .
The sermon was over at last and then followed a
prayer. . . . Forever blessed be the fathers of the
Episcopal Church for giving us a fixed liturgy! When
we met at dinner Mrs. F. exclaimed, "Now, G., you
heard him prove from the Bible that slavery is right
and that therefore secession is. Were you not convinced?" I said, "I was so busy thinking how completely it proved too that Brigham Young is right
about polygamy that it quite weakened the force of
the argument for me." This raised a laugh, and covered my retreat.

Jan. 26, 1861. — The solemn boom of cannon to-day announced that the convention have passed the ordinance of secession. We must take a reef in our patriotism and narrow it down to State limits. Mine still sticks out all around the borders of the State. It will be bad if New Orleans should secede from Louisiana and set up for herself. Then indeed I would be "cabined, cribbed, confined." The faces in the house are jubilant to-day. Why is it so easy for them and not for me to "ring out the old, ring in the new"? I am out of place.

Jan. 28, Monday. — Sunday has now got to be a day of special excitement. The gentlemen save all the sensational papers to regale us with at the late Sunday breakfast. Rob opened the battle yesterday morning by saying to me in his most aggressive manner, "G., I believe these are your sentiments"; and then he read aloud an article from the "Journal des Debats" expressing in rather contemptuous terms the fact that France will follow the policy of non-intervention. When I answered: "Well, what do you expect? This is not their quarrel," he raved at me, ending by a declaration that he would willingly pay my passage to foreign parts if I would like to go. "Rob," said his father, "keep cool; don't let that threat excite you. Cotton is king. Just wait till they feel the pinch a little; their tone will change." I went to Trinity Church. Some Union people who are not Episcopalians go there now because the pastor has not so much chance to rail at the Lord when things are not going to suit; but yesterday was a marked Sunday. The usual prayer for the President and Congress was changed to the "governor and people of this commonwealth and their representatives in convention assembled."

The city was very lively and noisy this evening with rockets and lights in honor of secession. Mrs. F., in common with the neighbors, illuminated. We walked out to see the houses of others gleaming amid the dark shrubbery like a fairy scene. The perfect stillness added to the effect, while the moon rose slowly with calm splendor. We hastened home to dress for a soirée, but on the stairs Edith said, "G., first come and help me dress Phœbe and Chloe [the negro servants]. There is a ball to-night in aristocratic colored society. This is Chloe's first introduction to New Orleans circles, and Henry Judson, Phœbe's husband, gave five dollars for a ticket for her." Chloe is a recent purchase from Georgia. We superintended their very stylish toilets, and Edith said, "G., run into your room, please, and write a pass for Henry. Put Mr. D.'s name to it." "Why, Henry is free," I said. — "That makes no difference; all colored people must have a pass if out late. They choose a master for protection and always carry his pass. Henry chose Mr. D., but he's lost the pass he had." When the pass was ready, a carriage dashed up to the back-gate and the party drove off in fine style.

At the soirée we had secession talk sandwiched everywhere; between the supper, and the music, and the dance; but midnight has come, and silence, and a few too brief hours of oblivion.

II.

THE VOLUNTEERS. — FORT SUMTER.

Feb. 24, 1861. — The toil of the week has ended. Nearly a month has passed since I wrote here. Events have crowded upon one another. A lowering sky closes in upon the gloomy evening, and a moaning wind is sobbing in every key. They seem in keeping with the national sorrow, and in lieu of other sympathy I am glad to have that of Nature to-night. On the 4th the cannon boomed in honor of Jefferson Davis's election, and day before yesterday Washington's Birthday was made the occasion of another grand display and illumination, in honor of the birth of a new nation and the breaking of that Union which he labored to cement. We drove to the race-course to see the review of troops. A flag was presented to the Washington Artillery by ladies. Senaator Judah Benjamin made an impassioned speech. The banner was orange satin on one side, crimson silk on the other, the pelican and brood embroidered in pale green and gold. Silver crossed cannon surmounted it, orange-colored fringe surrounded it, and crimson tassels drooped from it. It was a brilliant, unreal scene; with military bands clashing triumphant music, elegant vehicles, high-stepping horses, and lovely women richly appareled.

Wedding cards have been pouring in till the contagion has reached us; Edith will be married next

Thursday. The wedding dress is being fashioned, and the bridesmaids and groomsmen have arrived. Edith has requested me to be special mistress of ceremonies on Thursday evening, and I have told this terrible little rebel, who talks nothing but blood and thunder, yet faints at the sight of a worm, that if I fill that office no one shall mention war or politics during the whole evening, on pain of expulsion. The clock points to ten. I must lay the pen aside.

March 10, 1861. — The excitement in this house has risen to fever heat during the past week. The four gentlemen have each a different plan for saving the country, and now that the bridal bouquets have faded, the three ladies have again turned to public affairs; Lincoln's inauguration and the story of the disguise in which he traveled to Washington is a never-ending source of gossip. The family board being the common forum, each gentleman as he appears first unloads his pockets of papers from all the Southern States, and then his overflowing heart to his eager female listeners, who in turn relate, inquire, sympathize, or cheer. If I dare express a doubt that the path to victory will be a flowery one, eyes flash, cheeks burn, and tongues clatter, till all are checked up suddenly by a warning rap for "Order, order!" from the amiable lady presiding. Thus we swallow politics with every meal. We take a mouthful and read a telegram, one eye on table, the other on the paper. One must be made of cool stuff to keep calm and collected. I say but little. There is one great comfort; this war fever has banished small talk. The black servants move about quietly, never seeming to notice that this is all about them.

"How can you speak so plainly before them?" I say.

"Why, what matter? They know that we shall keep the whip-handle."

April 13, 1861. — More than a month has passed since the last date here. This afternoon I was seated on the floor covered with loveliest flowers, arranging a floral offering for the fair, when the gentlemen arrived (and with papers bearing the news of the fall of Fort Sumter, which, at her request, I read to Mrs. F.).

April 20. — The last few days have glided away in a halo of beauty. I can't remember such a lovely spring ever before. But nobody has time or will to enjoy it. War, war! is the one idea. The children play only with toy cannons and soldiers; the oldest inhabitant goes by every day with his rifle to practice; the public squares are full of companies drilling, and are now the fashionable resorts. We have been told that it is best for women to learn how to shoot too, so as to protect themselves when the men have all gone to battle. Every evening after dinner we adjourn to the back lot and fire at a target with pistols.

Yesterday I dined at Uncle Ralph's. Some members of the bar were present and were jubilant about their brand-new Confederacy. It would soon be the grandest government ever known. Uncle Ralph said solemnly, "No, gentlemen; the day we seceded the star of our glory set." The words sunk into my mind like a knell, and made me wonder at the mind that could recognize that and yet adhere to the doctrine of secession.

In the evening I attended a farewell gathering at a friend's whose brothers are to leave this week for Richmond. There was music. No minor chord was permitted.

III.

TRIBULATION.

April 25, 1861. — Yesterday I went with Cousin E. to have her picture taken. The picture-galleries are doing a thriving business. Many companies are ordered off to take possession of Fort Pickens (Florida), and all seem to be leaving sweethearts behind them. The crowd was in high spirits; they don't dream that any destinies will be spoiled. When I got home Edith was reading from the daily paper of the dismissal of Miss G. from her place as teacher for expressing abolition sentiments, and that she would be ordered to leave the city. Soon a lady came with a paper setting forth that she has established a "company" — we are nothing if not military — for making lint and getting stores of linen to supply the hospitals.

My name went down. If it had n't, my spirit would have been wounded as with sharp spears before night. Next came a little girl with a subscription paper to get a flag for a certain company. The little girls, especially the pretty ones, are kept busy trotting around with subscription lists. A gentleman leaving for Richmond called to bid me good-bye. We had a serious talk on the chances of his coming home maimed. He handed me a rose and went off gaily, while a vision came before me of the crowd of cripples that will be hobbling around when the war is over. It stayed with me all the afternoon while I shook hands with one after another in their shining gray and gold uniforms. Latest of all came little Guy, Mr. F.'s youngest clerk, the pet of the firm as well as of his home, a mere boy of sixteen. Such senseless sacrifices seem a sin. He chattered brightly, but lingered about, saying good-bye. He got through it bravely until Edith's husband incautiously said, " You did n't kiss your little sweetheart," as he always called Ellie, who had been allowed to sit up. He turned suddenly, broke into agonizing sobs and ran down the steps. I went right up to my room.

Suddenly the midnight stillness was broken by the sound of trumpets and flutes. It was a serenade, by her lover, to the young lady across the street. She leaves to-morrow for her home in Boston, he joins the Confederate army in Virginia. Among the callers yesterday she came and astonished us all by the change in her looks. She is the only person I have yet seen who seems to realize the horror that is coming. Was this pallid, stern-faced creature, the gentle, glowing Nellie whom we had welcomed and admired when she came early last fall with her parents to enjoy a Southern winter ?

May 10, 1861. — I am tired and ashamed of myself.

Last week I attended a meeting of the lint society to hand in the small contribution of linen I had been able to gather. We scraped lint till it was dark. A paper was shown, entitled the " Volunteer's Friend," started by the girls of the high school, and I was asked to help the girls with it. I positively declined. To-day I was pressed into service to make red flannel cartridge-bags for ten-inch columbiads. I basted while Mrs. S. sewed, and I felt ashamed to think that I had not the moral courage to say, "I don't approve of your war and won't help you, particularly in the murderous part of it."

May 27, 1861. — This has been a scenic Sabbath. Various companies about to depart for Virginia occupied the prominent churches to have their flags consecrated. The streets were resonant with the clangor of drums and trumpets. E. and myself went to Christ Church because the Washington Artillery were to be there.

June 13. — To-day has been appointed a Fast Day. I spent the morning writing a letter on which I put my first Confederate postage-stamp. It is of a brown color and has a large 5 in the center. To-morrow must be devoted to all my foreign correspondents before the expected blockade cuts us off.

June 29. — I attended a fine luncheon yesterday at one of the public schools. A lady remarked to a school official that the cost of provisions in the Confederacy was getting very high, butter, especially, being scarce and costly. " Never fear, my dear madame," he replied. " Texas alone can furnish butter enough to supply the whole Confederacy; we'll soon be getting it from there." It's just as well to have this sublime confidence.

July 15, 1861. — The quiet of midsummer reigns, but ripples of excitement break around us as the papers tell of skirmishes and attacks here and there in Virginia. "Rich Mountain" and "Carrick's Ford" were the last. "You see," said Mrs. D. at breakfast to-day, "my prophecy is coming true that Virginia will be the seat of war." "Indeed," I burst out, forgetting my resolution not to argue, "you may think yourselves lucky if this war turns out to have any seat in particular."

So far, no one especially connected with me has gone to fight. How glad I am for his mother's sake that Rob's lameness will keep him at home. Mr. F., Mr. S., and Uncle Ralph are beyond the age for active service, and Edith says Mr. D. can't go now. She is very enthusiastic about other people's husbands being enrolled, and regrets that her Alex is not strong enough to defend his country and his rights.

July 22. — What a day! I feel like one who has been out in a high wind, and cannot get my breath. The news-boys are still shouting with their extras, "Battle of Bull's Run! List of the killed! Battle oi Manassas! List of the wounded!" Tender-hearted Mrs. F. was sobbing so she could not serve the tea; but nobody cared for tea. "O G.!" she said, "three thousand of our own, dear Southern boys are lying out there." "My dear Fannie," spoke Mr. F., "they are heroes now. They died in a glorious cause, and it

is not in vain. This will end it. The sacrifice had
to be made, but those killed have gained immortal
names." Then Rob rushed in with a new extra, reading of the spoils captured, and grief was forgotten.
Words cannot paint the excitement. Rob capered
about and cheered; Edith danced around ringing the
dinner bell and shouting, "Victory!" Mrs. F. waved
a small Confederate flag, while she wiped her eyes,
and Mr. D. hastened to the piano and in his most brilliant style struck up "Dixie," followed by "My Maryland" and the "Bonnie Blue Flag."

"Do not look so gloomy, G.," whispered Mr. S.
"You should be happy to-night; for, as Mr. F. says,
now we shall have peace."

"And is that the way you think of the men of your
own blood and race?" I replied. But an utter scorn
choked me, and I walked out of the room. What proof
is there in this dark hour that they are not right?
Only the emphatic answer of my own soul. To-morrow
I will pack my trunk and accept the invitation to visit
at Uncle Ralph's country-house.

Sept. 25, 1861. (*Home again from " The Pines."*)
— When I opened the door of Mrs. F.'s room on my
return, the rattle of two sewing-machines and a blaze
of color met me.

"Ah! G., you are just in time to help us; these
are coats for Jeff Thompson's men. All the cloth in
the city is exhausted; these flannel-lined oilcloth
table-covers are all we could obtain to make overcoats
for Thompson's poor boys. They will be very warm
and serviceable."

"Serviceable, yes! The Federal army will fly when they see those coats! I only wish I could be with the regiment when these are shared around." Yet I helped make them.

Seriously, I wonder if any soldiers will ever wear these remarkable coats. The most bewildering combination of brilliant, intense reds, greens, yellows, and blues in big flowers meandering over as vivid grounds; and as no table-cover was large enough to make a coat, the sleeves of each were of a different color and pattern. However, the coats were duly finished. Then we set to work on gray pantaloons, and I have just carried a bundle to an ardent young lady who wishes to assist. A slight gloom is settling down, and the inmates here are not quite so cheerfully confident as in July.

IV.

A BELEAGUERED CITY.

Oct. 22, 1861. — When I came to breakfast this morning Rob was capering over another victory — Ball's Bluff. He would read me, "We pitched the Yankees over the bluff," and ask me in the next breath to go to the theater this evening. I turned on the poor fellow: "Don't tell me about your victories. You vowed by all your idols that the blockade would be raised by October 1, and I notice the ships are still serenely anchored below the city."

"G., you are just as pertinacious yourself in championing your opinions. What sustains you when no-body agrees with you ? "

I would not answer.

Oct. 28, 1861.—When I dropped in at Uncle Ralph's last evening to welcome them back, the whole family were busy at a great center-table copying sequestration acts for the Confederate Government. The property of all Northerners and Unionists is to be sequestrated, and Uncle Ralph can hardly get the work done fast enough. My aunt apologized for the rooms looking chilly; she feared to put the carpets down, as the city might be taken and burned by the Federals. "We are living as much packed up as possible. A signal has been agreed upon, and the instant the army approaches we shall be off to the country again."

Great preparations are being made for defense. At several other places where I called the women were almost hysterical. They seemed to look forward to being blown up with shot and shell, finished with cold steel, or whisked off to some Northern prison. When I got home Edith and Mr. D. had just returned also.

"Alex," said Edith, "I was up at your orange-lots to-day and the sour oranges are dropping to the ground, while they cannot get lemons for our sick soldiers."

"That 's my kind, considerate wife," replied Mr. D. "Why did n't I think of that before ? Jim shall fill some barrels to-morrow and take them to the hos-pitals as a present from you."

Nov. 10. — Surely this year will ever be memorable to me for its perfection of natural beauty. Never was sunshine such pure gold, or moonlight such transparent silver. The beautiful custom prevalent here of decking the graves with flowers on All Saint's day was well fulfilled, so profuse and rich were the blossoms. On All-hallow Eve Mrs. S. and myself visited a large cemetery. The chrysanthemums lay like great masses of snow and flame and gold in every garden we passed, and were piled on every costly tomb and lowly grave. The battle of Manassas robed many of our women in mourning, and some of these, who had no graves to deck, were weeping silently as they walked through the scented avenues.

A few days ago Mrs. E. arrived here. She is a widow, of Natchez, a friend of Mrs. F.'s, and is traveling home with the dead body of her eldest son, killed at Manassas. She stopped two days waiting for a boat, and begged me to share her room and read her to sleep, saying she could n't be alone since he was killed; she feared her mind would give way. So I read all the comforting chapters to be found till she dropped into forgetfulness, but the recollection of those weeping mothers in the cemetery banished sleep for me.

Nov. 26, 1861. — The lingering summer is passing into those misty autumn days I love so well, when there is gold and fire above and around us. But the glory of the natural and the gloom of the moral world agree not well together. This morning Mrs. F. came to my room in dire distress. "You see," she said, "cold weather is coming on fast, and our poor fellows are lying out at night with nothing to cover them. There is a wail for blankets, but there is not a blanket in town. I have gathered up all the spare bed-clothing, and now want every available rug or table-cover in the house. Can't I have yours, G.? We must make these small sacrifices of comfort and elegance, you know, to secure independence and freedom."

"Very well," I said, denuding the table. " This may do for a drummer boy."

Dec. 26, 1861. — The foul weather cleared off bright and cool in time for Christmas. There is a midwinter lull in the movement of troops. In the evening we went to the grand bazaar in the St. Louis Hotel, got up to clothe the soldiers. This bazaar has furnished the gayest, most fashionable war-work yet, and has kept social circles in a flutter of pleasant, heroic excitement all through December. Everything beautiful or rare garnered in the homes of the rich was given for exhibition, and in some cases for raffle and sale. There were many fine paintings, statues, bronzes, engravings, gems, laces — in fact, heirlooms, and bric-à-brac of all sorts. There were many lovely Creole girls present, in exquisite toilets, passing to and fro through the decorated rooms, listening to the band clash out the Anvil Chorus.

This morning I joined the B.'s and their party in a visit to the new fortifications below the city. It all looks formidable enough, but of course I am no judge of military defenses. We passed over the battle-ground where Jackson fought the English, and thinking of how he dealt with treason, one could almost fancy his unquiet ghost stalking about.

Jan. 2, 1862. — I am glad enough to bid '61 good-bye. Most miserable year of my life! What ages of thought and experience have I not lived in it.

Last Sunday I walked home from church with a young lady teacher in the public schools. The teachers have been paid recently in "shin-plasters." I don't understand the horrid name, but nobody seems to have any confidence in the scrip. In pure benevolence I advised my friend to get her money changed into coin, as in case the Federals took the city she would be in a bad fix, being in rather a lonely position. She turned upon me in a rage.

"You are a black-hearted traitor," she almost screamed at me in the street, this well-bred girl! "My money is just as good as coin you'll see! Go to Yankee land. It will suit you better with your sordid views and want of faith, than the generous South."

"Well," I replied, "when I think of going, I'll come to you for a letter of introduction to your grandfather in Yankee land." I said good-morning and turned down another street in a sort of a maze, trying to put myself in her place and see what there was sordid in my advice.

Luckily I met Mrs. B. to turn the current of thought. She was very merry. The city authorities have been searching houses for fire-arms. It is a good way to get more guns, and the homes of those men suspected of being Unionists were searched first. Of course they went to Dr. B.'s. He met them with his own delightful courtesy. "Wish to search for arms? Certainly, gentlemen." He conducted them through all the house with smiling readiness, and after what seemed a very thorough search bowed them politely out. His gun was all the time safely reposing between the canvas folds of a cot-bed which leaned folded up together against the wall, in the very room where they had ransacked the closets. Queerly, the rebel families have been the ones most anxious to conceal all weapons. They have dug pits quietly at night in the back yards, and carefully wrapping the weapons, buried them out of sight. Every man seems to think he will have some private fighting to do to protect his family.

V.

MARRIED.

Friday, Jan. 24, 1862. (On steamboat W., Mississippi River.) — With a changed name I open you once more, my journal. It was a sad time to wed, when one knew not how long the expected conscription would spare the bridegroom. The women-folk knew how to sympathize with a girl expected to prepare for her wedding in three days, in a blockaded city, and about to go far from any base of supplies. They all rallied round me with tokens of love and consideration, and sewed, shopped, mended, and packed, as if sewing soldier clothes. They decked the whole house and the church with flowers. Music breathed, wine sparkled, friends came and went. It seemed a dream, and comes up now and again out of the afternoon sunshine where I sit on deck. The steamboat slowly plows its way through lumps of floating ice, — a novel sight to me, — and I look forward wondering whether the new people I shall meet will be as fierce about the war as those in New Orleans. That past is to be all forgiven and forgotten; I understood thus the kindly acts that sought to brighten the threshold of a new life.

Feb. 15, 1862. (*Village of X.*) — We reached Arkansas Landing at nightfall. Mr. Y., the planter who owns the landing, took us right up to his residence. He ushered me into a large room where a couple of candles gave a dim light, and close to them, and sewing as if on a race with time, sat Mrs. Y. and a little negro girl, who was so black and sat so stiff and straight she looked like an ebony image. This was a large plantation; the Y.'s knew H. very well, and were very kind and cordial in their welcome and congratulations. Mrs. Y. apologized for continuing her work; the war had pushed them this year in getting the negroes clothed, and she had to sew by dim candles, as they could obtain no more oil. She asked if there were any new fashions in New Orleans.

Next morning we drove over to our home in this village. It is the county-seat, and was, till now, a good place for the practice of H.'s profession. It lies on the edge of a lovely lake. The adjacent planters count their slaves by the hundreds. Some of them live with a good deal of magnificence, using service of plate, having smoking-rooms for the gentlemen built off the house, and entertaining with great hospitality.

The Baptists, Episcopalians, and Methodists hold services on alternate Sundays in the court-house. All the planters and many others, near the lake shore, keep a boat at their landing, and a raft for crossing vehicles and horses. It seemed very piquant at first, this taking our boat to go visiting, and on moonlight nights it was charming. The woods around are lovelier than those in Louisiana, though one misses the moaning of the pines. There is fine fishing and hunting, but these cotton estates are not so pleasant to visit as sugar plantations.

But nothing else has been so delightful as, one morning, my first sight of snow and a wonderful, new, white world.

Feb. 27, 1862.—The people here have hardly felt the war yet. There are but two classes. The planters and the professional men form one; the very poor villagers the other. There is no middle class. Ducks and partridges, squirrels and fish, are to be had. H. has bought me a nice pony, and cantering along the shore of the lake in the sunset is a panacea for mental worry.

VI.

HOW IT WAS IN ARKANSAS.

March 11, 1862. — The serpent has entered our Eden. The rancor and excitement of New Orleans have invaded this place. If an incautious word betrays any want of sympathy with popular plans, one

is " traitorous," " ungrateful," " crazy." If one remains silent, and controlled, then one is " phlegmatic,"
" cool-blooded," " unpatriotic." Cool-blooded! Heav-
ens! if they only knew. It is very painful to see lovable and intelligent women rave till the blood mounts
to face and brain. The immediate cause of this access
of war fever has been the battle of Pea Ridge. They
scout the idea that Price and Van Dorn have been
completely worsted. Those who brought the news
were speedily told what they ought to say. " No,
it is only a serious check; they must have more
men sent forward at once. This country must do
its duty." So the women say another company *must*
be raised.

We were guests at a dinner-party yesterday. Mrs.
A. was very talkative. " Now, ladies, you must all
join in with a vim and help equip another company."

" Mrs. L.," she said, turning to me, " are you not
going to send your husband? Now use a young bride's
influence and persuade him; he would be elected one
of the officers." " Mrs. A.," I replied, longing to
spring up and throttle her, " the Bible says, ' When a
man hath married a new wife, he shall not go to war
for one year, but remain at home and cheer up his
wife.' " . . .

" Well, H.," I questioned, as we walked home after
crossing the lake, " can you stand the pressure, or
shall you be forced into volunteering?" " Indeed," he
replied, " I will not be bullied into enlisting by women,
or by men. I will sooner take my chance of conscription and feel honest about it. You know my attach-

ments, my interests are here; these are my people. I could never fight against them; but my judgment disapproves their course, and the result will inevitably be against us."

This morning the only Irishman left in the village presented himself to H. He has been our wood-sawyer, gardener, and factotum, but having joined the new company, his time recently has been taken up with drilling. H. and Mr. R. feel that an extensive vegetable garden must be prepared while he is here to assist or we shall be short of food, and they sent for him yesterday.

" So, Mike, you are really going to be a soldier ? "

" Yes, sor; but faith, Mr. L., I don't see the use of me going to shtop a bullet when sure an' I'm willin' for it to go where it plazes."

March 18, 1862. — There has been unusual gayety in this little village the past few days. The ladies from the surrounding plantations went to work to get up a festival to equip the new company. As Annie and myself are both brides recently from the city, requisition was made upon us for engravings, costumes, music, garlands, and so forth. Annie's heart was in the work; not so with me. Nevertheless, my pretty things were captured, and shone with just as good a grace last evening as if willingly lent. The ball was a merry one. One of the songs sung was "Nellie Gray," in which the most distressing feature of slavery is bewailed so pitifully. To sing this at a festival for raising money to clothe soldiers fighting to perpetuate that very thing was strange.

March 20, 1862. — A man professing to act by General Hindman's orders is going through the country impressing horses and mules. The overseer of a certain estate came to inquire of H. if he had not a legal right to protect the property from seizure. Mr. L. said yes, unless the agent could show some better credentials than his bare word. This answer soon spread about, and the overseer returned to report that it excited great indignation, especially among the company of new volunteers. H. was pronounced a traitor, and they declared that no one so untrue to the Confederacy should live there. When H. related the circumstance at dinner, his partner, Mr. R., became very angry, being ignorant of H.'s real opinions. He jumped up in a rage and marched away to the village thoroughfare. There he met a batch of the volunteers, and said, "We know what you have said of us, and I have come to tell you that you are liars, and you know where to find us."

Of course I expected a difficulty ; but the evening passed, and we retired undisturbed. Not long afterward a series of indescribable sounds broke the stillness of the night, and the tramp of feet was heard outside the house. Mr. R. called out, "It's a serenade, H. Get up and bring out all the wine you have." Annie and I peeped through the parlor window, and lo ! it was the company of volunteers and a diabolical band composed of bones and broken-winded brass instruments. They piped and clattered and whined for some time, and then swarmed in, while we ladies retreated and listened to the clink of glasses.

March 22, 1862. — H., Mr. R., and Mike have been very busy the last few days getting the acre of kitchen-garden plowed and planted. The stay-law has stopped all legal business, and they have welcomed this work. But to-day a thunderbolt fell in our household. Mr. R. came in and announced that he has agreed to join the company of volunteers. Annie's Confederate principles would not permit her to make much resistance, and she has been sewing and mending as fast as possible to get his clothes ready, stopping now and then to wipe her eyes. Poor Annie! She and Max have been married only a few months longer than we have; but a noble sense of duty animates and sustains her.

VII.

THE FIGHT FOR FOOD AND CLOTHING.

April 1, 1862. — The last ten days have brought changes in the house. Max R. left with the company to be mustered in, leaving with us his weeping Annie. Hardly were her spirits somewhat composed when her brother arrived from Natchez to take her home. This morning he, Annie, and Reeney, the black handmaiden, posted off. Out of seven of us only H., myself, and Aunt Judy are left. The absence of Reeney will not be the one least noted. She was as precious an imp as any Topsy ever was. Her tricks were endless and her innocence of them amazing. When sent out to bring in eggs she would take them from nests where hens were hatching, and embryo chickens would be served up at breakfast, while Reeney stood by grinning to see them opened; but when accused she was imperturbable. "Laws, Mis' L., I nebber done bin nigh dem hens. Mis' Annie, you can go count dem dere eggs." That when counted they were found minus the number she had brought had no effect on her stolid denial. H. has plenty to do finishing the garden all by himself, but the time rather drags for me.

April 13, 1862. — This morning I was sewing up a rent in H.'s garden-coat, when Aunt Judy rushed in.

"Laws! Mis' L., here's Mr. Max and Mis' Annie done come back!" A buggy was coming up with Max, Annie, and Reeney.

"Well, is the war over?" I asked.

"Oh, I got sick!" replied our returned soldier, getting slowly out of the buggy.

He was very thin and pale, and explained that he took a severe cold almost at once, had a mild attack of pneumonia, and the surgeon got him his discharge as unfit for service. He succeeded in reaching Annie, and a few days of good care made him strong enough to travel back home.

"I suppose, H., you've heard that Island No. 10 is gone?"

Yes, we heard that much, but Max had the particulars, and an exciting talk followed. At night H. said to me, "G., New Orleans will be the next to go, you'll see, and I want to get there first; this stagnation here will kill me."

April 28, 1862. — This evening has been very lovely, but full of a sad disappointment. H. invited me to drive. As we turned homeward he said:

"Well, my arrangements are completed. You can begin to pack your trunks to-morrow, and I shall have a talk with Max."

Mr. R. and Annie were sitting on the gallery as I ran up the steps.

"Heard the news ? " they cried.

"No! What news ? "

"New Orleans is taken! All the boats have been run up the river to save them. No more mails."

How little they knew what plans of ours this dashed away. But our disappointment is truly an infinitesimal drop in the great waves of triumph and despair surging to-night in thousands of hearts.

April 30. — The last two weeks have glided quietly away without incident except the arrival of new neighbors — Dr. Y., his wife, two children, and servants. That a professional man prospering in Vicksburg should come now to settle in this retired place looks queer. Max said:

"H., that man has come here to hide from the conscript officers. He has brought no end of provisions, and is here for the war. He has chosen well, for this county is so cleaned of men it won't pay to send the conscript officers here."

Our stores are diminishing and cannot be replenished from without; ingenuity and labor must evoke them. We have a fine garden in growth, plenty of chickens, and hives of bees to furnish honey in lieu of sugar. A good deal of salt meat has been stored in the smoke-house, and, with fish in the lake, we expect to keep the wolf from the door. The season for game is about over, but an occasional squirrel or duck comes to the larder, though the question of ammunition has to be considered. What we have may be all we can have, if the war last five years longer; and they say they are prepared to hold out till the crack of doom. Food, however, is not the only want. I never realized before the varied needs of civilization. Every day something is "out." Last week but two bars of soap remained, so we began to save bones and ashes. Annie said: "Now, if we only had some china-berry trees here we should n't need any other grease. They are making splendid soap at Vicksburg with china-balls. They just put the berries into the lye and it eats them right up and makes a fine soap." I did long for some china-berries to make this experiment. H. had laid in what seemed a good supply of kerosene, but it is nearly gone, and we are down to two candles kept for an emergency. Annie brought a receipt from Natchez for making candles of rosin and wax, and with great forethought brought also the wick and rosin. So yesterday we tried making candles. We had no molds, but Annie said the latest style in Natchez was to make a waxen rope by dipping, then wrap it round a corn-cob. But H. cut smooth blocks of wood about four inches square, into which he set a polished cylinder about four inches high. The waxen ropes were coiled round the cylinder like a serpent, with the head raised about two inches ; as the light burned down to the cylinder, more of the rope was unwound. To-day the vinegar was found to be all gone and we have started to make some. For tyros we succeed pretty well.

VIII.

DROWNED OUT AND STARVED OUT.

May 9, 1862. — A great misfortune has come upon us all. For several days every one has been uneasy about the unusual rise of the Mississippi and about a rumor that the Federal forces had cut levees above to swamp the country. There is a slight levee back of the village, and H. went yesterday to examine it. It looked strong and we hoped for the best. About dawn this morning a strange gurgle woke me. It had a pleasing, lulling effect. I could not fully rouse at first, but curiosity conquered at last, and I called H.

"Listen to that running water; what is it?" He sprung up, listened a second, and shouted : "Max, get up! The water is on us!" They both rushed off to the lake for the skiff. The levee had not broken. The water was running clean over it and through the garden fence so rapidly that by the time I dressed and got outside Max was paddling the pirogue they had brought in among the pea-vines, gathering all the ripe peas left above the water. We had enjoyed one mess and he vowed we should have another.

H. was busy nailing a raft together while he had a

dry place to stand on. Annie and I, with Reeney,
had to secure the chickens, and the back piazza was
given up to them. By the time a hasty breakfast
was eaten the water was in the kitchen. The stove
and everything there had to be put up in the dining-
room. Aunt Judy and Reeney had likewise to move
into the house, their floor also being covered with
water. The raft had to be floated to the store-house
and a platform built, on which everything was ele-
vated. At evening we looked round and counted the
cost. The garden was utterly gone. Last evening
we had walked round the strawberry beds that fringed
the whole acre and tasted a few just ripe. The hives
were swamped. Many of the chickens were drowned.
Sancho had been sent to high ground where he could
get grass. In the village every green thing was swept
away. Yet we were better off than many others; for
this house, being raised, we have escaped the water
indoors. It just laves the edge of the galleries.

May 26, 1862. — During the past week we have
lived somewhat like Venetians, with a boat at front
steps and a raft at the back. Sunday H. and I took
skiff to church. The clergyman, who is also tutor at
a planter's across the lake, preached to the few who
had arrived in skiffs. We shall not try it again, it is
so troublesome getting in and out at the court-house
steps. The imprisonment is hard to endure. It
threatened to make me really ill, so every evening
H. lays a thick wrap in the pirogue, I sit on it and we
row off to the ridge of dry land running along the
lake-shore and branching off to a strip of woods also

out of water. Here we disembark and march up
and down till dusk. A great deal of the wood got
wet and has to be laid out to dry on the galleries,
with clothing, and everything that must be dried.
One's own trials are intensified by the worse suffering
around that we can do nothing to relieve.

Max has a puppy named after General Price. The
gentlemen had both gone up town yesterday in the
skiff when Annie and I heard little Price's despairing
cries from under the house, and we got on the raft to
find and save him. We wore light morning dresses
and slippers, for shoes are becoming precious. Annie
donned a Shaker and I a broad hat. We got the raft
pushed out to the center of the grounds opposite the
house and could see Price clinging to a post; the next
move must be to navigate the raft up to the side of
the house and reach for Price. It sounds easy; but
poke around with our poles as wildly or as scientifi-
cally as we might, the raft would not budge. The
noonday sun was blazing right overhead and the
muddy water running all over slippered feet and
dainty dresses. How long we staid praying for rescue,
yet wincing already at the laugh that would come
with it, I shall never know. It seemed like a day
before the welcome boat and the "Ha, ha!" of H. and
Max were heard. The confinement tells severely on
all the animal life about us. Half the chickens are
dead and the other half sick.

The days drag slowly. We have to depend mainly
on books to relieve the tedium, for we have no piano;
none of us like cards; we are very poor chess-players,

and the chess-set is incomplete. When we gather round the one lamp — we dare not light any more — each one exchanges the gems of thought or mirthful ideas he finds. Frequently the gnats and the mosquitoes are so bad we cannot read at all. This evening, till a strong breeze blew them away, they were intolerable. Aunt Judy goes about in a dignified silence, too full for words, only asking two or three times, "W'at I dun tole you fum de fust?" The food is a trial. This evening the snaky candles lighted the glass and silver on the supper-table with a pale gleam and disclosed a frugal supper indeed — tea without milk (for all the cows are gone), honey, and bread. A faint ray twinkled on the water swishing against the house and stretching away into the dark woods. It looked like civilization and barbarism met together. Just as we sat down to it, some one passing in a boat shouted that Confederates and Federals were fighting at Vicksburg.

Monday, June 2, 1862. — On last Friday morning, just three weeks from the day the water rose, signs of its falling began. Yesterday the ground appeared, and a hard rain coming down at the same time washed off much of the unwholesome débris. To-day is fine, and we went out without a boat for a long walk.

June 13. — Since the water ran off, we have, of course, been attacked by swamp fever. H. succumbed first, then Annie, Max next, and then I. Luckily, the new Dr. Y. had brought quinine with him, and we took heroic doses. Such fever never burned in my veins before or sapped strength so rapidly, though probably the want of good food was a factor. The two or three other professional men have left. Dr. Y. alone remains. The roads now being dry enough, H. and Max started on horseback, in different directions, to make an exhaustive search for supplies. H. got back this evening with no supplies.

June 15, 1862. — Max got back to-day. He started right off again to cross the lake and interview the planters on that side, for they had not suffered from overflow.

June 16. — Max got back this morning. H. and he were in the parlor talking and examining maps together till dinner-time. When that was over they laid the matter before us. To buy provisions had proved impossible. The planters across the lake had decided to issue rations of corn-meal and peas to the villagers whose men had all gone to war, but they utterly refused to sell anything. "They said to me," said Max, "'We will not see your family starve, Mr. R.; but with such numbers of slaves and the village poor to feed, we can spare nothing for sale.'" "Well, of course," said H., "we do not purpose to stay here and live on charity rations. We must leave the place at all hazards. We have studied out every route and made inquiries everywhere we went. We shall have to go down the Mississippi in an open boat as far as Fetler's Landing (on the eastern bank). There we can cross by land and put the boat into Steele's Bayou, pass thence to the Yazoo River, from there to Chickasaw Bayou, into McNutt's Lake, and land near my uncle's in Warren County."

June 20, 1862. — As soon as our intended departure was announced, we were besieged by requests for all sorts of things wanted in every family — pins, matches, gunpowder, and ink. One of the last cases H. and Max had before the stay-law stopped legal business was the settlement of an estate that included a country store. The heirs had paid in chattels of the store. These had remained packed in the office. The main contents of the cases were hardware; but we found treasure indeed — a keg of powder, a case of matches, a paper of pins, a bottle of ink. Red ink is now made out of poke-berries. Pins are made by capping thorns with sealing-wax, or using them as nature made them. These were articles money could not get for us. We would give our friends a few matches to save for the hour of tribulation. The paper of pins we divided evenly, and filled a bank-box each with the matches. H. filled a tight tin case apiece with powder for Max and himself and sold the rest, as we could not carry any more on such a trip. Those who did not hear of this in time offered fabulous prices afterwards for a single pound. But money has not its old attractions. Our preparations were delayed by Aunt Judy falling sick of swamp fever.

Friday, June 27. — As soon as the cook was up again, we resumed preparations. We put all the clothing in order and had it nicely done up with the last of the soap and starch. "I wonder," said Annie, "when I shall ever have nicely starched clothes after these? They had no starch in Natchez or Vicksburg when I was there." We are now furbishing up dresses suitable for such rough summer travel. While we sat at work yesterday the quiet of the clear, calm noon was broken by a low, continuous roar like distant thunder. To-day we are told it was probably cannon at Vicksburg. This is a great distance, I think, to have heard it — over a hundred miles.

H. and Max have bought a large yawl and are busy on the lake bank repairing it and fitting it with lockers. Aunt Judy's master has been notified when to send for her; a home for the cat Jeff has been engaged; Price is dead, and Sancho sold. Nearly all the furniture is disposed of, except things valued from association, which will be packed in H.'s office and left with some one likely to stay through the war. It is hardest to leave the books.

Tuesday, July 8, 1862. — We start to-morrow. Packing the trunks was a problem. Annie and I are allowed one large trunk apiece, the gentlemen a smaller one each, and we a light carpet-sack apiece for toilet articles. I arrived with six trunks and leave with one! We went over everything carefully twice, rejecting, trying to shake off the bonds of custom and get down to primitive needs. At last we made a judicious selection. Everything old or worn was left; everything merely ornamental, except good lace, which was light. Gossamer evening dresses were all left. I calculated on taking two or three books that would bear the most reading if we were again shut up where none could be had, and so, of course, took Shakspere first. Here I was interrupted to go and pay a farewell visit, and when we returned Max had packed and nailed the

cases of books to be left. Chance thus limited my
choice to those that happened to be in my room —
"Paradise Lost," the "Arabian Nights," a volume of
Macaulay's History that I was reading, and my prayer-
book. To-day the provisions for the trip were cooked:
the last of the flour was made into large loaves of
bread; a ham and several dozen eggs were boiled; the
few chickens that have survived the overflow were
fried; the last of the coffee was parched and ground;
and the modicum of the tea was well corked up. Our
friends across the lake added a jar of butter and two
of preserves. H. rode off to X. after dinner to con-
clude some business there, and I sat down before a
table to tie bundles of things to be left. The sunset
glowed and faded and the quiet evening came on calm
and starry. I sat by the window till evening deepened
into night, and as the moon rose I still looked a reluc-
tant farewell to the lovely lake and the grand woods,
till the sound of H.'s horse at the gate broke the spell.

IX.

HOMELESS AND SHELTERLESS.

Thursday, July 10, 1862. (—— *Plantation.*) — Yesterday about 4 o'clock we walked to the lake and embarked. Provisions and utensils were packed in the
lockers, and a large trunk was stowed at each end. The
blankets and cushions were placed against one of them,
and Annie and I sat on them Turkish fashion. Near the

center the two smaller trunks made a place for Reeney. Max and H. were to take turns at the rudder and oars. The last word was a fervent God-speed from Mr. E., who is left in charge of all our affairs. We believe him to be a Union man, but have never spoken of it to him. We were gloomy enough crossing the lake, for it was evident the heavily laden boat would be difficult to manage. Last night we staid at this plantation, and from the window of my room I see the men unloading the boat to place it on the cart, which a team of oxen will haul to the river. These hospitable people are kindness itself, till you mention the war.

Saturday, July 12, 1862. (Under a cotton-shed on the bank of the Mississippi River.) — Thursday was a lovely day, and the sight of the broad river exhilarating. The negroes launched and reloaded the boat, and when we had paid them and spoken good-bye to them we felt we were really off. Every one had said that if we kept in the current the boat would almost go of itself, but in fact the current seemed to throw it about, and hard pulling was necessary. The heat of the sun was very severe, and it proved impossible to use an umbrella or any kind of shade, as it made steering more difficult. Snags and floating timbers were very troublesome. Twice we hurried up to the bank out of the way of passing gunboats, but they took no notice of us. When we got thirsty, it was found that Max had set the jug of water in the shade of a tree and left it there. We must dip up the river water or go without. When it got too dark to travel safely we disembarked.

Reeney gathered wood, made a fire and some tea, and we had a good supper. We then divided, H. and I remaining to watch the boat, Max and Annie on shore. She hung up a mosquito-bar to the trees and went to bed comfortably. In the boat the mosquitoes were horrible, but I fell asleep and slept till voices on the bank woke me. Annie was wandering disconsolate round her bed, and when I asked the trouble, said, "Oh, I can't sleep there! I found a toad and a lizard in the bed." When dropping off again, H. woke me to say he was very sick; he thought it was from drinking the river water. With difficulty I got a trunk opened to find some medicine. While doing so a gunboat loomed up vast and gloomy, and we gave each other a good fright. Our voices doubtless reached her, for instantly every one of her lights disappeared and she ran for a few minutes along the opposite bank. We momently expected a shell as a feeler.

At dawn next morning we made coffee and a hasty breakfast, fixed up as well as we could in our sylvan dressing-rooms, and pushed on, for it is settled that traveling between eleven and two will have to be given up unless we want to be roasted alive. H. grew worse. He suffered terribly, and the rest of us as much to see him pulling in such a state of exhaustion. Max would not trust either of us to steer. About eleven we reached the landing of a plantation. Max walked up to the house and returned with the owner, an old gentleman living alone with his slaves. The housekeeper, a young colored girl, could not be surpassed in her graceful efforts to make us comfortable and anticipate every want. I was so anxious about H. that I remember nothing except that the cold drinking-water taken from a cistern beneath the building, into which only the winter rains were allowed to fall, was like an elixir. They offered luscious peaches that, with such water, were nectar and ambrosia to our parched lips. At night the housekeeper said she was sorry they had no mosquito-bars ready and hoped the mosquitoes would not be thick, but they came out in legions. I knew that on sleep that night depended recovery or illness for H. and all possibility of proceeding next day. So I sat up fanning away mosquitoes that he might sleep, toppling over now and then on the pillows till roused by his stirring. I contrived to keep this up till, as the chill before dawn came, they abated and I got a short sleep. Then, with the aid of cold water, a fresh toilet, and a good breakfast, I braced up for another day's baking in the boat.

[If I had been well and strong as usual the discomforts of such a journey would not have seemed so much to me; but I was still weak from the effects of the fever, and annoyed by a worrying toothache which there had been no dentist to rid me of in our village.[1]]

Having paid and dismissed the boat's watchman, we started and traveled till eleven to-day, when we stopped at this cotton-shed. When our dais was spread and lunch laid out in the cool breeze, it seemed a blessed spot. A good many negroes came offering

---

[1] Restored omission. See page 262.

chickens and milk in exchange for tobacco, which we had not. We bought some milk with money.

A United States transport just now steamed by and the men on the guards cheered and waved to us. We all replied but Annie. Even Max was surprised into an answering cheer, and I waved my handkerchief with a very full heart as the dear old flag we have not seen for so long floated by; but Annie turned her back.

Sunday, July 13, 1862. (Under a tree on the east bank of the Mississippi.) — Late on Saturday evening we reached a plantation whose owner invited us to spend the night at his house. What a delightful thing is courtesy ! The first tone of our host's welcome indicated the true gentleman. We never leave the oars with the watchman; Max takes those, Annie and I each take a band-box, H. takes my carpet-sack, and Reeney brings up the rear with Annie's. It is a funny procession. Mr. B.'s family were absent, and as we sat on the gallery talking it needed only a few minutes to show this was a " Union man." His home was elegant and tasteful, but even here there was neither tea nor coffee.

About eleven we stopped here in this shady place. While eating lunch the negroes again came imploring for tobacco. Soon an invitation came from the house for us to come and rest. We gratefully accepted, but found the idea of rest for warm, tired travelers was for us to sit in the parlor on stiff chairs while the whole family trooped in, cool and clean in fresh toilets, to stare and question. We soon returned to the trees;

however, they kindly offered corn-meal pound-cake and beer, which were excellent. If we reach Fetler's Landing to-night, the Mississippi-River part of the journey is concluded. Eight gunboats and one transport have passed us. Getting out of their way has been troublesome. Our gentlemen's hands are badly blistered.

Tuesday, July 15, 1862.—Sunday night about ten we reached the place where, according to our map, Steele's Bayou comes nearest to the Mississippi, and where the landing should be, but when we climbed the steep bank there was no sign of habitation. Max walked off into the woods on a search, and was gone so long we feared he had lost his way. He could find no road. H. suggested shouting and both began. At last a distant halloo replied, and by cries the answerer was guided to us. A negro said "Who are you? What do you want?" "Travelers seeking shelter for the night." He came forward and said that was the right place, his master kept the landing, and he would watch the boat for five dollars. He showed the road, and said his master's house was one mile off and another house two miles. We mistook and went to the one two miles off. There a legion of dogs rushed at us, and several great, tall, black fellows surrounded us till the master was roused. He put his head through the window and said,— "I'll let nobody in. The Yankees have been here and took twenty-five of my negroes to work on their fortifications, and I've no beds nor anything for anybody." At 1 o'clock we reached Mr. Fetler's, who was pleasant, and said we should have the best he had. The bed into whose grateful soft-

ness I sank was piled with mattresses to within two
or three feet of the ceiling, and, with no step-ladder,
getting in and out was a problem. This morning we
noticed the high-water mark, four feet above the lower
floor. Mrs. Fetler said they had lived up-stairs several
weeks.

X.

FRIGHTS AND PERILS IN STEELE'S BAYOU.

*Wednesday, July 16, 1862. (Under a tree on the
bank of Steele's Bayou.)* — Early this morning our boat
was taken out of the Mississippi and put on Mr. Fetler's ox-cart. After breakfast we followed on foot.
The walk in the woods was so delightful that all were
disappointed when a silvery gleam through the trees
showed the bayou sweeping along, full to the banks,
with dense forest trees almost meeting over it. The
boat was launched, calked, and reloaded, and we were
off again. Towards noon the sound of distant cannon
began to echo around, probably from Vicksburg again.
About the same time we began to encounter rafts.
To get around them required us to push through brush
so thick that we had to lie down in the boat. The
banks were steep and the land on each side a bog.
About 1 o'clock we reached this clear space with
dry shelving banks and disembarked to eat lunch. To
our surprise a neatly dressed woman came tripping
down the declivity bringing a basket. She said she
lived above and had seen our boat. Her husband was

in the army, and we were the first white people she had talked to for a long while. She offered some corn-meal pound-cake and beer, and as she climbed back told us to "look out for the rapids." H. is putting the boat in order for our start and says she is waving good-bye from the bluff above.

Thursday, July 17, 1862. (*On a raft in Steele's Bayou.*) — Yesterday we went on nicely awhile and at afternoon came to a strange region of rafts, extending about three miles, on which persons were living. Many saluted us, saying they had run away from Vicksburg at the first attempt of the fleet to shell it. On one of these rafts, about twelve feet square,[1] bagging had been hung up to form three sides of a tent. A bed was in one corner, and on a low chair, with her provisions in jars and boxes grouped round her, sat an old woman feeding a lot of chickens. They were strutting about oblivious to the inconveniences of war, and she looked serenely at ease.

Having moonlight, we had intended to travel till late. But about ten o'clock, the boat beginning to go with great speed, H., who was steering, called to Max:

"Don't row so fast; we may run against something."

" I 'm hardly pulling at all."

"Then we 're in what she called the rapids !"

The stream seemed indeed to slope downward, and in a minute a dark line was visible ahead. Max tried to turn, but could not, and in a second more we dashed

---

[1] More likely twelve yards. — G. W. C.

against this immense raft, only saved from breaking up by the men's quickness. We got out upon it and ate supper. Then, as the boat was leaking and the current swinging it against the raft, H. and Max thought it safer to watch all night, but told us to go to sleep. It was a strange spot to sleep in — a raft in the middle of a boiling stream, with a wilderness stretching on either side. The moon made ghostly shadows and showed H., sitting still as a ghost, in the stern of the boat, while mingled with the gurgle of the water round the raft beneath was the boom of cannon in the air, solemnly breaking the silence of night. It drizzled now and then, and the mosquitoes swarmed over us. My fan and umbrella had been knocked overboard, so I had no weapon against them. Fatigue, however, overcomes everything, and I contrived to sleep.

H. roused us at dawn. Reeney found light-wood enough on the raft to make a good fire for coffee, which never tasted better. Then all hands assisted in unloading; a rope was fastened to the boat, Max got in, H. held the rope on the raft, and, by much pulling and pushing, it was forced through a narrow passage to the farther side. Here it had to be calked, and while that was being done we improvised a dressing-room in the shadow of our big trunks. (During the trip I had to keep the time, therefore properly to secure belt and watch was always an anxious part of my toilet.) The boat is now repacked, and while Annie and Reeney are washing cups I have scribbled, wishing much that mine were the hand of an artist.

Friday morning, July 18, 1862. (*House of Col. K., on Yazoo River.*) — After leaving the raft yester-day all went well till noon, when we came to a nar-row place where an immense tree lay clear across the stream. It seemed the insurmountable obstacle at last. We sat despairing what to do, when a man appeared beside us in a pirogue. So sudden, so silent was his arrival that we were thrilled with surprise. He said if we had a hatchet he could help us. His fairy bark floated in among the branches like a bubble, and he soon chopped a path for us, and was delighted to get some matches in return. He said the cannon we heard yesterday were in an engagement with the ram *Arkansas*, which ran out of the Yazoo that morning. We did not stop for dinner to-day, but ate a hasty lunch in the boat, after which nothing but a small piece of bread was left. About two we reached the forks, one of which ran to the Yazoo, the other to the Old River. Max said the right fork was our road; H. said the left, that there was an error in Max's map; but Max steered into the right fork. After pulling about three miles he admitted his mistake and turned back; but I shall never forget Old River. It was the vision of a drowned world, an illimitable waste of dead waters, stretching into a great, silent, desolate forest. A horror chilled me and I begged them to row fast out of that terrible place.

Just as we turned into the right way, down came the rain so hard and fast we had to stop on the bank. It defied trees or umbrellas and nearly took away the breath. The boat began to fill, and all five of us had to bail as fast as possible for the half-hour the sheet of water was pouring down. As it abated a cold breeze sprung up that, striking our wet clothes, chilled us to the bone. All were shivering and blue — no, I was green. Before leaving Mr. Fetler's Wednesday morning I had donned a dark-green calico. I wiped my face with a handkerchief out of my pocket, and face and hands were all dyed a deep green. When Annie turned round and looked at me she screamed and I realized how I looked; but she was not much better, for of all dejected things wet feathers are the worst, and the plumes in her hat were painful.

About five we reached Colonel K.'s house, right where Steele's Bayou empties into the Yazoo. We had both to be fairly dragged out of the boat, so cramped and weighted were we by wet skirts. The family were absent, and the house was headquarters for a squad of Confederate cavalry, which was also absent. The old colored housekeeper received us kindly and lighted fires in our rooms to dry the clothing. My trunk had got cracked on top, and all the clothing to be got at was wet. H. had dropped his in the river while lifting it out, and his clothes were wet. A spoonful of brandy apiece was left in the little flask, and I felt that mine saved me from being ill. Warm blankets and the brandy revived us, and by supper-time we got into some dry clothes.

Just then the squad of cavalry returned; they were only a dozen, but they made much uproar, being in great excitement. Some of them were known to Max and H., who learned from them that a gunboat was coming to shell them out of this house. Then ensued a clatter such as twelve men surely never made before — rattling about the halls and galleries in heavy boots and spurs, feeding horses, calling for supper, clanking swords, buckling and unbuckling belts and pistols. At last supper was dispatched, and they mounted and were gone like the wind. We had a quiet supper and good night's rest in spite of the expected shells, and did not wake till ten to-day to realize we were not killed. About eleven breakfast was furnished. Now we are waiting till the rest of our things are dried to start on our last day of travel by water.

Sunday, July 20, 1862. — A little way down the Yazoo on Friday we ran into McNutt's Lake, thence into Chickasaw Bayou, and at dark landed at Mrs. C.'s farm, the nearest neighbors of H.'s uncle. The house was full of Confederate sick, friends from Vicksburg, and while we ate supper all present poured out the story of the shelling and all that was to be done at Vicksburg. Then our stuff was taken from the boat, and we finally abandoned the stanch little craft that had carried us for over one hundred and twenty-five miles in a trip occupying nine days. The luggage in a wagon, and ourselves packed in a buggy, were driven for four or five miles, over the roughest road I ever traveled, to the farm of Mr. B., H.'s uncle, where we arrived at midnight and hastened to hide in bed the utter exhaustion of mind and body. Yesterday we were too tired to think, or to do anything but to eat peaches.

XI.

WILD TIMES IN MISSISSIPPI.

THIS morning there was a most painful scene. Annie's father came into Vicksburg, ten miles from here, and learned of our arrival from Mrs. C.'s messenger. He sent out a carriage to bring Annie and Max to town that they might go home with him, and with it came a letter for me from friends on the Jackson Railroad, written many weeks before. They had heard that our village home was under water, and invited us to visit them. The letter had been sent to Annie's people to forward, and thus had reached us. This decided H., as the place was near New Orleans, to go there and wait the chance of getting into that city. Max, when he heard this from H., lost all self-control and cried like a baby. He stalked about the garden in the most tragic manner, exclaiming:

"Oh! my soul's brother from youth up is a traitor! A traitor to his country!"

Then H. got angry and said, "Max, don't be a fool!"

"Who has done this?" bawled Max. "You felt with the South at first; who has changed you?"

"Of course I feel *for* the South now, and nobody has changed me but the logic of events, though the twenty-negro law has intensified my opinions. I can't see why I, who have no slaves, must go to fight for them, while every man who has twenty may stay at home."

I, also, tried to reason with Max and pour oil on his wound. "Max, what interest has a man like you, without slaves, in a war for slavery? Even if you had them, they would not be your best property. That lies in your country and its resources. Nearly all the world has given up slavery; why can't the South do the same and end the struggle? It has shown you what the South needs, and if all went to work with united hands the South would soon be the greatest country on earth. You have no right to call H. a traitor; it is we who are the true patriots and lovers of the South."

This had to come, but it has upset us both. H. is deeply attached to Max, and I can't bear to see a cloud between them. Max, with Annie and Reeney, drove off an hour ago, Annie so glad at the prospect of again seeing her mother that nothing could cloud her day. And so the close companionship of six months, and of dangers, trials, and pleasures shared together, is over.

Oak Ridge, July 26, 1862, Saturday. — It was not till Wednesday that H. could get into Vicksburg, ten miles distant, for a passport, without which we could not go on the cars. We started Thursday morning. I had to ride seven miles on a hard-trotting horse to the nearest station. The day was burning at white heat. When the station was reached my hair was down, my hat on my neck, and my feelings were indescribable.

On the train one seemed to be right in the stream of war, among officers, soldiers, sick men and cripples, adieus, tears, laughter, constant chatter, and, strangest of all, sentinels posted at the locked car-doors demanding passports. There was no train south from Jackson that day, so we put up at the Bowman House. The excitement was indescribable. All the world appeared to be traveling through Jackson. People were besieging the two hotels, offering enormous prices for the privilege of sleeping anywhere under a roof. There were many refugees from New Orleans, among them some acquaintances of mine. The peculiar style of [women's] dress necessitated by the exigencies of war gave the crowd a very striking appearance. In single suits I saw sleeves of one color, the waist of another, the skirt of another; scarlet jackets and gray skirts; black waists and blue skirts; black skirts and gray waists; the trimming chiefly gold braid and buttons, to give a military air. The gray and gold uniforms of the officers, glittering between, made up a carnival of color. Every moment we saw strange meetings and partings of people from all over the South. Conditions of time, space, locality, and estate were all loosened; everybody seemed floating he knew not whither, but determined to be jolly, and keep up an excitement. At supper we had tough steak, heavy, dirty-looking bread, Confederate coffee. The coffee was made of either parched rye or cornmeal, or of sweet potatoes cut in small cubes and roasted. This was the favorite. When flavored with "coffee essence," sweetened with sorghum, and tinctured with chalky milk, it made a curious beverage, which, after tasting, I preferred not to drink. Every one else was drinking it, and an acquaintance said, "Oh, you 'll get bravely over that. I used to be a Jewess about pork, but now we just kill a hog and eat it, and kill another and do the same. It 's all we have."

Friday morning we took the down train for the station near my friend's house. At every station we had to go through the examination of passes, as if in a foreign country.

The conscript camp was at Brookhaven, and every man had been ordered to report there or to be treated as a deserter. At every station I shivered mentally, expecting H. to be dragged off. Brookhaven was also the station for dinner. I choked mine down, feeling the sword hanging over me by a single hair. At sunset we reached our station. The landlady was pouring tea when we took our seats and I expected a treat, but when I tasted it it was sassafras tea, the very odor of which sickens me. There was a general surprise when I asked to exchange it for a glass of water; every one was drinking it as if it were nectar. This morning we drove out here.

My friend's little nest is calm in contrast to the tumult not far off.

Yet the trials of war are here too. Having no matches, they keep fire, carefully covering it at night, for Mr. G. has no powder, and cannot flash the gun into combustibles as some do. One day they had to go with the children to the village, and the servant let the fire go out. When they returned at nightfall, wet and hungry, there was neither fire nor food. Mr. G.

had to saddle the tired mule and ride three miles
for a pan of coals, and blow them, all the way back,
to keep them alight. Crockery has gradually been
broken and tin-cups rusted out, and a visitor told me
they had made tumblers out of clear glass bottles by
cutting them smooth with a heated wire, and that
they had nothing else to drink from.

Aug. 11, 1862. — We cannot get to New Orleans.
A special passport must be shown, and we are told
that to apply for it would render H. very likely to be
conscripted. I begged him not to try; and as we
hear that active hostilities have ceased at Vicksburg,
he left me this morning to return to his uncle's and
see what the prospects are there. I shall be in misery
about conscription till he returns.

Sunday, Sept. 7. (Vicksburg, Washington Hotel.) —
H. did not return for three weeks. An epidemic
disease broke out in his uncle's family and two children died. He staid to assist them in their trouble.
Tuesday evening he returned for me and we reached
Vicksburg yesterday. It was my first sight of the
"Gibraltar of the South." Looking at it from a slight
elevation suggests the idea that the fragments left from
world-building had tumbled into a confused mass of
hills, hollows, hillocks, banks, ditches, and ravines,
and that the houses had rained down afterwards.
Over all there was dust impossible to conceive. The
bombardment has done little injury. People have
returned and resumed business. A gentleman asked
H. if he knew of a nice girl for sale. I asked if he
did not think it impolitic to buy slaves now.

"Oh, not young ones. Old ones might run off when the enemy's lines approach ours, but with young ones there is no danger."

We had not been many hours in town before a position was offered to H. which seemed providential. The chief of a certain department was in ill-health and wanted a deputy. It secures him from conscription, requires no oath, and pays a good salary. A mountain seemed lifted off my heart.

Thursday, Sept. 18, 1862. (*Thanksgiving Day.*) — We staid three days at the Washington Hotel; then a friend of H.'s called and told him to come to his house till he could find a home. Boarding-houses have all been broken up, and the army has occupied the few houses that were for rent. To-day H. secured a vacant room for two weeks in the only boarding-house.

Oak Haven, Oct. 3. — To get a house in V. proved impossible, so we agreed to part for a time till H. could find one. A friend recommended this quiet farm, six miles from —— (a station on the Jackson Railroad). On last Saturday H. came with me as far as Jackson and put me on the other train for the station.

On my way hither a lady, whom I judged to be a Confederate "blockade runner," told me of the tricks resorted to to get things out of New Orleans, including this : A very large doll was emptied of its bran, filled with quinine, and elaborately dressed. When the owner's trunk was opened, she declared with tears that the doll was for a poor crippled girl, and it was passed.

This farm of Mr. W.'s[1] is kept with about forty negroes. Mr. W., nearly sixty, is the only white man on it. He seems to have been wiser in the beginning than most others, and curtailed his cotton to make room for rye, rice, and corn. There is a large vegetable garden and orchard; he has bought plenty of stock for beef and mutton, and laid in a large supply of sugar. He must also have plenty of ammunition, for a man is kept hunting and supplies the table with delicious wild turkeys and other game. There is abundance of milk and butter, hives for honey, and no end of pigs. Chickens seem to be kept like game in parks, for I never see any, but the hunter shoots them, and eggs are plentiful. We have chicken for breakfast, dinner, and supper, fried, stewed, broiled, and in soup, and there is a family of ten. Luckily I never tire of it. They make starch out of corn-meal by washing the meal repeatedly, pouring off the water and drying the sediment. Truly the uses of corn in the Confederacy are varied. It makes coffee, beer, whisky, starch, cake, bread. The only privations here are the lack of coffee, tea, salt, matches, and good candles. Mr. W. is now having the dirt-floor of his smoke-house dug up and boiling from it the salt that has dripped into it for years. To-day Mrs. W. made tea out of dried blackberry leaves, but no one liked it. The beds, made out of equal parts of cotton and corn-shucks, are the most elastic I ever slept in. The ser-

---

[1] On this plantation, and in this domestic circle, I myself afterward sojourned, and from them enlisted in the Confederate army. The initials are fictitious, but the description is perfect. — G. W. C.

vants are dressed in gray homespun. Hester, the chambermaid, has a gray gown so pretty that I covet one like it. Mrs. W. is now arranging dyes for the thread to be woven into dresses for herself and the girls. Sometimes her hands are a curiosity.

The school at the nearest town is broken up and Mrs. W. says the children are growing up heathens. Mr. W. has offered me a liberal price to give the children lessons in English and French, and I have accepted transiently.

Oct. 28, 1862. — It is a month to-day since I came here. I only wish H. could share these benefits — the nourishing food, the pure aromatic air, the sound sleep away from the fevered life of Vicksburg. He sends me all the papers he can get hold of, and we both watch carefully the movements reported, lest an army should get between us. The days are full of useful work, and in the lovely afternoons I take long walks with a big dog for company. The girls do not care for walking. In the evening Mr. W. begs me to read aloud all the war news. He is fond of the "Memphis Appeal," which has moved from town to town so much that they call it the "Moving Appeal." I sit in a low chair by the fire, as we have no other light to read by. Sometimes traveling soldiers stop here, but that is rare.

Oct. 31. — Mr. W. said last night the farmers felt uneasy about the "Emancipation Proclamation" to take effect in December. The slaves have found it out, though it had been carefully kept from them.

"Do yours know it?" I asked.

"Oh, yes. Finding it to be known elsewhere, I told it to mine with fair warning what to expect if they tried to run away. The hounds are not far off."

The need of clothing for their armies is worrying them too. I never saw Mrs. W. so excited as on last evening. She said the provost-marshal at the next town had ordered the women to knit so many pairs of socks.

"Just let him try to enforce it and they'll cow-hide him. He'll get none from me. I'll take care of my own friends without an order from him."

"Well," said Mr. W., "if the South is defeated and the slaves set free, the Southern people will all become atheists, for the Bible justifies slavery and says it shall be perpetual."

"You mean, if the Lord does not agree with you, you'll repudiate him."

"Well, we'll feel it's no use to believe in anything."

At night the large sitting-room makes a striking picture. Mr. W., spare, erect, gray-headed, patriarchal, sits in his big chair by the odorous fire of pine logs and knots roaring up the vast fireplace. His driver brings to him the report of the day's picking and a basket of snowy cotton for the spinning. The hunter brings in the game. I sit on the other side to read. The great spinning wheels stand at the other end of the room, and Mrs. W. and her black satellites, the heads of the elderly women in bright bandanas, are hard at work. Slender and auburn-haired, she steps back and forth out of shadow into shine following the thread with graceful movements. Some card the cotton, some reel it into hanks. Over all the firelight glances, now touching the golden curls of little John toddling about, now the brown heads of the girls stooping over their books, now the shadowy figure of little Jule, the girl whose duty it is to supply the fire with rich pine to keep up the vivid light. If they would only let the child sit down! But that is not allowed, and she gets sleepy and stumbles and knocks her head against the wall and then straightens up again. When that happens often it drives me off. Sometimes while I read the bright room fades and a vision rises of figures clad in gray and blue lying pale and stiff on the blood-sprinkled ground.

Nov. 15, 1862. — Yesterday a letter was handed me from H. Grant's army was moving, he wrote, steadily down the Mississippi Central and might cut the road at Jackson. He has a house and will meet me in Jackson to-morrow.

When Bessie J. and I went in to dinner to-day, a stranger was sitting by Mr. W.; a dark, heavy-looking man who said but little. I excused myself to finish packing. Presently Bessie rushed upstairs flushed and angry.

" I shall give Mr. W. a piece of my mind. He must have taken leave of his senses ! "

" What is the matter, Bessie ? "

" Why, G., don't you know whom you've been sitting at table with ? "

" That stranger, you mean; I suppose Mr. W. forgot to introduce him."

" Forgot ! He knew better than to introduce him !

That man is a negro-chaser. He 's got his blood-hounds here now."

" Did you see the dogs ? "

" No, I asked Hester if he had them, and she said, 'Yes.' Think of Mr. W. bringing him to table with us. If my brothers knew it there would be a row."

" Where are your brothers ? At college still ? "

" No, in the army; Pa told them they 'd have to come and fight to save their property. His men cost him twelve to fifteen hundred dollars apiece and are too valuable to lose."

" Well, I would n't worry about this man, he may be useful some day to save that kind of property."

" Of course, you can take it easily, you 're going away ; but if Mr. W. thinks I 'm going to sit at table with that wretch he 's vastly mistaken."

Nov. 20, 1862. (*Vicksburg.*) — A fair morning for my journey back to Vicksburg. The autumn woods were shining through a veil of silvery mist and the spicy breezes blew cool and keen from the heart of the pines, a friend sat beside me, a husband's welcome awaited me. General Pemberton, recently appointed to the command at Vicksburg, was on the train; also the gentleman who in New Orleans had told us we should have all the butter we wanted from Texas. On the cars, as elsewhere, the question of food alternated with news of the war.

When we ran into the Jackson station H. was on the platform, and I gladly learned that we could go right on. A runaway negro, an old man, ashy colored from fright and exhaustion, with his hands chained, was being dragged along by a common-looking man. Just as we started out of Jackson the conductor led in a young woman sobbing in a heart-broken manner. Her grief seemed so overpowering, and she was so young and helpless, that every one was interested. Her husband went into the army in the opening of the war, just after their marriage, and she had never heard from him since. After months of weary searching she learned he had been heard of at Jackson, and came full of hope, but found no clue. The sudden breaking down of her hope was terrible. The conductor placed her in care of a gentleman going her way and left her sobbing. At the next station the conductor came to ask her about her baggage. She raised her head to try and answer. "Don't cry so, you'll find him yet." She gave a start, jumped from her seat with arms flung out and eyes staring. "There he is now!" she cried. Her husband stood before her.

The gentleman beside her yielded his seat, and as hand grasped hand a hysterical gurgle gave place to a look like Heaven's peace. The low murmur of their talk began, and when I looked round at the next station they had bought pies and were eating them together like happy children.

Midway between Jackson and Vicksburg we reached the station near where Annie's parents were staying. I looked out, and there stood Annie with a little sister on each side of her, brightly smiling at us. Max had written to H., but we had not seen them since our parting. There was only time for a word and the train flashed away.

XII.

VICKSBURG.

WE reached Vicksburg that night and went to
H.'s room. Next morning the cook he had engaged
arrived, and we moved into this house. Martha's
ignorance keeps me busy, and H. is kept close at
his office.

January 7th, 1863. — I have had little to record
recently, for we have lived to ourselves, not visiting
or visited. Every one H. knows is absent, and I
know no one. H. tells me of the added triumph
since the repulse of Sherman in December, and the
one paper published here shouts victory as much as
its gradually diminishing size will allow. Paper
is a serious want. There is a great demand for
envelopes in the office where H. is. He found and
bought a lot of thick and smooth colored paper, cut a
tin pattern, and we have whiled away some long evenings making envelopes. I have put away a package
of the best to look at when we are old. The books I
brought from Arkansas have proved a treasure, but
we can get no more. I went to the only book-store
open; there were none but Mrs. Stowe's "Sunny
Memories of Foreign Lands." The clerk said I could
have that cheap, because he could n't sell her books, so
I am reading it now. The monotony has only been
broken by letters from friends here and there in the
Confederacy. One of these letters tells of a Federal

raid and says, " But the worst thing was, they would take every tooth-brush in the house, because we can't buy any more; and one cavalry man put my sister's new bonnet on his horse, and said 'Get up, Jack,' and her bonnet was gone."

Feb. 25th, 1863. — A long gap in my journal, because H. has been ill unto death with typhoid fever. I nearly broke down from loss of sleep, there being no one to relieve me. It was terrible to be alone at night with a patient in delirium, and no one within call. To wake Martha was simply impossible. I got the best doctor here, but when convalescence began the question of food was a trial. I got with great difficulty two chickens. The doctor made the drug-store sell two of their six bottles of port; he said his patient's life depended on it. An egg is a rare and precious thing. Meanwhile the Federal fleet has been gathering, has anchored at the bend, and shells are thrown in at intervals.

March 20th. — The slow shelling of Vicksburg goes on all the time, and we have grown indifferent. It does not at present interrupt or interfere with daily avocations, but I suspect they are only getting the range of different points; and when they have them all complete, showers of shot will rain on us all at once. Non combatants have been ordered to leave or prepare accordingly. Those who are to stay are having caves built. Cave-digging has become a regular business; prices range from twenty to fifty dollars, according to size of cave. Two diggers worked at ours a week and charged thirty dollars. It is well made in the hill that slopes just in the rear of the house, and well propped with thick posts, as they all are. It has a shelf, also, for holding a light or water. When we went in this evening and sat down, the earthy, suffocating feeling, as of a living tomb, was dreadful to me. I fear I shall risk death outside rather then melt in that dark furnace. The hills are so honeycombed with caves that the streets look like avenues in a cemetery. The hill called the Sky-parlor has become quite a fashionable resort for the few upper-circle families left here. Some officers are quartered there, and there is a band and a field-glass. Last evening we also climbed the hill to watch the shelling, but found the view not so good as on a quiet hill nearer home. Soon a lady began to talk to one of the officers: "It is such folly for them to waste their ammunition like that. How can they ever take a town that has such advantages for defense and protection as this? We'll just burrow into these hills and let them batter away as hard as they please."

"You are right, madam; and besides, when our women are so willing to brave death and endure discomfort, how can we ever be conquered?"

Soon she looked over with significant glances to where we stood, and began to talk at H.

"The only drawback," she said, "are the contemptible men who are staying at home in comfort when they ought to be in the army if they had a spark of honor."

I cannot repeat all, but it was the usual tirade. It is strange I have met no one yet who seems to comprehend an honest difference of opinion, and stranger yet that the ordinary rules of good breeding are now so entirely ignored. As the spring comes on one has the craving for fresh, green food that a monotonous diet produces. There was a bed of radishes and onions in the garden, that were a real blessing. An onion salad, dressed only with salt, vinegar, and pepper, seemed a dish fit for a king, but last night the soldiers quartered near made a raid on the garden and took them all.

April 2d, 1863. — We have had to move, and have thus lost our cave. The owner of the house suddenly returned and notified us that he intended to bring his family back; did n't think there 'd be any siege. The cost of the cave could go for the rent. That means he has got tired of the Confederacy and means to stay here and thus get out of it. This house was the only one to be had. It was built by ex-Senator G., and is so large our tiny household is lost in it. We only use the lower floor. The bell is often rung by persons who take it for a hotel and come beseeching food at any price. To-day one came who would not be denied. "We do not keep a hotel, but would willingly feed hungry soldiers if we had the food." "I have been traveling all night and am starving; will pay any price for just bread." I went to the dining-room and found some biscuits, and set out two, with a large piece of corn-bread, a small piece of bacon, some nice sirup, and a pitcher of water. I locked the door of the safe and left him to enjoy his lunch. After he left I found he had broken open the safe and taken the remaining biscuits.

April 28th, 1863. — What shall we eat? what shall we drink? and wherewithal shall we be clothed? We have no prophet of the Lord at whose prayer the meal and oil will not waste. As to wardrobe, I have learned to darn like an artist. Making shoes is now another accomplishment. Mine were in tatters. H. came across a moth-eaten pair that he bought me, giving ten dollars, I think, and they fell into rags when I tried to wear them; but the soles were good, and that has helped me to shoes. A pair of old coat-sleeves — nothing is thrown away now — was in my trunk. I cut an exact pattern from my old shoes, laid it on the sleeves, and cut out thus good uppers and sewed them carefully; then soaked the soles and sewed the cloth to them. I am so proud of these home-made shoes that I think I'll put them in a glass case when the war is over, as an heirloom. H. says he has come to have an abiding faith that everything he needs to wear will come out of that trunk while the war lasts. It is like a fairy-casket. I have but a dozen pins remaining, I gave so many away. Every time these are used they are straightened and kept from rust. All these curious labors are performed while the shells are leisurely screaming through the air; but as long as we are out of range we don't worry. For many nights we have had but little sleep because the Federal gun-boats have been running past the batteries. The uproar when this is happening is phenomenal. The first night the thundering artillery burst the bars of sleep, we thought it an attack by the river. To get into garments and rush upstairs

was the work of a moment. From the upper gallery
we have a fine view of the river, and soon a red glare
lit up the scene and showed a small boat towing two
large barges, gliding by. The Confederates had set
fire to a house near the bank. Another night, eight
boats ran by, throwing a shower of shot, and two burning houses made the river clear as day. One of the
batteries has a remarkable gun they call "Whistling
Dick," because of the screeching, whistling sound it
gives, and certainly it does sound like a tortured thing.
Added to all this is the indescribable Confederate yell,
which is a soul-harrowing sound to hear. I have
gained respect for the mechanism of the human ear,
which stands it all without injury. The streets are
seldom quiet at night; even the dragging about of
cannon makes a din in these echoing gullies. The
other night we were on the gallery till the last of
the eight boats got by. Next day a friend said to H.,
"It was a wonder you did n't have your heads taken
off last night. I passed and saw them stretched over
the gallery, and grape-shot were whizzing up the street
just on a level with you." The double roar of batteries and boats was so great, we never noticed the
whizzing. Yesterday the *Cincinnati* attempted to go
by in daylight, but was disabled and sunk. It was a
pitiful sight; we could not see the finale, though we
saw her rendered helpless.

XIII.

PREPARATIONS FOR THE SIEGE.

Vicksburg, May 1st, 1863. — Ever since we were
deprived of our cave, I had been dreading that H.
would suggest sending me to the country, where his
relatives live. As he could not leave his position and
go also without being conscripted, and as I felt certain
an army would get between us, it was no part of my
plan to be obedient. A shell from one of the prac-
ticing mortars brought the point to an issue yesterday
and settled it. Sitting at work as usual, listening to
the distant sound of bursting shells, apparently aimed
at the court-house, there suddenly came a nearer explosion; the house shook, and a tearing sound was
followed by terrified screams from the kitchen. I
rushed thither, but met in the hall the cook's little
girl America, bleeding from a wound in the forehead,
and fairly dancing with fright and pain, while she
uttered fearful yells. I stopped to examine the wound,
and her mother bounded in, her black face ashy from
terror. "Oh! Miss G., my child is killed and the
kitchen tore up." Seeing America was too lively to
have been killed, I consoled Martha and hastened
to the kitchen. Evidently a shell had exploded just
outside, sending three or four pieces through. When
order was restored I endeavored to impress on Martha's
mind the uselessness of such excitement. Looking
round at the close of the lecture, there stood a group

of Confederate soldiers laughing heartily at my sermon and the promising audience I had. They chimed
in with a parting chorus:

"Yes, it's no use hollerin', old lady."

"Oh! H.," I exclaimed, as he entered soon after,
"America is wounded."

"That is no news; she has been wounded by traitors
long ago."

"Oh, this is real, living, little, black America. I
am not talking in symbols. Here are the pieces of
shell, the first bolt of the coming siege."

"Now you see," he replied, "that this house will
be but paper to mortar-shells. You must go into the
country."

The argument was long, but when a woman is obsti-
nate and eloquent, she generally conquers. I came
off victorious, and we finished preparations for the
siege to-day. Hiring a man to assist, we descended
to the wine-cellar, where the accumulated bottles told
of festive hours long since departed. To empty this
cellar was the work of many hours. Then in the
safest corner a platform was laid for our bed, and in
another portion one arranged for Martha. The dun-
geon, as I call it, is lighted only by a trap-door, and
is very damp. The next question was of supplies. I
had nothing left but a sack of rice-flour, and no manner
of cooking I had heard or invented contrived to make
it eatable. A column of recipes for making delicious
preparations of it had been going the rounds of Confederate papers. I tried them all; they resulted only
in brick-bats, or sticky paste. H. sallied out on a

hunt for provisions, and when he returned the dis-
proportionate quantity of the different articles pro-
voked a smile. There was a *hogshead* of sugar, a
barrel of sirup, ten pounds of bacon and pease, four
pounds of wheat-flour, and a small sack of corn-meal,
a little vinegar, and actually some spice! The wheat-
flour he purchased for ten dollars as a special favor
from the sole remaining barrel for sale. We decided
that must be kept for sickness. The sack of meal, he
said, was a case of corruption, though a special provi-
dence to us. There is no more for sale at any price,
but, said he, "a soldier who was hauling some of the
Government sacks to the hospital offered me this for
five dollars, if I could keep a secret. When the meal
is exhausted, perhaps we can keep alive on sugar.
Here are some wax candles; hoard them like gold."
He handed me a parcel containing about two pounds
of candles, and left me to arrange my treasures. It
would be hard for me to picture the memories those
candles called up. The long years melted away, and I

> " Trod again my childhood's track
> And felt its very gladness."

In those childish days, whenever came dreams of
household splendor or festal rooms or gay illumina-
tions, the lights in my vision were always wax candles
burning with a soft radiance that enchanted every
scene. . . . And, lo! here on this spring day of '63,
with war raging through the land, I was in a fine
house, and had my wax candles sure enough, but,
alas! they were neither cerulean blue nor rose-tinted,

but dirty brown; and when I lighted one, it spluttered and wasted like any vulgar tallow thing, and lighted only a desolate scene in the vast handsome room. They were not so good as the waxen rope we had made in Arkansas. So, with a long sigh for the dreams of youth, I return to the stern present in this besieged town, my only consolation to remember the old axiom, "A city besieged is a city taken," — so if we live through it we shall be out of the Confederacy. H. is very tired of having to carry a pass around in his pocket and go every now and then to have it renewed. We have been so very free in America, these restrictions are irksome.

May 9th, 1863. — This morning the door-bell rang a startling peal. Martha being busy, I answered it. An orderly in gray stood with an official envelope in his hand.

" Who lives here ? "

" Mr. L."

Very imperiously — " Which Mr. L. ? "

" Mr. H. L."

" Is he here ? "

" No."

" Where can he be found ? "

" At the office of Deputy ——."

"I 'm not going there. This is an order from General Pemberton for you to move out of this house in two hours. He has selected it for headquarters. He will furnish you with wagons."

" Will he furnish another house also ? "

"Of course not."

"Has the owner been consulted?"

"He has not; that is of no consequence; it has been taken. Take this order."

"I shall not take it, and I shall not move, as there is no place to move to but the street."

"Then I'll take it to Mr. L."

"Very well, do so."

As soon as Mr. Impertine walked off I locked, bolted, and barred every door and window. In ten minutes H. came home.

"Hold the fort till I've seen the owner and the general," he said, as I locked him out.

Then Dr. B.'s remark in New Orleans about the effect of Dr. C.'s fine presence on the Confederate officials there came to my mind. They are influenced in that way, I thought; I look rather shabby now, I will dress. I made an elaborate toilet, put on the best and most becoming dress I had, the richest lace, the handsomest ornaments, taking care that all should be appropriate to a morning visit; dressed my hair in the stateliest braids, and took a seat in the parlor ready for the fray. H. came to the window and said:

"Landlord says, 'Keep them out. Wouldn't let them have his house at any price.' He is just riding off to the country and can't help us now. Now I'm going to see Major C., who sent the order."

Next came an officer, banged at the door till tired, and walked away. Then the orderly came again and beat the door — same result. Next, four officers with bundles and lunch-baskets, followed by a wagon-load of furniture. They went round the house, tried every door, peeped in the windows, pounded and rapped, while I watched them through the blind-slats. Presently the fattest one, a real Falstaffian man, came back to the front door and rung a thundering peal. I saw the chance for fun and for putting on their own grandiloquent style. Stealing on tiptoe to the door, I turned the key and bolt noiselessly, and suddenly threw wide back the door, and appeared behind it. He had been leaning on it, and nearly pitched forward with an "Oh! what's this?" Then seeing me as he straightened up, "Ah, madam!" almost stuttering from surprise and anger, "are you aware I had the right to break down this door if you had n't opened it?"

"That would make no difference to me. I'm not the owner. You or the landlord would pay the bill for the repairs."

"Why did n't you open the door?"

"Have I not done so as soon as you rung? A lady does not open the door to men who beat on it. Gentlemen usually ring; I thought it might be stragglers pounding."

"Well," growing much blander, "we are going to send you some wagons to move; you must get ready."

"With pleasure, if you have selected a house for me. This is too large; it does not suit me."

"No, I did n't find a house for you."

"You surely don't expect *me* to run about in the dust and shelling to look for it, and Mr. L. is too busy."

"Well, madam, then we must share the house. We will take the lower floor."

"I prefer to keep the lower floor myself; you surely

don't expect *me* to go up and down stairs when you are so light and more able to do it."

He walked through the hall, trying the doors. "What room is that?"—"The parlor." "And this?" —"My bedroom." "And this?"—"The dining-room."

"Well, madam, we'll find you a house and then come and take this."

"Thank you, colonel. I shall be ready when you find the house. Good morning, sir."

I heard him say as he ran down the steps, "We must go back, captain; you see I didn't know they were this kind of people."

Of course the orderly had lied in the beginning to scare me, for General Pemberton is too far away from Vicksburg to send such an order. He is looking about for General Grant. We are told he has gone out to meet Johnston; and together they expect to annihilate Grant's army and free Vicksburg forever. There is now a general hospital opposite this house and a small-pox hospital next door. War, famine, pestilence, and fire surround us. Every day the band plays in front of the small-pox hospital. I wonder if it is to keep up their spirits? One would suppose quiet would be more cheering.

May 17th, 1863.—Hardly was our scanty breakfast over this morning when a hurried ring drew us both to the door. Mr. J., one of H.'s assistants, stood there in high excitement.

"Well, Mr. L., they are upon us; the Yankees will be here by this evening."

" What do you mean ? "

" That Pemberton has been whipped at Baker's Creek and Big Black, and his army are running back here as fast as they can come and the Yanks after them, in such numbers nothing can stop them. Has n't Pemberton acted like a fool ? "

" He may not be the only one to blame," replied H.

" They 're coming along the Big B. road, and my folks went down there to be safe, you know ; now they 're right in it. I hear you can't see the armies for the dust ; never was anything else known like it. But I must go and try to bring my folks back here."

What struck us both was the absence of that concern to be expected, and a sort of relief or suppressed pleasure. After twelve some worn-out-looking men sat down under the window.

" What is the news ? " I inquired.

" Ritreat, ritreat ! " they said, in broken English — they were Louisiana Acadians.

About 3 o'clock the rush began. I shall never forget that woful sight of a beaten, demoralized army that came rushing back, — humanity in the last throes of endurance. Wan, hollow-eyed, ragged, footsore, bloody, the men limped along unarmed, but followed by siege-guns, ambulances, gun-carriages, and wagons in aimless confusion. At twilight two or three bands on the court-house hill and other points began playing Dixie, Bonnie Blue Flag, and so on, and drums began to beat all about ; I suppose they were rallying the scattered army.

XIV.

THE SIEGE ITSELF.

May 28th, 1863. — Since that day the regular siege
has continued. We are utterly cut off from the world,
surrounded by a circle of fire. The fiery shower of
shells goes on day and night. H.'s occupation, of
course, is gone, his office closed. Every man has to
carry a pass in his pocket. People do nothing but
eat what they can get, sleep when they can, and dodge
the shells. There are three intervals when the shelling stops, either for the guns to cool or for the gun-
ners' meals, I suppose, — about eight in the morning,
the same in the evening, and at noon. In that time
we have both to prepare and eat ours. Clothing cannot be washed or anything else done. On the 19th
and 22d, when the assaults were made on the lines, I
watched the soldiers cooking on the green opposite.
The half-spent balls coming all the way from those
lines were flying so thick that they were obliged to
dodge at every turn. At all the caves I could see
from my high perch, people were sitting, eating their
poor suppers at the cave doors, ready to plunge in
again. As the first shell again flew they dived, and
not a human being was visible. The sharp crackle
of the musketry-firing was a strong contrast to the
scream of the bombs. I think all the dogs and cats
must be killed or starved, we don't see any more pitiful animals prowling around. . . . The cellar is so

damp and musty the bedding has to be carried out and
laid in the sun every day, with the forecast that it
may be demolished at any moment. The confinement
is dreadful. To sit and listen as if waiting for death
in a horrible manner would drive me insane. I don't
know what others do, but we read when I am not
scribbling in this. H. borrowed somewhere a lot of
Dickens's novels, and we reread them by the dim
light in the cellar. When the shelling abates H. goes
to walk about a little or get the "Daily Citizen,"
which is still issuing a tiny sheet at twenty-five and
fifty cents a copy. It is, of course, but a rehash of
speculations which amuses half an hour. To-day we
heard while out that expert swimmers are crossing
the Mississippi on logs at night to bring and carry
news to Johnston. I am so tired of corn-bread, which
I never liked, that I eat it with tears in my eyes. We
are lucky to get a quart of milk daily from a family
near who have a cow they hourly expect to be killed. I
send five dollars to market each morning, and it buys
a small piece of mule-meat. Rice and milk is my main
food; I can't eat the mule-meat. We boil the rice and
eat it cold with milk for supper. Martha runs the
gauntlet to buy the meat and milk once a day in a
perfect terror. The shells seem to have many different
names; I hear the soldiers say, "That's a mortar-shell.
There goes a Parrott. That's a rifle-shell." They are
all equally terrible. A pair of chimney-swallows have
built in the parlor chimney. The concussion of the
house often sends down parts of their nest, which they
patiently pick up and reascend with.

Friday, June 5th, 1863. (*In the cellar.*) — Wednesday evening H. said he must take a little walk, and went while the shelling had stopped. He never leaves me alone long, and when an hour had passed without his return I grew anxious; and when two hours, and the shelling had grown terrific, I momentarily expected to see his mangled body. All sorts of horrors fill the mind now, and I am so desolate here; not a friend. When he came he said that passing a cave where there were no others near, he heard groans, and found a shell had struck above and caused the cave to fall in on the man within. He could not extricate him alone, and had to get help and dig him out. He was badly hurt, but not mortally. I felt fairly sick from the suspense.

Yesterday morning a note was brought H. from a bachelor uncle out in the trenches, saying he had been taken ill with fever, and could we receive him if he came? H. sent to tell him to come, and I arranged one of the parlors as a dressing-room for him, and laid a pallet that he could move back and forth to the cellar. He did not arrive, however. It is our custom in the evening to sit in the front room a little while in the dark, with matches and candles held ready in hand, and watch the shells, whose course at night, is shown by the fuse. H. was at the window and suddenly sprang up, crying, "Run!" — "Where?" — "*Back!*"

I started through the back room, H. after me. I was just within the door when the crash came that threw me to the floor. It was the most appalling sensation I'd ever known. Worse than an earthquake, which I've also experienced. Shaken and deafened I picked myself up; H. had struck a light to find me. I lighted mine, and the smoke guided us to the parlor I had fixed for Uncle J. The candles were useless in the dense smoke, and it was many minutes before we could see. Then we found the entire side of the room torn out. The soldiers who had rushed in said, " This is an eighty-pound Parrott." It had entered through the front and burst on the pallet-bed, which was in tatters; the toilet service and everything else in the room was smashed. The soldiers assisted H. to board up the break with planks to keep out prowlers, and we went to bed in the cellar as usual. This morning the yard is partially plowed by two shells that fell there in the night. I think this house, so large and prominent from the river, is perhaps mistaken for headquarters and specially shelled. As we descend at night to the lower regions, I think of the evening hymn that grandmother taught me when a child:

> " Lord, keep us safe this night,
>   Secure from all our fears;
> May angels guard us while we sleep,
>   Till morning light appears."

June 7th, 1863. (In the cellar.) — I feel especially grateful that amid these horrors we have been spared that of suffering for water. The weather has been dry a long time, and we hear of others dipping up the water from ditches and mud-holes. This place has two large underground cisterns of good cool water, and every night in my subterranean dressing-room a tub of cold water is the nerve-calmer that sends me to sleep in spite of the roar. One cistern I had to give up to the soldiers, who swarm about like hungry animals seeking something to devour. Poor fellows! my heart bleeds for them. They have nothing but spoiled, greasy bacon, and bread made of musty pea-flour, and but little of that. The sick ones can't bolt it. They come into the kitchen when Martha puts the pan of corn-bread in the stove, and beg for the bowl she has mixed it in. They shake up the scrapings with water, put in their bacon, and boil the mixture into a kind of soup, which is easier to swallow than pea-bread. When I happen in they look so ashamed of their poor clothes. I know we saved the lives of two by giving a few meals. To-day one crawled upon the gallery to lie in the breeze. He looked as if shells had lost their terrors for his dumb and famished misery. I've taught Martha to make first-rate corn-meal gruel, because I can eat meal easier that way than in hoe-cake, and I prepared him a saucerful, put milk and sugar and nutmeg — I've actually got a nutmeg. When he ate it the tears ran from his eyes. "Oh, madam, there was never anything so good! I shall get better."

June 9th, 1863. — The churches are a great resort for those who have no caves. People fancy they are not shelled so much, and they are substantial and the pews good to sleep in. We had to leave this house last night, they were shelling our quarter so heavily. The night before, Martha forsook the cellar for a church. We went to H.'s office, which was com-

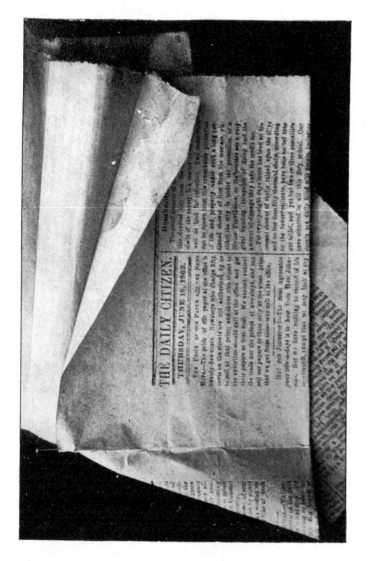

PRINTED ON WALL PAPER IN THE SIEGE OF VICKSBURG.

paratively quiet last night. H. carried the bank box;
I the case of matches; Martha the blankets and pillows, keeping an eye on the shells. We slept on piles
of old newspapers. In the streets the roar seems so
much more confusing, I feel sure I shall run right into
the way of a shell. They seem to have five different sounds from the second of throwing them to the
hollow echo wandering among the hills, which sounds
the most blood-curdling of all.

June 13th, 1863. — Shell burst just over the roof
this morning. Pieces tore through both floors down
into the dining-room. The entire ceiling of that room
fell in a mass. We had just left it. Every piece of
crockery on the table was smashed. The "Daily Citizen" to-day is a foot and a half long and six inches
wide. It has a long letter from a Federal officer, P.
P. Hill, who was on the gun-boat *Cincinnati*, that was
sunk May 27th. Says it was found in his floating
trunk. The editorial says, "The utmost confidence
is felt that we can maintain our position until succor
comes from outside. The undaunted Johnston is at
hand."

June 18th. — To-day the "Citizen" is printed on
wall paper; therefore has grown a little in size. It
says, "But a few days more and Johnston will be
here"; also that "Kirby Smith has driven Banks
from Port Hudson," and that "the enemy are throwing incendiary shells in."

June 20th. — The gentleman who took our cave
came yesterday to invite us to come to it, because; he
said, "it's going to be very bad to-day." I don't know

why he thought so.   We went, and found his own and
another family in it; sat outside and watched the
shells till we concluded the cellar was as good a place
as that hill-side.   I fear the want of good food is
breaking down H.   I know from my own feelings
of weakness, but mine is not an American constitu-
tion and has a recuperative power that his has not.

June 21st, 1863. — I had gone upstairs to-day during the interregnum to enjoy a rest on my bed and
read the reliable items in the "Citizen," when a shell
burst right outside the window in front of me.   Pieces
flew in, striking all round me, tearing down masses of
plaster that came tumbling over me.   When H. rushed
in I was crawling out of the plaster, digging it out of
my eyes and hair.   When he picked up beside my
pillow a piece as large as a saucer, I realized my narrow escape.   The window-frame began to smoke, and
we saw the house was on fire.   H. ran for a hatchet
and I for water, and we put it out.   Another (shell)
came crashing near, and I snatched up my comb and
brush and ran down here.   It has taken all the afternoon to get the plaster out of my hair, for my hands
were rather shaky.

June 25th. — A horrible day.   The most horrible
yet to me, because I've lost my nerve.   We were all
in the cellar, when a shell came tearing through the
roof, burst upstairs, and tore up that room, the pieces
coming through both floors down into the cellar.   One
of them tore open the leg of H.'s pantaloons.   This
was tangible proof the cellar was no place of protection from them.   On the heels of this came Mr. J.,

to tell us that young Mrs. P. had had her thigh-bone crushed. When Martha went for the milk she came back horror-stricken to tell us the black girl there had her arm taken off by a shell. For the first time I quailed. I do not think people who are physically brave deserve much credit for it; it is a matter of nerves. In this way I am constitutionally brave, and seldom think of danger till it is over; and death has not the terrors for me it has for some others. Every night I had lain down expecting death, and every morning rose to the same prospect, without being unnerved. It was for H. I trembled. But now I first seemed to realize that something worse than death might come; I might be crippled, and not killed. Life, without all one's powers and limbs, was a thought that broke down my courage. I said to H., " You must get me out of this horrible place; I cannot stay; I know I shall be crippled." Now the regret comes that I lost control, for H. is worried, and has lost his composure, because my coolness has broken down.

July 1st, 1863. — Some months ago, thinking it might be useful, I obtained from the consul of my birthplace, by sending to another town, a passport for foreign parts. H. said if we went out to the lines we might be permitted to get through on that. So we packed the trunk, got a carriage, and on the 30th drove out there. General V. offered us seats in his tent. The rifle-bullets were whizzing so *zip, zip* from the sharp-shooters on the Federal lines that involuntarily I moved on my chair. He said, "Don't be alarmed; you are out of range. They are firing at our mules yonder." His horse, tied by the tent door, was quivering all over, the most intense exhibition of fear I'd ever seen in an animal. General V. sent out a flag of truce to the Federal headquarters, and while we waited wrote on a piece of silk paper a few words. Then he said, "My wife is in Tennessee. If you get through the lines, give her this. They will search you, so I will put it in this toothpick." He crammed the silk paper into a quill toothpick, and handed it to H. It was completely concealed. The flag-of-truce officer came back flushed and angry. "General Grant says that no human being shall pass out of Vicksburg; but the lady may feel sure danger will soon be over. Vicksburg will surrender on the 4th."

"Is that so, general?" inquired H. "Are arrangements for surrender made?"

"We know nothing of the kind. Vicksburg will not surrender."

"Those were General Grant's exact words, sir," said the flag-officer. "Of course it is nothing but their brag."

We went back sadly enough, but to-day H. says he will cross the river to General Porter's lines and try there; I shall not be disappointed.

July 3d, 1863. — H. was going to headquarters for the requisite pass, and he saw General Pemberton crawling out of a cave, for the shelling has been as hot as ever. He got the pass, but did not act with his usual caution, for the boat he secured was a miserable, leaky one — a mere trough. Leaving Martha in charge, we went to the river, had our trunks put in the boat, and embarked; but the boat became utterly unmanageable, and began to fill with water rapidly. H. saw that we could not cross it and turned to come back; yet in spite of that the pickets at the battery fired on us. H. raised the white flag he had, yet they fired again, and I gave a cry of horror that none of these dreadful things had wrung from me. I thought H. was struck. When we landed H. showed the pass, and said that the officer had told him the battery would be notified we were to cross. The officer apologized and said they were not notified. He furnished a cart to get us home, and to-day we are down in the cellar again, shells flying as thick as ever. Provisions are so nearly gone, except the hogshead of sugar, that a few more days will bring us to starvation indeed. Martha says rats are hanging dressed in the market for sale with mule meat, — there is nothing else. The officer at the battery told me he had eaten one yesterday. We have tried to leave this Tophet and failed, and if the siege continues I must summon that higher kind of courage — moral bravery — to subdue my fears of possible mutilation.

XV.

GIBRALTAR FALLS.

July 4th, 1863. — It is evening. All is still. Silence and night are once more united. I can sit at the table in the parlor and write. Two candles are lighted. I would like a dozen. We have had wheat supper and wheat bread once more. H. is leaning back in the rocking-chair; he says:

"G., it seems to me I can hear the silence, and feel it too. It wraps me like a soft garment; how else can I express this peace?"

But I must write the history of the last twenty-four hours. About five yesterday afternoon, Mr. J., H.'s assistant, who, having no wife to keep him in, dodges about at every change and brings us the news, came to H. and said:

"Mr. L., you must both come to our cave to-night. I hear that to-night the shelling is to surpass anything yet. An assault will be made in front and rear. You know we have a double cave; there is room for you in mine, and mother and sister will make a place for Mrs. L. Come right up; the ball will open about seven."

We got ready, shut up the house, told Martha to go to the church again if she preferred it to the cellar, and walked up to Mr. J.'s. When supper was eaten, all secure, and the ladies in their cave night toilet, it was just six, and we crossed the street to the cave opposite. As I crossed a mighty shell flew screaming over my head. It was the last thrown into Vicksburg. We lay on our pallets waiting for the expected roar, but no sound came except the chatter from the neighboring caves, and at last we dropped asleep. I woke at dawn stiff. A draught from the funnel-shaped opening had been blowing on me all night. Every one was expressing surprise at the quiet. We started

for home and met the editor of the "Daily Citizen."
H. said:

"This is strangely quiet, Mr. L."

"Ah, sir," shaking his head gloomily, " I 'm afraid
the last shell has been thrown into Vicksburg."

"Why do you fear so ?"

"It is surrender. At six last evening a man went
down to the river and blew a truce signal; the shelling
stopped at once."

When I entered the kitchen a soldier was there waiting for the bowl of scrapings. (They took turns for it.)

"Good-morning, madam," he said; "we won't bother
you much longer. We can't thank you enough for
letting us come, for getting this soup boiled has helped
some of us to keep alive, but now all this is over."

"Is it true about the surrender ?"

"Yes; we have had no official notice, but they are
paroling out at the lines now, and the men in Vicksburg will never forgive Pemberton. An old granny!
A child would have known better than to shut men
up in this cursed trap to starve to death like useless
vermin." His eyes flashed with an insane fire as he
spoke. "Have n't I seen my friends carted out three
or four in a box, that had died of starvation! Nothing else, madam! Starved to death because we had
a fool for a general."

"Don't you think you 're rather hard on Pemberton?
He thought it his duty to wait for Johnston."

"Some people may excuse him, ma'am, but we 'll
curse him to our dying day. Anyhow, you 'll see the
blue-coats directly."

Breakfast dispatched, we went on the upper gallery. The street was deserted, save by a few people carrying home bedding from their caves. Among these was a group taking home a little creature, born in a cave a few days previous, and its wan-looking mother. About 11 o'clock a man in blue came sauntering along, looking about curiously. Then two followed him, then another.

"H., do you think these can be the Federal soldiers?"

"Why, yes; here come more up the street."

Soon a group appeared on the court-house hill, and the flag began slowly to rise to the top of the staff. As the breeze caught it, and it sprang out like a live thing exultant, H. drew a long breath of contentment.

"Now I feel once more at home in my own country."

In an hour more a grand rush of people set in toward the river, — foremost among them the gentleman who took our cave; all were flying as if for life.

"What can this mean, H.? Are the populace turning out to greet the despised conquerors?"

"Oh," said H., springing up, "look! It is the boats coming around the bend."

Truly, it was a fine spectacle to see that fleet of transports sweep around the curve and anchor in the teeth of the batteries so lately vomiting fire. Presently Mr. J. passed and called:

"Are n't you coming, Mr. L.? There's provisions on those boats: coffee and flour. 'First come, first served,' you know."

"Yes, I'll be there pretty soon," replied H.

But now the new-comers began to swarm into our yard, asking H. if he had coin to sell for green-backs. He had some, and a little bartering went on with the new greenbacks. H. went out to get provisions. When he returned a Confederate officer came with him. H. went to the box of Confed-erate money and took out four hundred dollars, and the officer took off his watch, a plain gold one, and laid it on the table, saying, "We have not been paid, and I must get home to my family." H. added a five-dollar greenback to the pile, and wished him a happy meeting. The townsfolk continued to dash through the streets with their arms full, canned goods predominating. Towards five Mr. J. passed again. "Keep on the lookout," he said; "the army of occu-pation is coming along," and in a few minutes the head of the column appeared. What a contrast to the suffering creatures we had seen so long were these stalwart, well-fed men, so splendidly set up and ac-coutered! Sleek horses, polished arms, bright plumes, — this was the pride and panoply of war. Civiliza-tion, discipline, and order seemed to enter with the measured tramp of those marching columns; and the heart turned with throbs of added pity to the worn men in gray, who were being blindly dashed against this embodiment of modern power. And now this "silence that is golden" indeed is over all, and my limbs are unhurt, and I suppose if I were Catholic, in my fervent gratitude, I would hie me with a rich offering to the shrine of "our Lady of Mercy."

July 7th, 1863. — I did not enjoy quiet long. First came Martha, who announced her intention of going to search for her sons, as she was free now. I was hardly able to stand since the severe cold taken in the cave that night, but she would not wait a day. A colored woman came in wanting a place, and said she had asked her mistress for wages and her mistress had turned her out. I was in no condition to stand upon ceremony then, and engaged her at once, but hear to-day that I am thoroughly pulled to pieces in Vicksburg circles; there is no more salvation for me. Next came two Federal officers and wanted rooms and board. To have some protection was a necessity; both armies were still in town, and for the past three days every Confederate soldier I see has a cracker in his hand. There is hardly any water in town, no prospect of rain, and the soldiers have emptied one cistern in the yard already and begun on the other. The colonel put a guard at the gate to limit the water given. Next came the owner of the house and said we must move; he wanted the house, but it was so big he'd just bring his family in; we could stay till we got one. They brought boarders with them too, and children. Men are at work all over the house shoveling up the plaster before repairing. Upstairs they are pouring it by bucketfuls through the windows. Colonel D. brought work for H. to help with from headquarters. Making out the paroles and copying them has taken so long they wanted help. I am surprised and mortified to find that two-thirds of all the men who have signed made their mark; they cannot write. I

Hd Qrs. Dist. of the Tenn
Tupelo. Aug. 6. 1862

Captain.

The Maj. for Comg directs me
to say that he submits it altogether to
your own discretion, whether you make
the attempt to capture Genl Grant, or
not — While the exploit would be very
brilliant if successful, you must re
-member that failure might be disastrous
to you & your men — The General com
-mends your activity & energy & expects you
to continue to shew their qualities —

I am very respectfully
Yr obt svt:
Thomas Snead
A A G.

Capt Geo. L. Baxter.
Army Maryland Scouts

never thought there was so much ignorance in the South. One of the men at headquarters took a fancy to H. and presented him with a portfolio, that he said he had captured when the Confederates evacuated their headquarters at Jackson. It contained mostly family letters written in French, and a few official papers. Among them was the following note, which I will copy here, and file away the original as a curiosity when the war is over.

HEADQUARTERS DEPT. OF TENN.
TUPELO, Aug. 6, 1862.

CAPT.: The Major-General Commanding directs me to say that he submits it altogether to your own discretion whether you make the attempt to capture General Grant or not. While the exploit would be very brilliant if successful, you must re- member that failure might be disastrous to you and your men. The General commends your activity and energy and expects you to continue to show these qualities.

I am, very respectfully, yr. obt. svt.

Thomas L. Snead, A. A. G.

CAPT. GEO. L. BAXTER,
Commanding Beauregard Scouts.

I would like to know if he tried it and came to grief or abandoned the project. As letters can now get through to New Orleans, I wrote there.

July 14th, 1863. — Moved yesterday into a house I call "Fair Rosamond's bower" because it would take a clue of thread to go through it without getting lost. One room has five doors opening into the house, and no windows. The stairs are like ladders, and the colonel's contraband valet won't risk his neck taking down water, but pours it through the windows on people's heads. We shan't stay in it. Men are at work closing up the caves; they had become hiding-places for trash. Vicksburg is now like one vast hospital — every one is getting sick or is sick. My cook was taken to-day with bilious fever, and nothing but will keeps me up.

July 23d, 1863. — We moved again two days ago.

Aug. 20. — Sitting in my easy chair to-day, looking out upon a grassy slope of the hill in the rear of this house, I have looked over this journal as if in a dream; for since the last date sickness and sorrow have been with me. I feel as if an angry wave had passed over me bearing away strength and treasure. For on one day there came to me from New Orleans the news of Mrs. B.'s death, a friend whom no tie of blood could have made nearer. The next day my beautiful boy ended his brief life of ten days and died in my arms. My own illness caused him to perish; the fatal cold in the cave was the last straw that broke down strength. The colonel's sweet wife has come, and I do not lack now for womanly com-panionship. She says that with such a pre-natal experience perhaps death was the best for him. I try to think so, and to be glad that H. has not been ill, though I see the effects. This book is exhausted, and I wonder whether there will be more adventures by flood and field to cause me to begin another.